IMAGES
of America

QUINCY
ILLINOIS

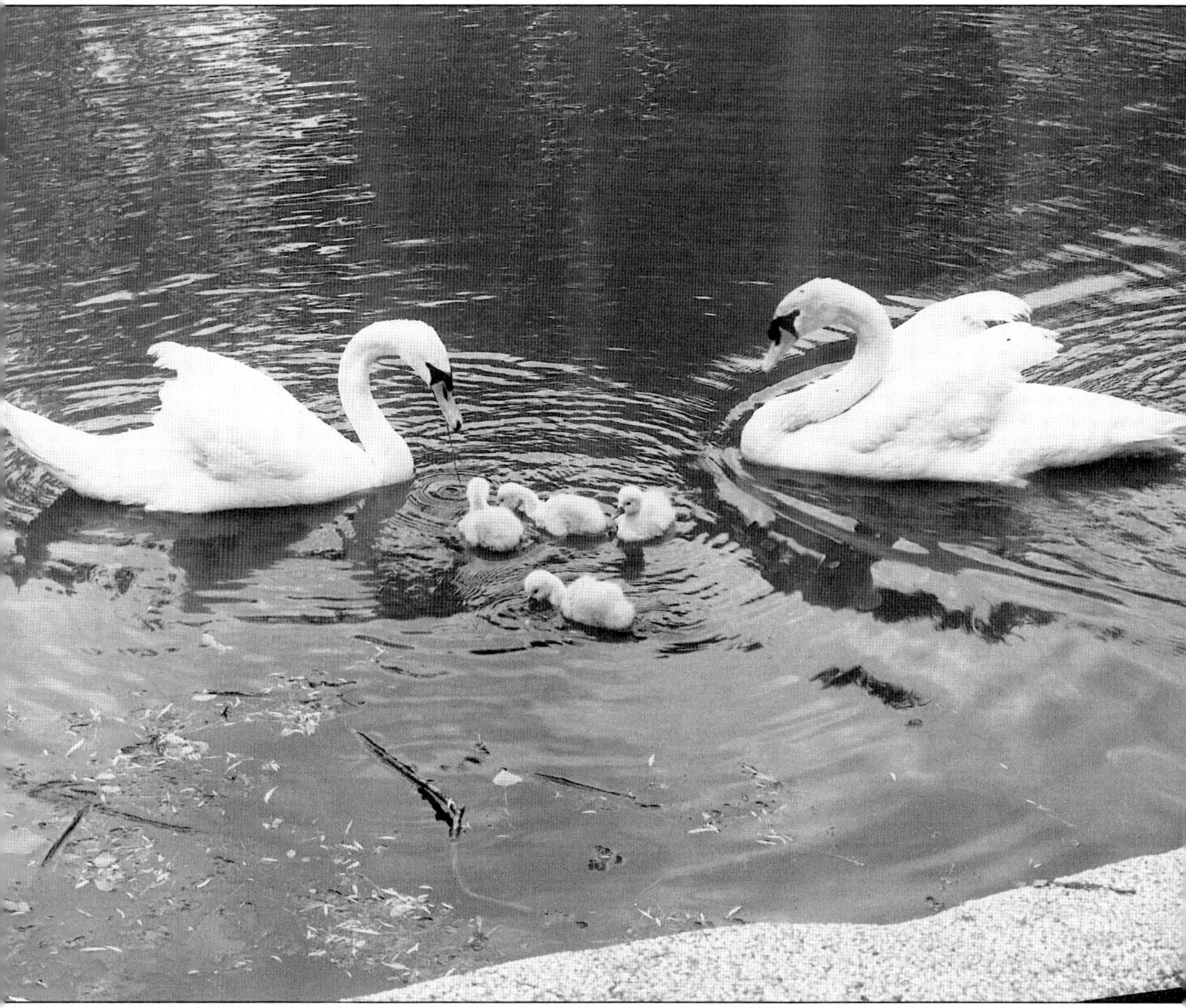

This peaceful scene of swans, geese, or ducks on the lake of the Illinois Veterans Home greets visitors to the grounds of the home in the summertime. In 1885, the State of Illinois passed legislation to establish and maintain a soldiers' home. The site selected was the farmland of E.A. Dudley, located north of Quincy. The Soldiers and Sailors Home was dedicated in October 1886; General Charles Lippincott was the first superintendent. The Dudley home was used as the managing officer's home, as it is today. The administration building was among the first erected, along with 17 cottages, a heating plant, dairy, and hospital. Lippincott Hall was completed in 1900, and other buildings, including a museum, have been added over the years. Later the name was changed to Veterans Home. For many years the home has also had a deer park, which in recent years has been expanded to include many other animals.

IMAGES
of America

QUINCY
ILLINOIS

Carl and Shirley Landrum

ARCADIA
PUBLISHING

ISBN 978-0-7385-0127-7

Published by Arcadia Publishing
Charleston, South Carolina

Printed in the United States of America

Library of Congress Catalog Card Number: 99-63804

For all general information contact Arcadia Publishing at:
Telephone 843-853-2070
Fax 843-853-0044
E-mail sales@arcadiapublishing.com
For customer service and orders:
Toll-Free 1-888-313-2665

Visit us on the Internet at www.arcadiapublishing.com

Contents

ACKNOWLEDGMENTS

No photographic history could be done without the help of many people. The pictures have come from many sources, and it would be impossible to give credit to all, but we would like to thank those people who contributed to Carl's collection and who thought that the pictures, clippings, and other memorabilia should be saved, but could not keep them themselves.

Thanks also goes to Judy Nelson of the *Quincy Herald-Whig* and Iris Nelson of the Quincy Public Library for their assistance in helping to identify photographs and providing accurate information for the captions.

Also, a special thanks goes to Phil Germann, executive director of the Historical Society of Quincy and Adams County, for serving as copy editor.

Introduction

Quincy, Illinois, is located on the Mississippi River, about 20 miles north of Hannibal, Missouri, and a hundred miles west of the state capitol, Springfield.

The town of Quincy and Adams County were named for President John Quincy Adams. The Quincy town square was named John's Square; it was later renamed Washington Square before becoming Washington Park.

It all started in 1822, when John Wood built a cabin at the foot of what would become Delaware Street, near the Mississippi River, and the village grew eastward.

The Mississippi River provided transportation in the early days, followed by the railroad system. Eventually a network of highways and air traffic would carry many passengers, but the river and the railroads are still indispensable in handling the city's freight.

In the beginning, cabins were built on the riverfront, but as the city grew, more and more homes were built on the bluffs overlooking the river. The Villa Kathrine, a Moorish castle, is the only one of its kind on the Mississippi. George Metz built it in 1900.

Pioneers have included immigrants from Germany (many who came to America to escape military service), the Irish, and Americans from Kentucky and Virginia. Many were lured to the area by reports of a lush land called the "Jewel of the West" and later "the Gem City."

Industrialists came from New York and other eastern states and were responsible for many of the stately homes we see on Maine Street and the adjacent streets today.

Early industry included pork packing, tobacco processing, papermaking, stove making, carriage making, the ice industry, and lumberyards. Of course, as the city grew, so did its need for schools, utilities, health facilities, and cultural activities, which have been added.

Each generation has watched changes take place that transformed a small village into a city's major resource, and that is why we feel it is important to remember the progress of the city through its citizens.

Carl's last pictorial book, *Quincy, A Pictorial History*, is no longer available, and there still seems to be a demand for such a book. For that reason we have decided to publish another pictorial history. For this book, we have chosen images from Carl's collection of photographs, most of them places and people no longer here, and many unpublished before now. For those who grew up here, it is their "home forever," whether they stay or live elsewhere. It is a book of remembrances for them, but also a book designed to help the newcomer to Quincy develop an appreciation for the city.

The images cover the city from the beginning to the 1960s. For the most part, they have come from family or business collections, given to us so that they would be preserved as a part of history.

The book is loosely divided into time spans. Of course it is not possible to present a complete history of a city in a book of this size, but, if it is true that "a photograph is worth a thousand words," then perhaps we have told at least a good portion of Quincy's history.

One

EARLY QUINCY

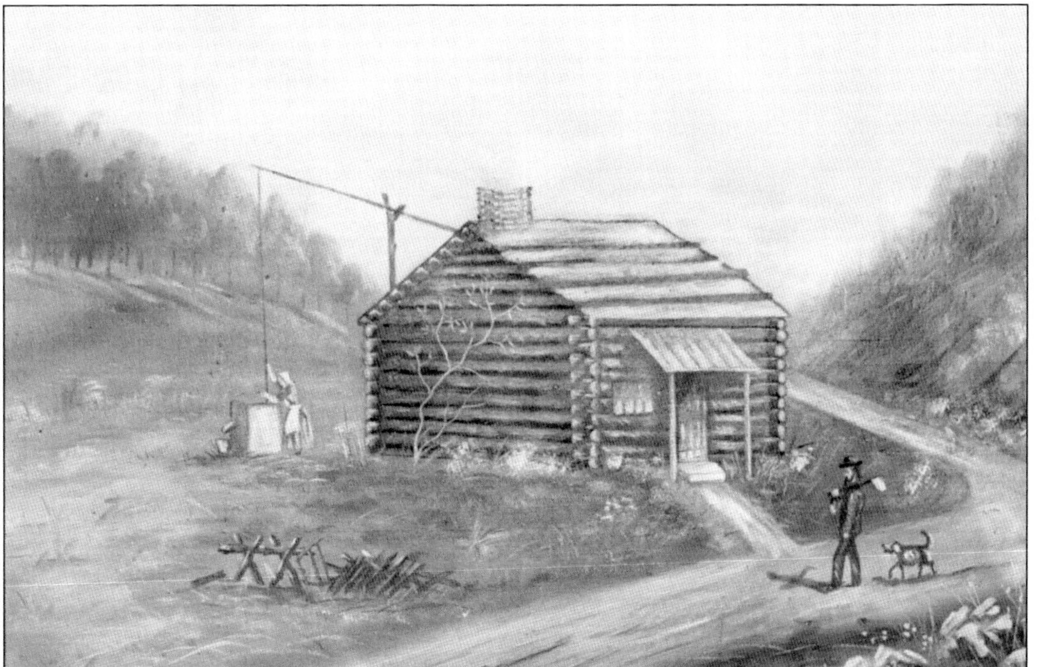

John Wood built the first cabin in Quincy at the foot of Delaware in 1822. This image is from an oil painting done at a later date. Wood later built a second cabin at 12th and State Streets, where he owned extensive land. When the first mail came to Quincy in 1825, the post office was a pine chest in Wood's first cabin.

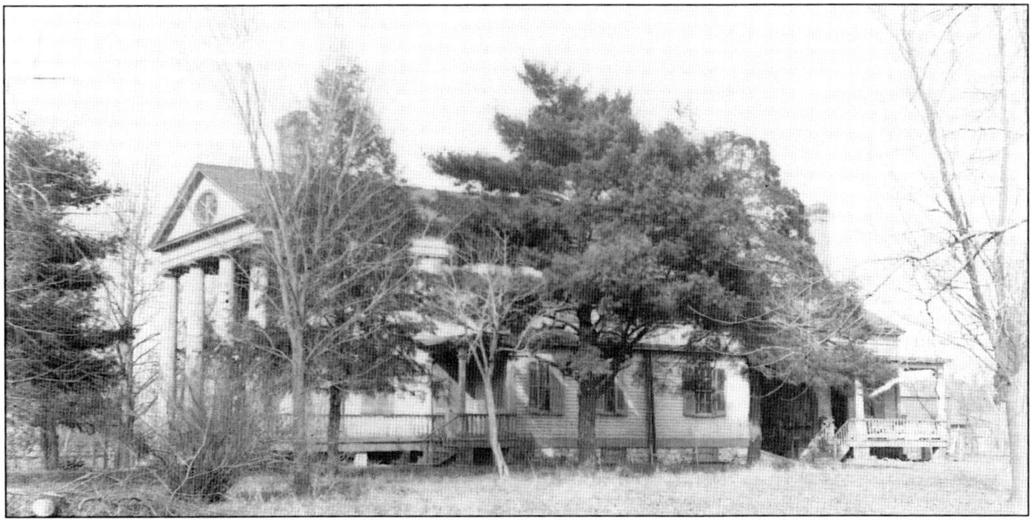

John Wood built the first mansion, in 1835, on the north side of State Street between 11th and 12th Streets. It was moved across a hedge in the spring of 1864 to its present location at 425 South 12th Street. At one time it was used as a rooming house and allowed to deteriorate, as shown in this photo *c.* 1900. When the Historical Society of Quincy and Adams County purchased the building, it underwent a complete restoration to become the beautiful structure it is today.

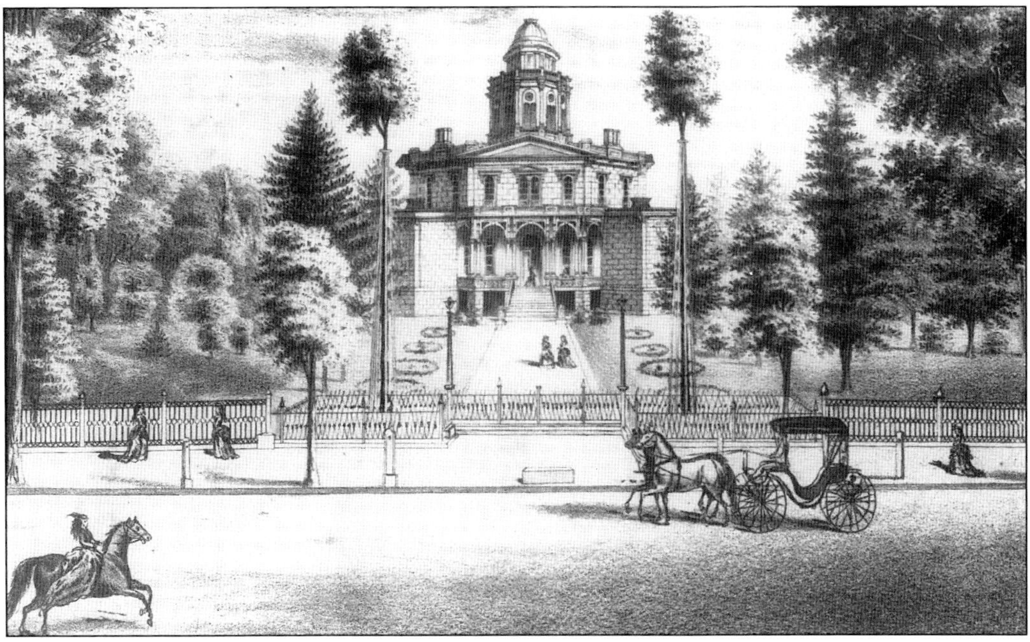

This drawing shows John Wood's octagonal mansion on the north side of State Street between Eleventh and Twelfth Streets. Started during the Civil War, it was not completed until after the war. It was built at an approximate cost of $250,000. The huge dome attracted attention to the building but had to be removed after being damaged in a storm. The fancy scrollwork on stone throughout the building was all chiseled out by hand. Chaddock College occupied the structure in the 1880s; St. Peter Catholic Church later used it for a grade school. It was razed in 1951.

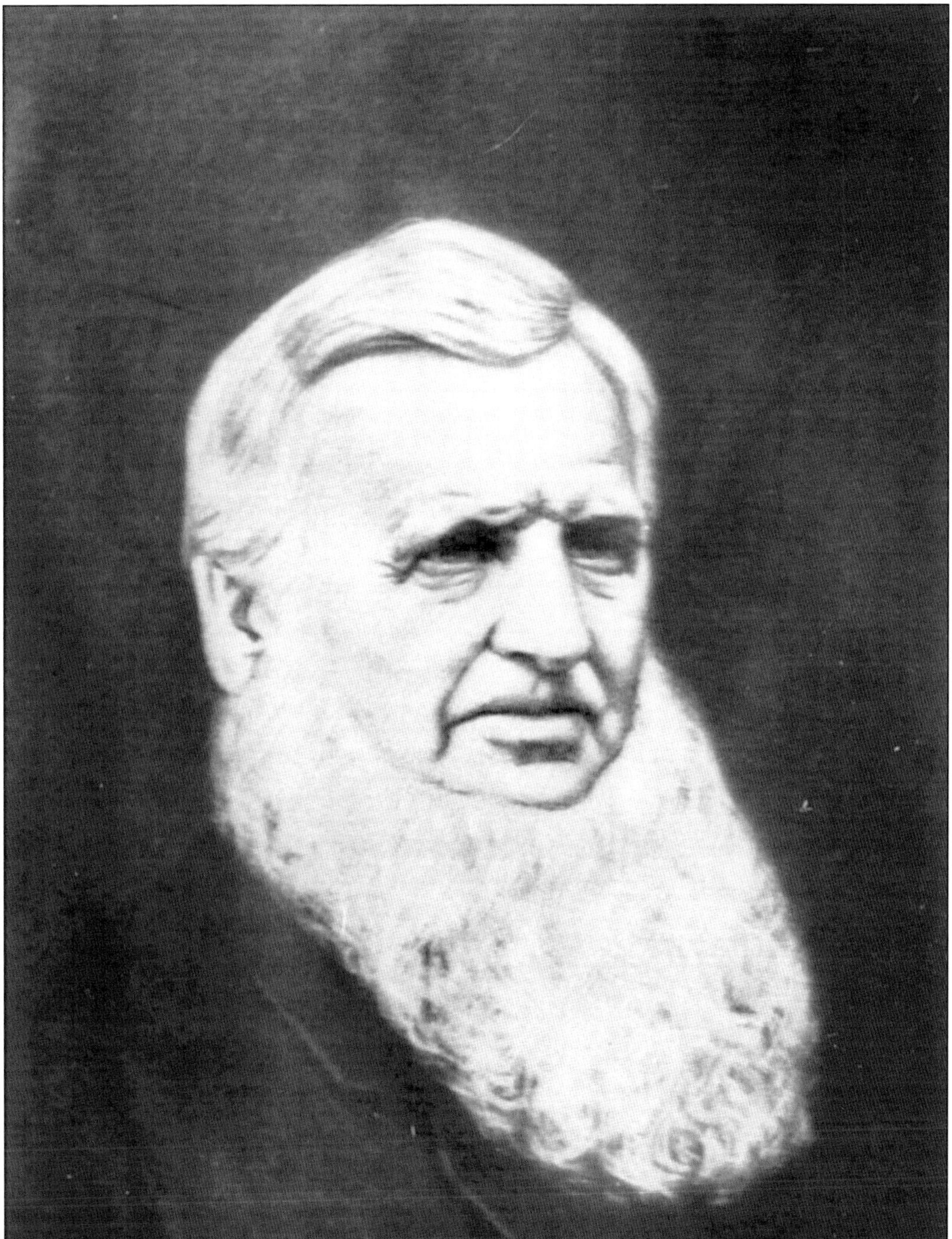

Founder of Quincy Governor John Wood was lieutenant governor and later Illinois state governor after Governor Bissell's death. Wood was a mayor of Quincy, quartermaster general for the state (which supplied equipment for the Union troops), and a friend of President Abraham Lincoln. Wood was born in Moravia, New York, in 1798, and came west as a young man. He died June 4, 1880, and is buried in Woodland Cemetery, the land for which he donated.

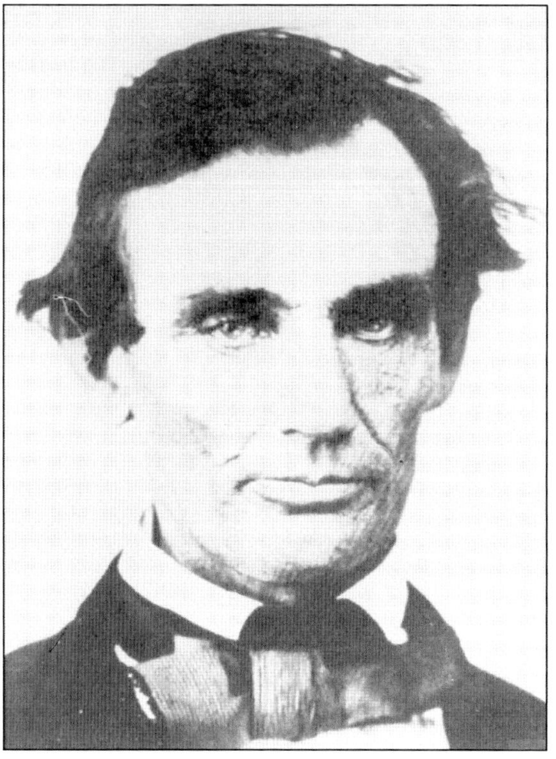

This ambrotype of Abraham Lincoln was taken during the Senate campaign in Pittsfield, Illinois, on October 1, 1858, just before the debate with Douglas in Galesburg, Illinois. The picture shows the deeply serious, almost sad expression of his eyes, which prevailed whenever he was photographed. Lincoln had just said he did not believe the extinction of slavery could possibly be sudden.

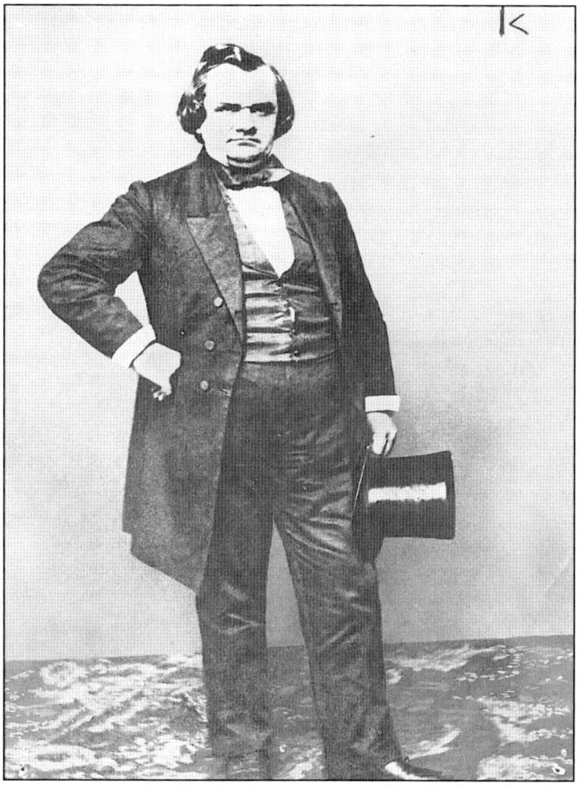

Sen. Stephen A. Douglas, only five feet, four inches tall, was known as "The Little Giant," and was Lincoln's opponent in the campaign of 1858 in Illinois and the famous Lincoln-Douglas Debates. After the series of debates, Douglas was elected to the United States Senate but died in office in 1861.

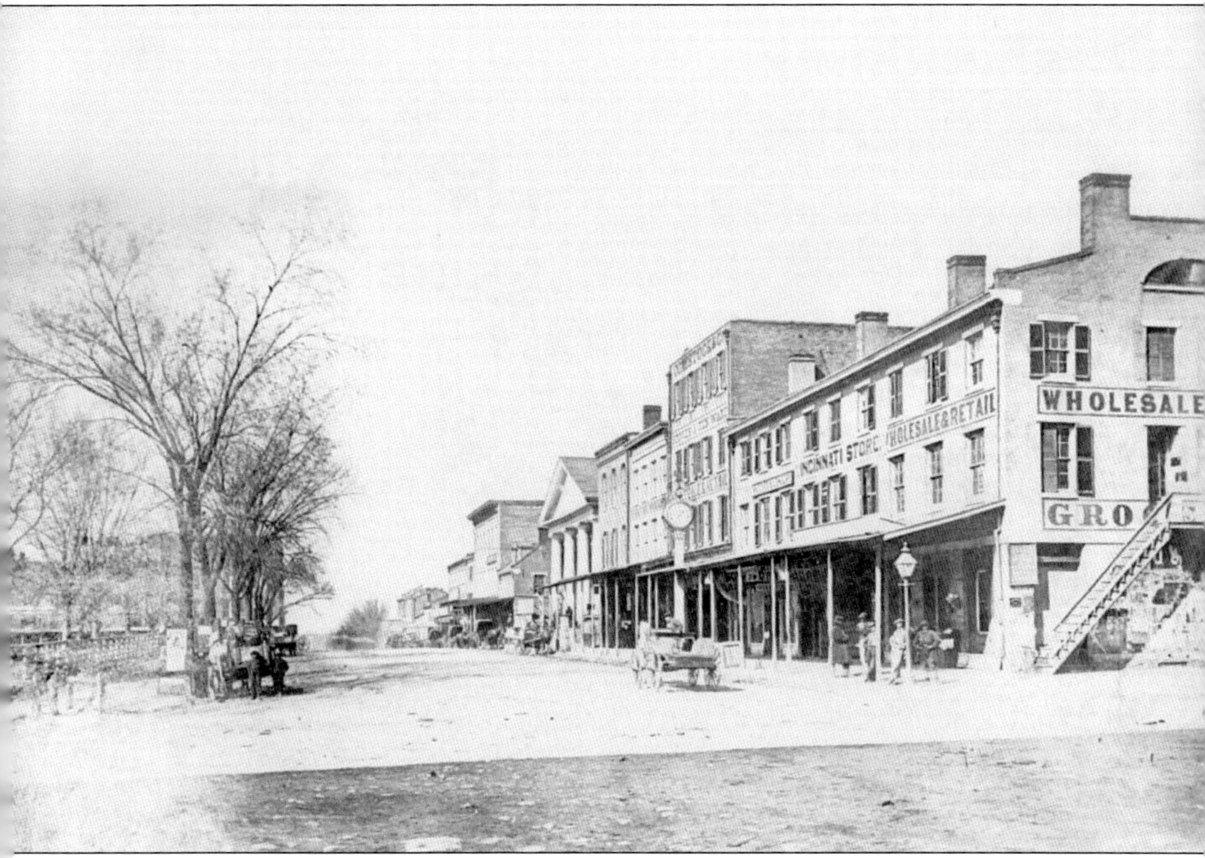

This view of Fifth Street looks north from Maine Street in the 1860s. This scene resembled that of the famous Lincoln-Douglas Debate in Quincy on October 13, 1858. The debate was held in Washington Park, seen on the left. The fence surrounding the park was built in 1841 to keep out cows and horses.

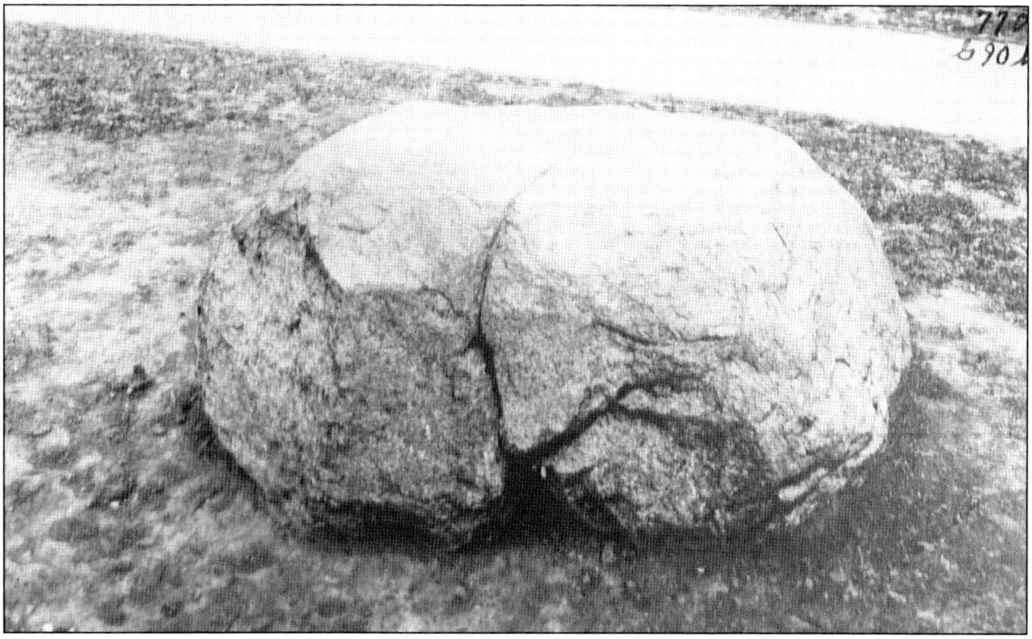

The 50th anniversary of the Lincoln-Douglas Debate was observed on October 13, 1908, in Washington Park. Many observers of the debate in 1858 also attended this memorial. A boulder was placed on the site with the inscription, as seen below: "Lincoln-Douglas Debate Oct. 13, 1858."

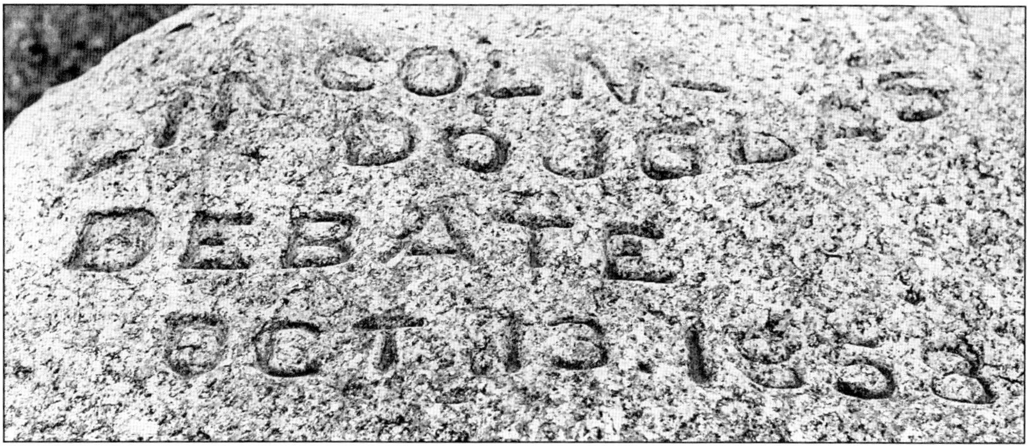

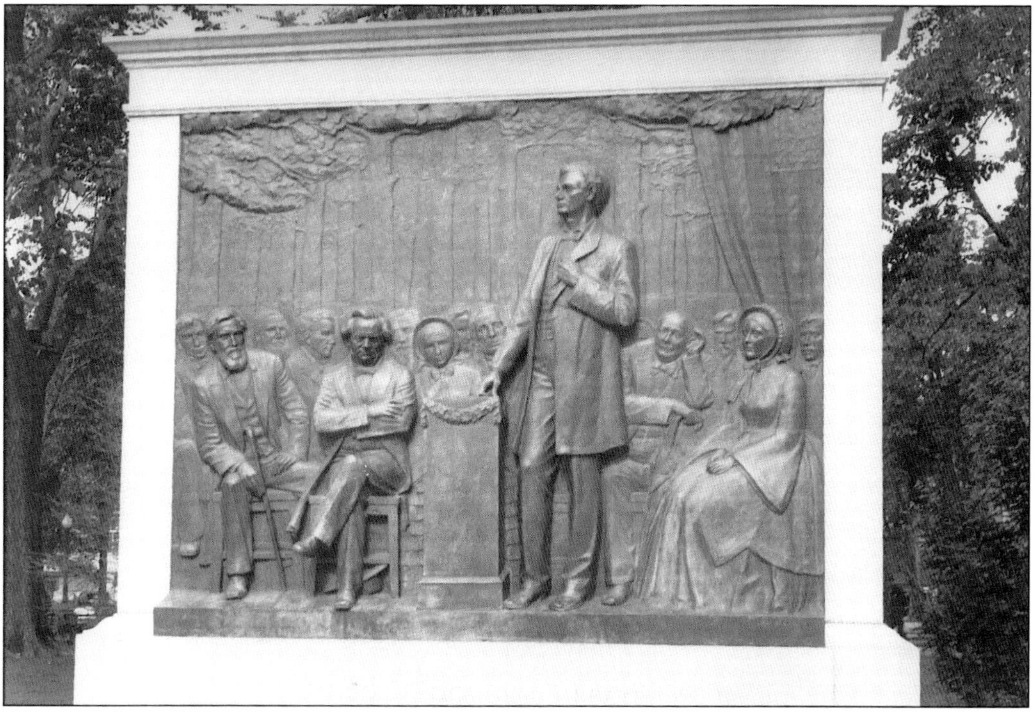

The Lincoln-Douglas plaque in Washington Park was dedicated on October 13, 1936. Governor Henry Horner and Lorado Taft, the sculptor of the plaque, were in attendance at the dedication. In order to place the plaque on the site of the Lincoln-Douglas Debate, it was necessary to move a statue of Governor John Wood to the west side of Washington Park.

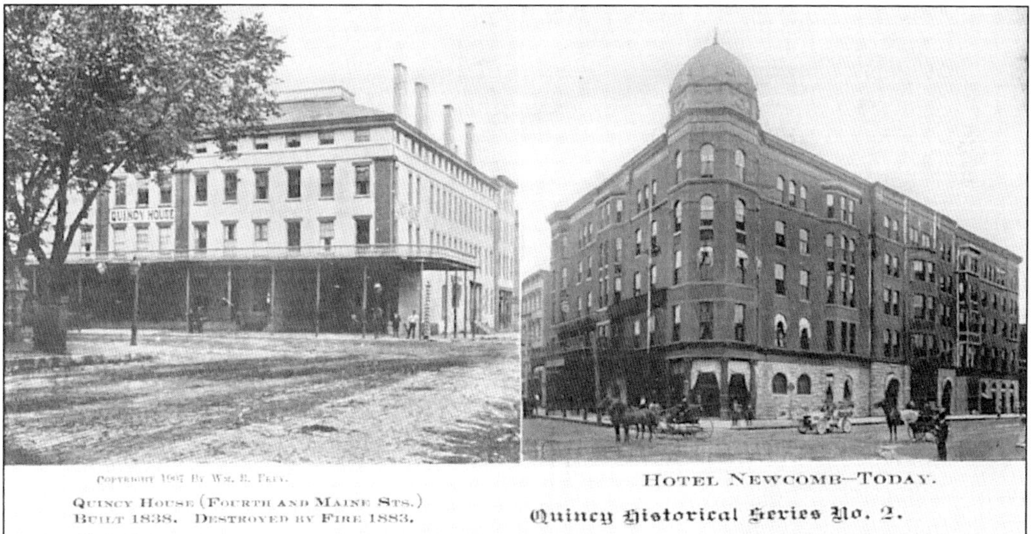

The Quincy House (on the left) was on the southeast corner of Fourth and Maine Streets. It was opened on November 8, 1838, and was considered the finest hotel this side of Pittsburgh. The hotel was destroyed by fire on January 19, 1883. Charles Howland was the architect and builder. The Hotel Newcomb (right) was constructed on this site in 1889; the structure is still standing today.

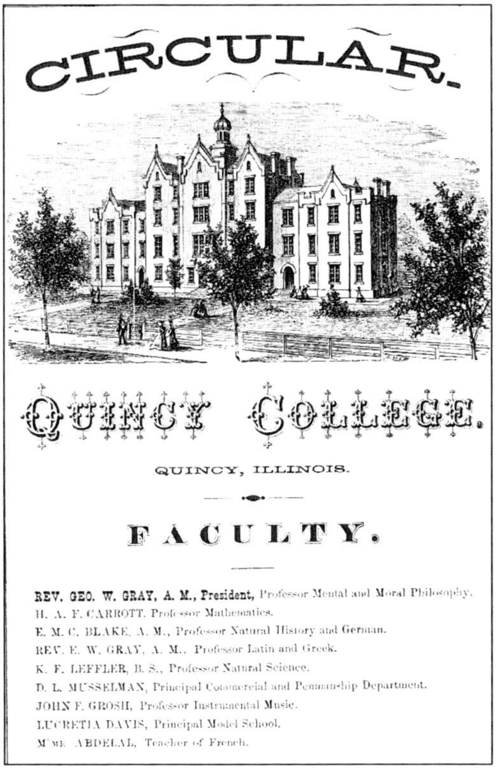

CIRCULAR.

QUINCY COLLEGE.

QUINCY, ILLINOIS.

FACULTY.

REV. GEO. W. GRAY, A. M., President, Professor Mental and Moral Philosophy.
H. A. F. CARROTT, Professor Mathematics.
E. M. C. BLAKE, A. M., Professor Natural History and German.
REV. E. W. GRAY, A. M., Professor Latin and Greek.
K. F. LEFFLER, B. S., Professor Natural Science.
D. L. MUSSELMAN, Principal Commercial and Penmanship Department.
JOHN F. GROSH, Professor Instrumental Music.
LUCRETIA DAVIS, Principal Model School.
M'ME ABDELAL, Teacher of French.

This is the front page of a circular distributed by the Quincy College, the old Methodist, German, and English College. Quincy College should not be confused with the Franciscan Quincy College at 18th and College Streets. D.L. Musselman of the Principal Commercial and Penmanship Department was on the faculty. He later organized the Gem City Business College.

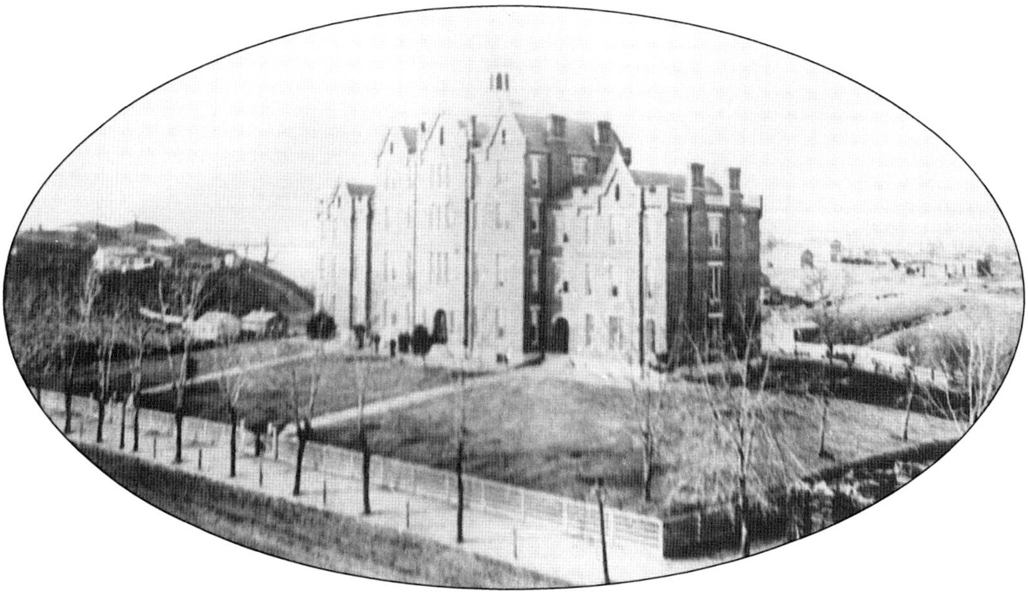

The Methodist, German, and English College, later Jefferson School, was on Spring between Third and Fourth Streets. It was built before the Civil War and continued in operation until 1872, when it merged with Johnson College of Macon, Missouri. In 1875, the college building was purchased by the City for use as a school and was renamed Jefferson School. Johnson College then bought the Governor John Wood mansion near Twelfth and State Streets and moved there.

Two

Civil War Era

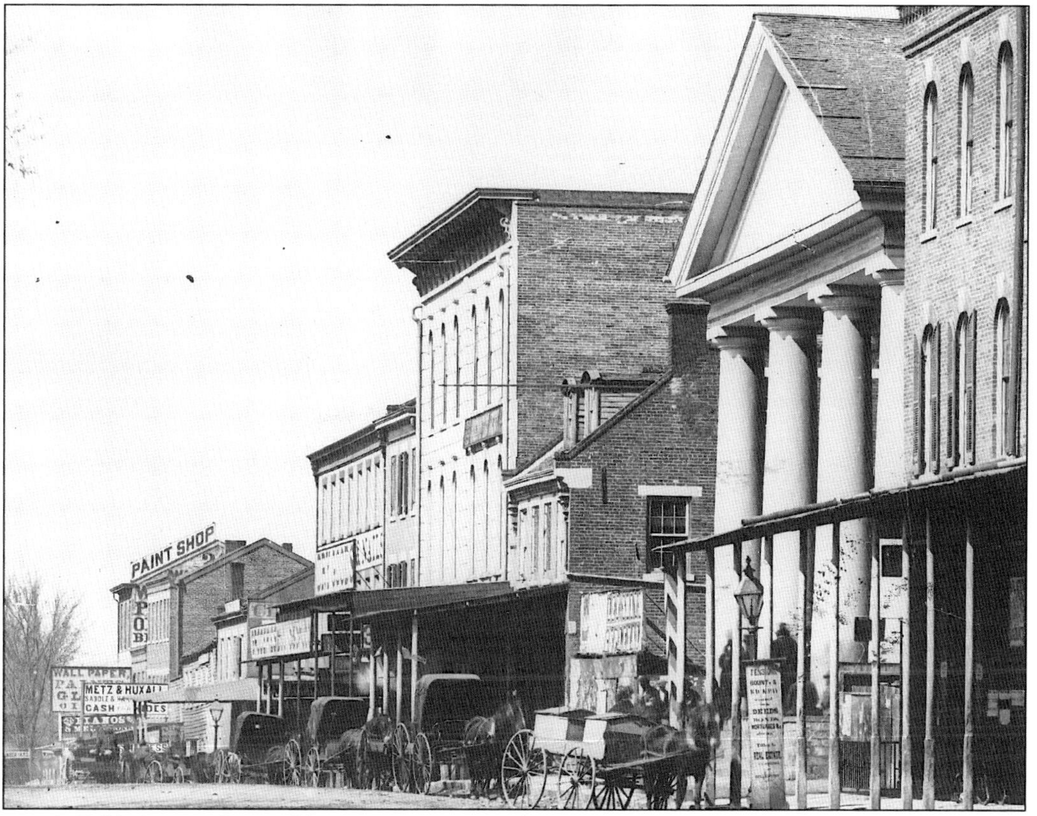

North Fifth Street, located between Maine and Hampshire Streets, shows the second Adams County courthouse, built after the first courthouse burned in 1835. The first courthouse was a log cabin located just north of Fifth and Maine Streets. When the second courthouse burned in 1875, the third courthouse was built on Jefferson Square between Vermont and Broadway, and Fifth and Sixth Streets. This picture, taken in 1861, also shows the house directly north of the courthouse where Governor Carlin lived when in Quincy.

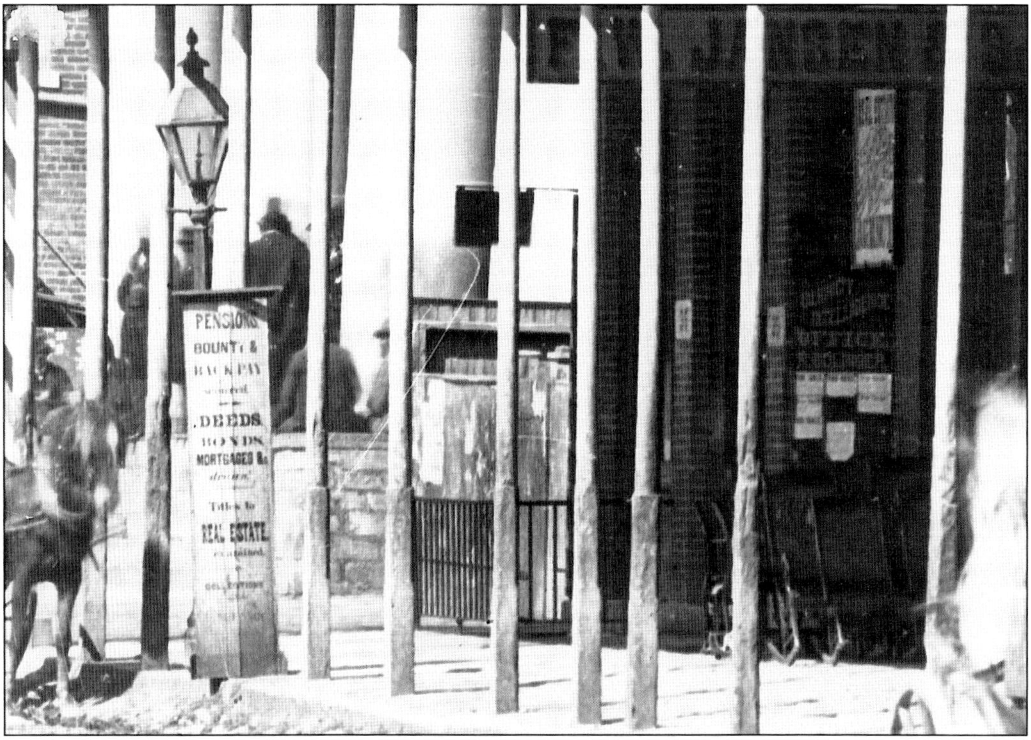

This blow-up of the preceding picture shows the building south of the courthouse, which housed R. Bolinger, Quincy Intelligence Office, 35 North Fifth, and Jansen Furniture Co., 36 North Fifth (old numbering system). The sign reads: "Pensions, Bounty & Back Pay, Deeds, Bonds, Mortgages, Titles for Real Estate Examined, Also Collections."

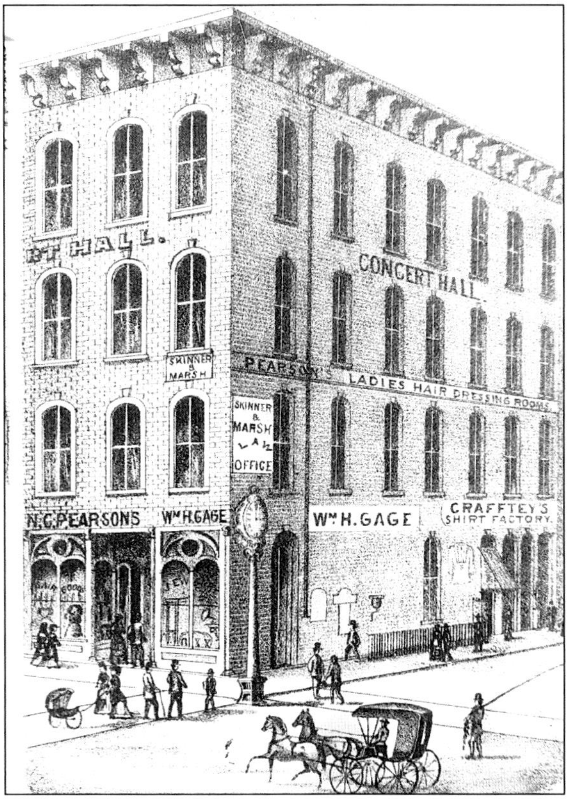

The concert hall building, located on the southeast corner of Fifth and Maine Streets, was erected by Ferdinand Flach in 1858. Skinner & Marsh Law Office occupied the second floor. Skinner was the son-in-law of Orville H. Browning. William H. Gage, Jewelry, and N.G. Pearson's Ladies Hair Dressing Rooms were on the first floor.

This picture of Abraham Lincoln was taken in the fall of 1861, before the effects of the Civil War could be seen in his face. As the war progressed and the casualties were reported to Mr. Lincoln, his face appeared more sad and gaunt. More than 600,000 Americans died in the war, almost as many as in all other American wars combined.

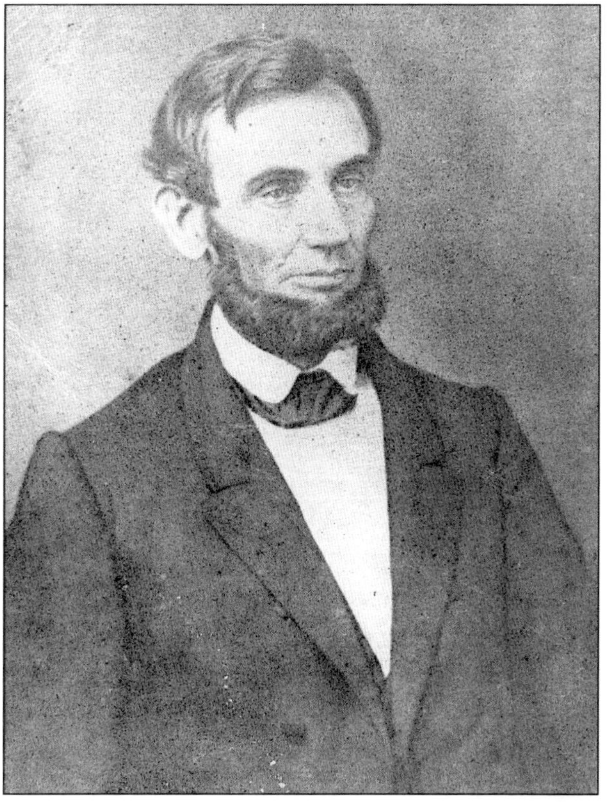

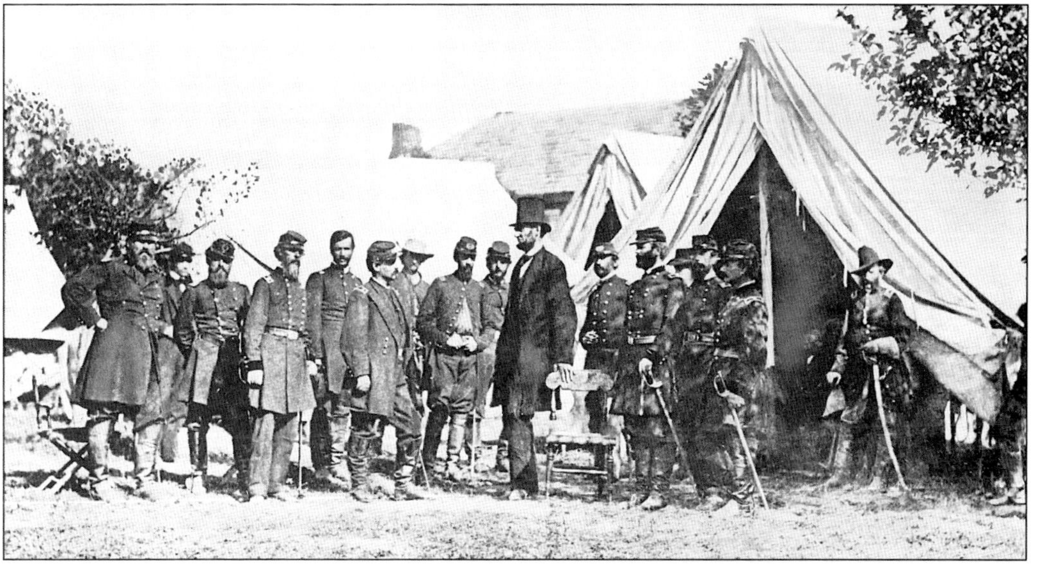

This photograph, by Mathew B. Brady, was made on the Antietam battlefield near Sharpsburg, Maryland, c. October 2, 1862. The September 17, 1862 Battle of Antietam was one of the bloodiest battles of the Civil War. Under the command of Major General George McClellan, the Union Army of the Potomac halted Confederate General Robert E. Lee's invasion of Maryland. Two weeks after the battle, President Lincoln visited General McClellan's camp and stayed for several days.

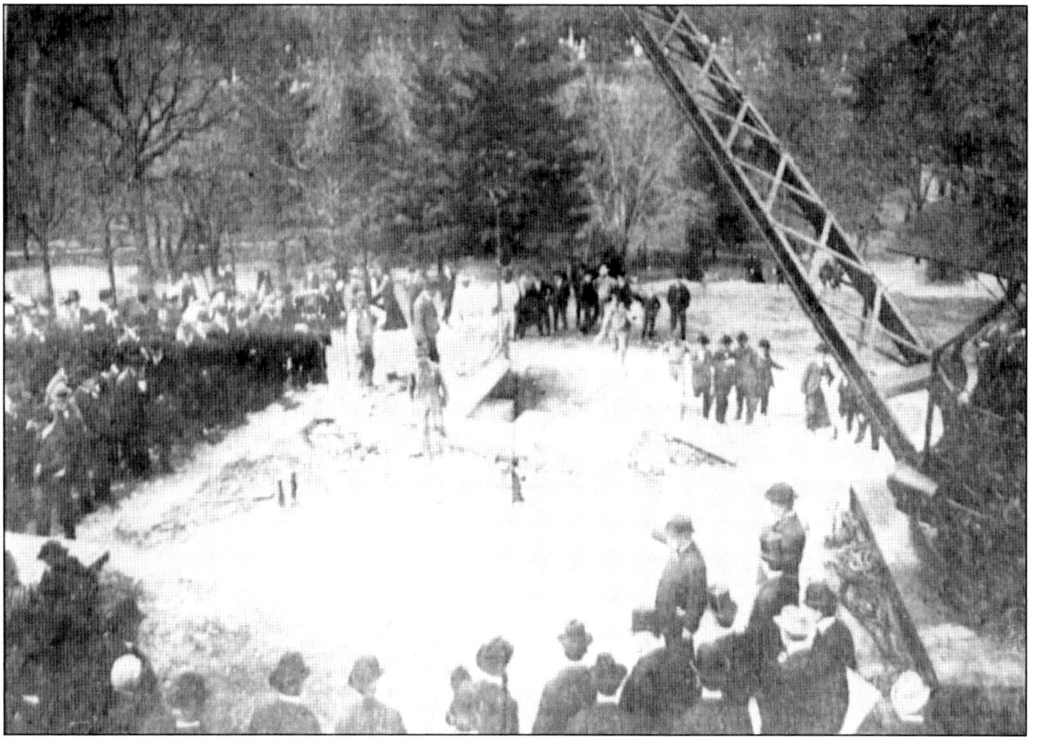

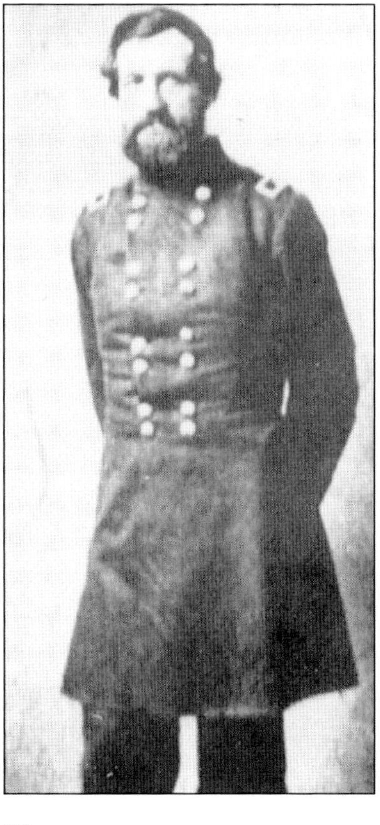

In April 1865, five days after the Confederate surrender, Abraham Lincoln was shot while at Ford's Theater by John Wilkes Booth, and died the next morning. His body was brought back to Springfield and placed in a temporary vault in Oak Ridge Cemetery. Later, when a monument was erected to his memory, Lincoln's body was moved to his permanent resting space. By the turn of the century, the tomb was in disrepair and had to be reconstructed by the J.S. Culver Construction Company of Springfield. This picture, taken April 24, 1901, shows the transferal of the Lincoln family bodies from their temporary vault to the rebuilt Lincoln tomb.

Major Gen. James D. Morgan, a prominent Quincy citizen, served his country during the Civil War without furlough from the beginning of the war until the end. He had also served as captain of the Quincy Grays during the Mormon difficulties in Hancock County in 1844-45, helping to maintain order after the murder of Joseph Smith and his brother in Carthage, Illinois.

In Quincy's early days, young men joined military companies as much as they join service clubs today. The Quincy City Guards won this prize cup from the Quincy Blues, commanded by Benjamin F. Prentiss, at a target shooting May 1, 1857. The City Guards presented the prize to their commander, Capt. James D. Morgan.

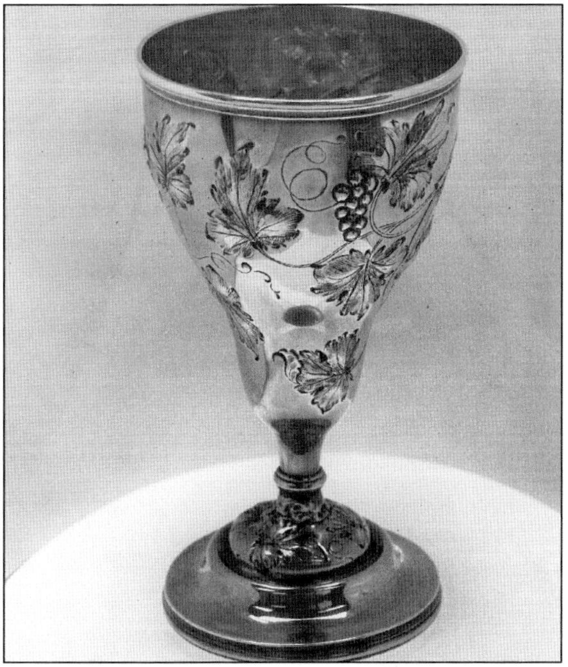

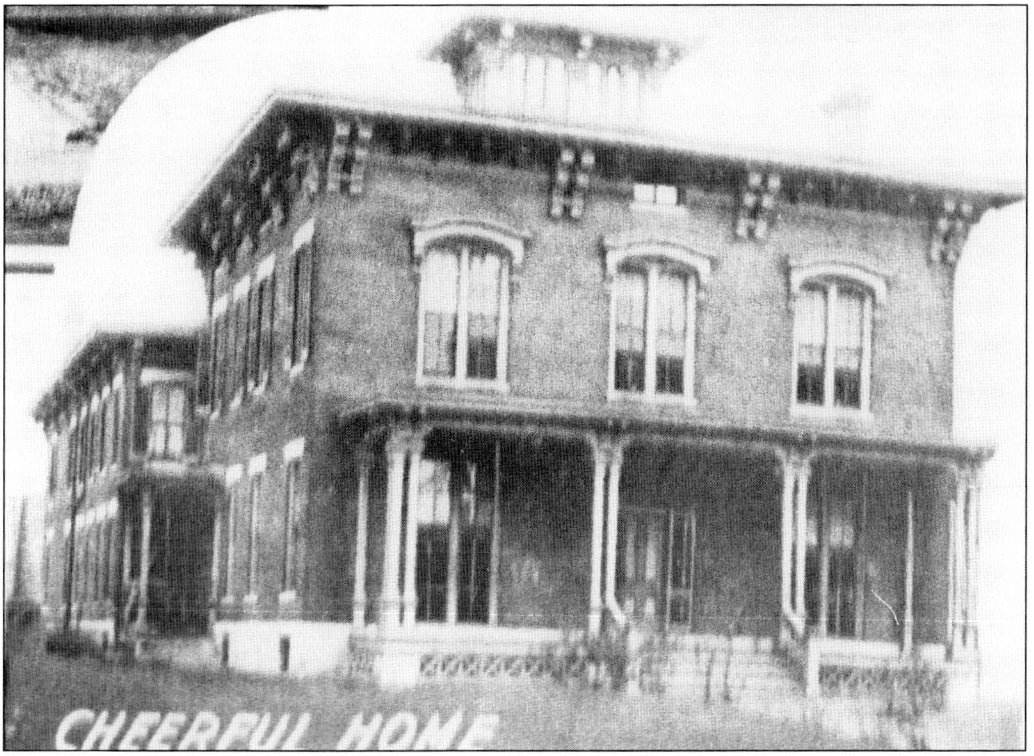

The James D. Morgan and Edward Wells families lived in this house at 421 Jersey. James D. Morgan came to Quincy in 1826 and opened a cooper shop in partnership with Edward Wells, a friend from Boston. In 1901, Lorenzo Bull purchased the house from the Wells estate for the Cheerful Home. Today it houses the Y.W.C.A.

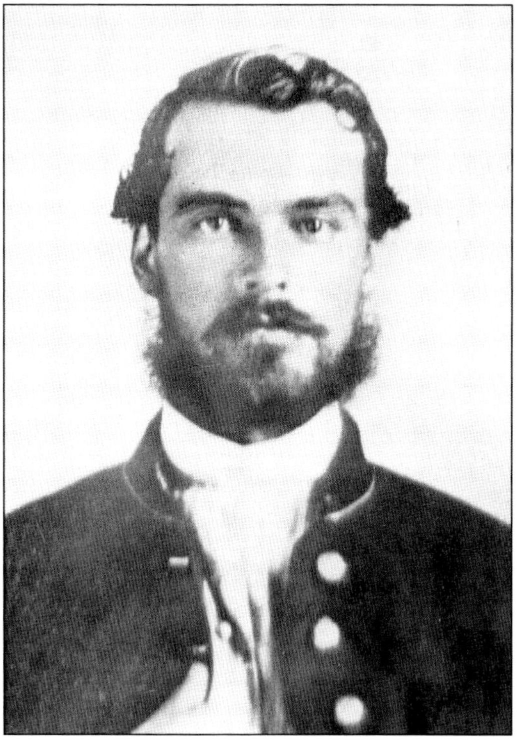

Elias Orton was a musician in Company B, 50th Illinois Infantry Volunteers. This was an Adams County regiment organized at Quincy in August 1861, made up entirely of Adams County men. They were mustered into federal service on September 12 of that year.

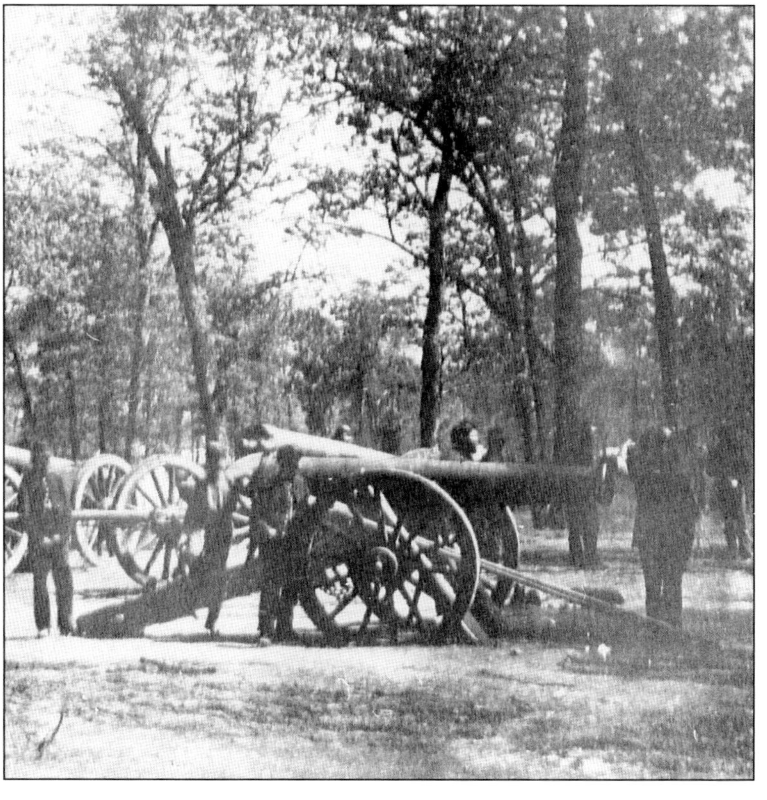

The 50th Illinois Infantry unit left Quincy in October 1861 on the steamer *Black Hawk* for Hannibal. In January 1862, they were ordered to Cairo, Illinois, and then to Tennessee, where they took part in the Battle of Shiloh. The Union forces drove the Confederate forces back; "Hornet's Nest" and "Bloody Pond" were names given to engagements during the battle.

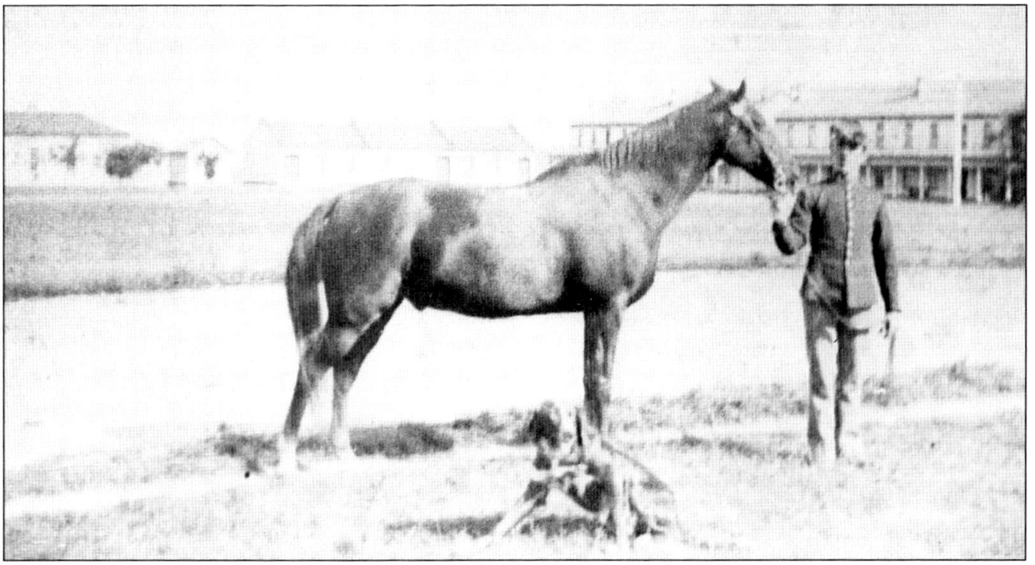

The uniforms of the 50th consisted of a gray hat, dark blue coat, and sky blue pants. After receiving their new uniforms they marched through the streets resplendent in their attire. This soldier, with horse and mascot, is unidentified.

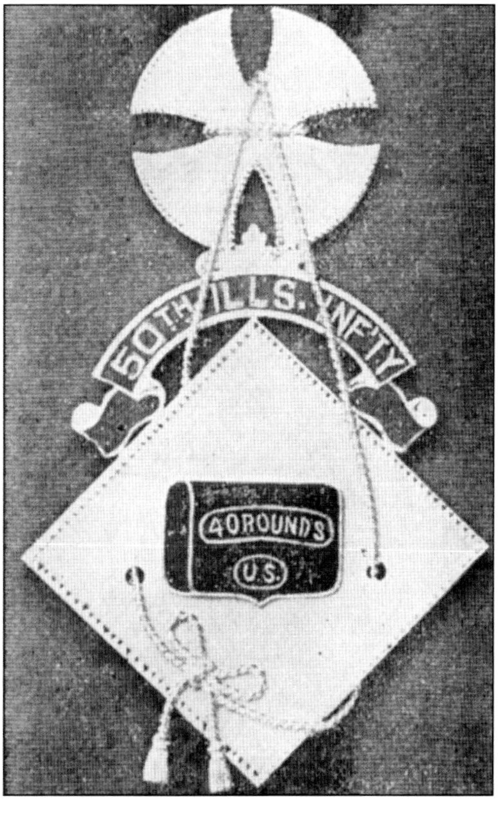

This is the chevron of the 50th Illinois Infantry. Doctor Moses M. Bane held the position of colonel, William Swarthout was lieutenant colonel, J.W. Randall was major, and Jefferson Brown was adjutant of the regiment. At the close of the war, the 50th won the drill contest in Louisville before returning home.

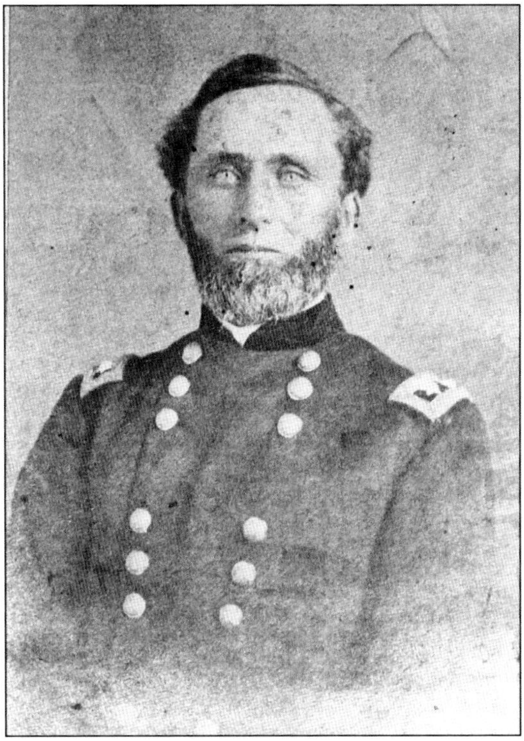

Major Gen. Benjamin Mayberry Prentiss was a hero of the Battle of Shiloh at Pittsburg Landing, Tennessee. He was one of the volunteers when President Lincoln called for recruits in 1861. He and his men were captured and imprisoned in Alabama and also in the Libby prison in Richmond. He was exchanged for a Confederate general in 1862 and saw further duty in 1863.

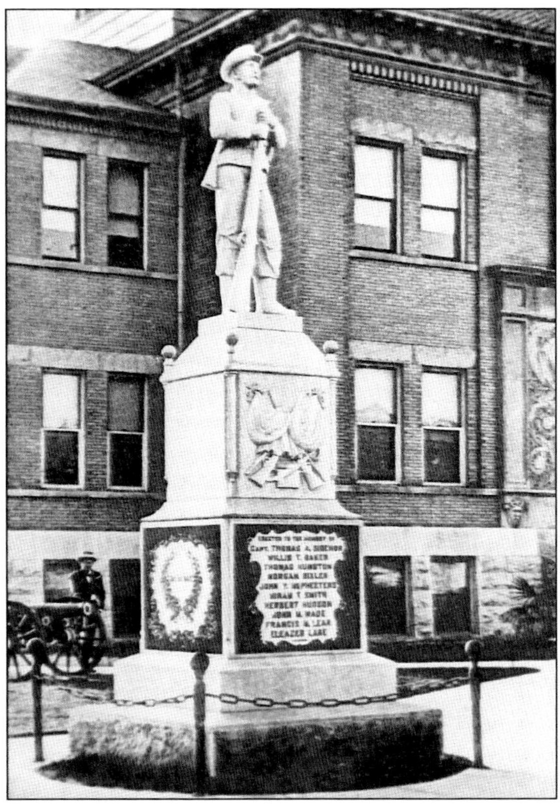

During the fall of 1862, Colonel Porter led guerrilla warfare in Missouri around Macon, Memphis, Palmyra, and Hannibal. On October 12, Porter was given notice that unless a Mr. Allsman, a Union man and non-combatant whom Porter had captured, was released, ten guerrilla prisoners from Palmyra and Hannibal would be shot. When Allsman was not returned, ten prisoners were selected, taken to the old fair grounds at Palmyra, and shot. This monument remembering those men was later erected in the courthouse square in Palmyra.

Three

POST CIVIL WAR 1899

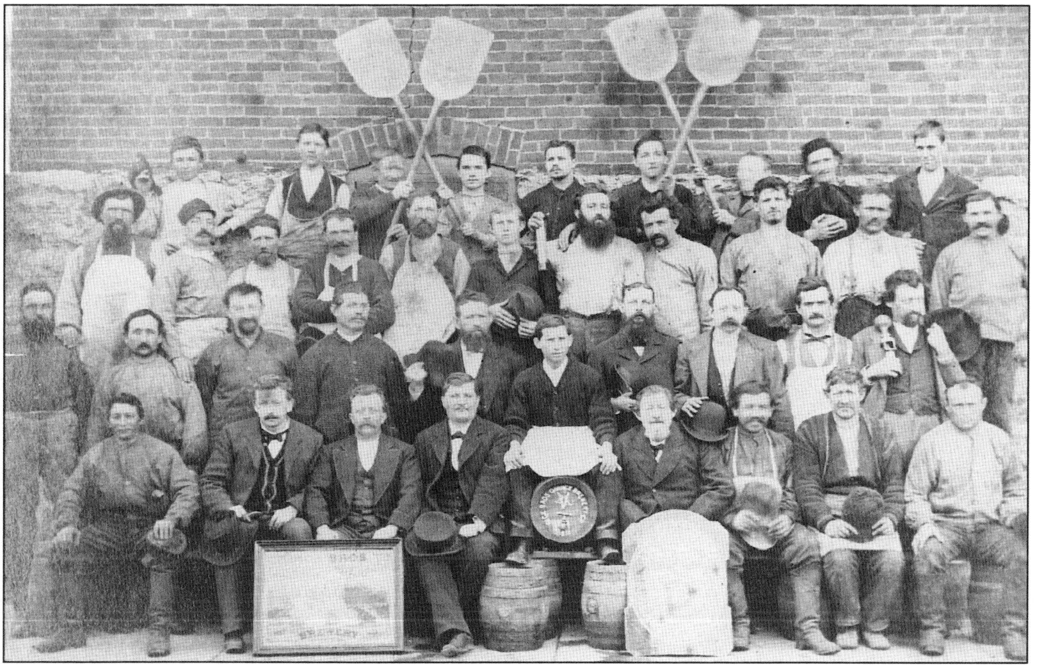

The Dick brothers, Matthew, John, and Jacob came to Quincy in 1856 from Belleville, Illinois. They bought land on the south side of York between Ninth and Tenth Streets, where there was a bubbling spring. They built their first brewery, the City Brewery, which they later renamed Dick Bros. In the beginning, the three Dick brothers did all the work, but as the business grew, so did the work force. This photograph, believed to be in the 1880s, shows the Dick Bros. work force. In later years, as they began shipping their product all over the southwest part of the country, they employed hundreds of men.

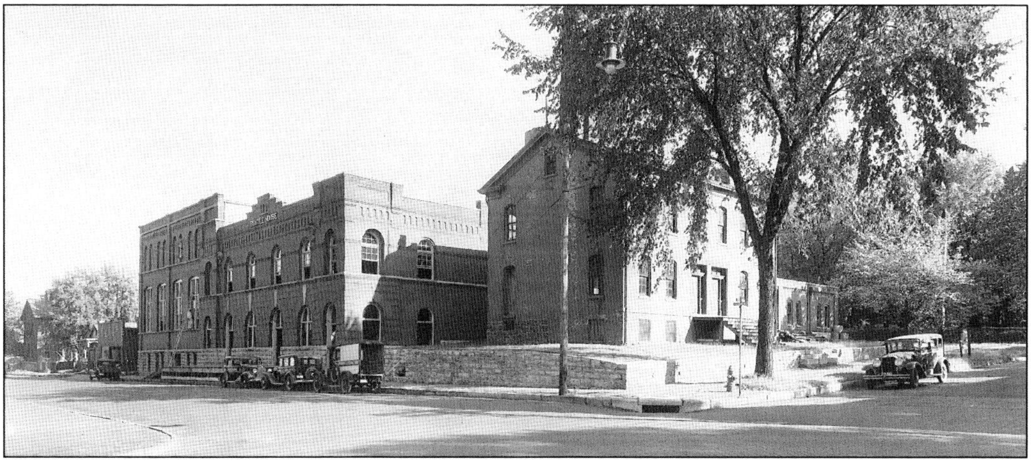

The Dick brothers first erected a small building on the south side of York and installed a large kettle, into which went the spring water, hops, and malt; under this kettle they built a fire. This small shack was eventually replaced by several other buildings, and the kettle by a huge kettle that brewed 275 barrels every 24 hours. The Dick family home was built next to the brewery and is shown in this photograph taken in the late 1920s or early 1930s before the house was razed in 1939.

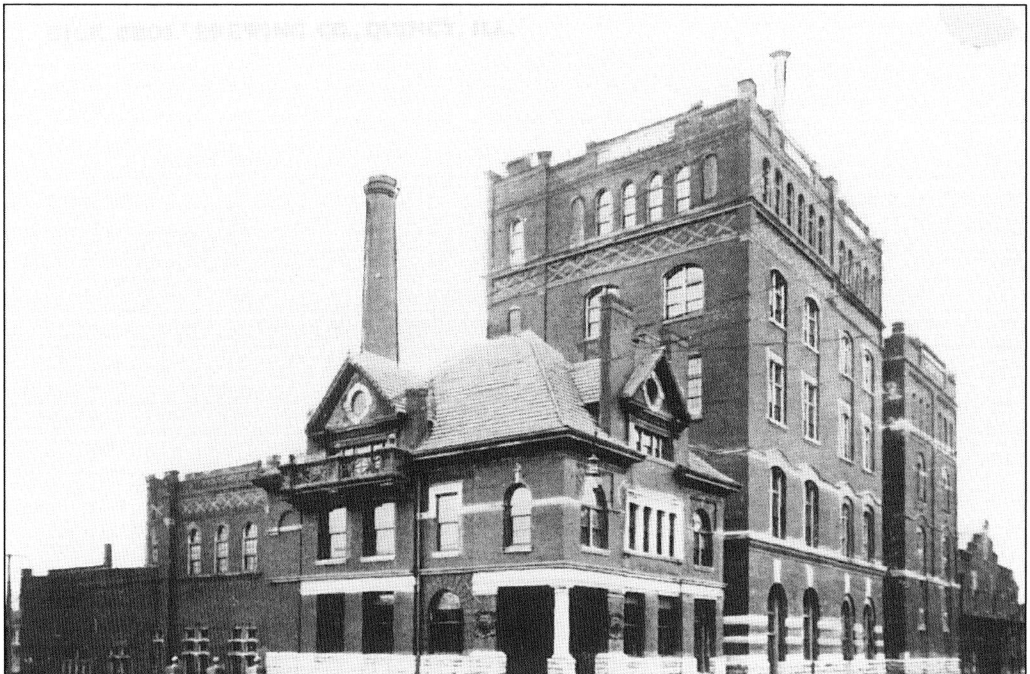

Before 1875, the operation of the brewery was almost entirely on the south side of York, at which time construction was started on the north side of York to expand the business. This picture shows the office on the corner, the brewhouse to the right, and the stock house next to it. The caverns under the original building continued to be used for some time for cooling and aging. However, with the development of refrigeration, brewing became a year-round business, and the old caverns were abandoned.

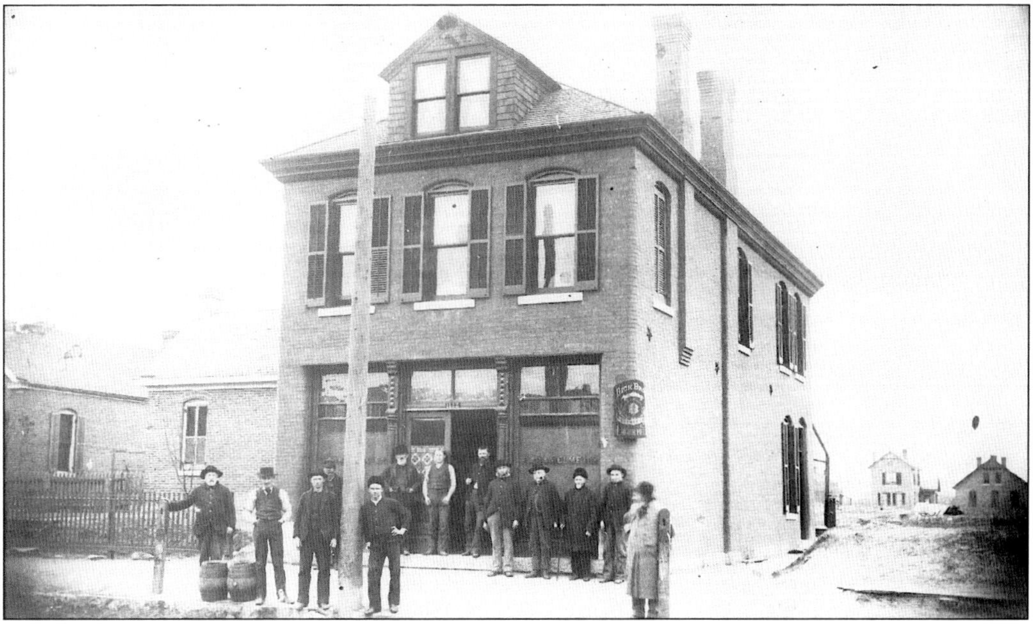

Around the turn of the century, there were about 145 saloons in Quincy, one in every block, it seemed. This photograph shows the Frank Bromelmeyer Saloon, 1112 North Tenth Street, in 1898. The Volstead Act, which became effective January 16, 1920, made it unlawful to sell distilled spirits as a beverage in any way.

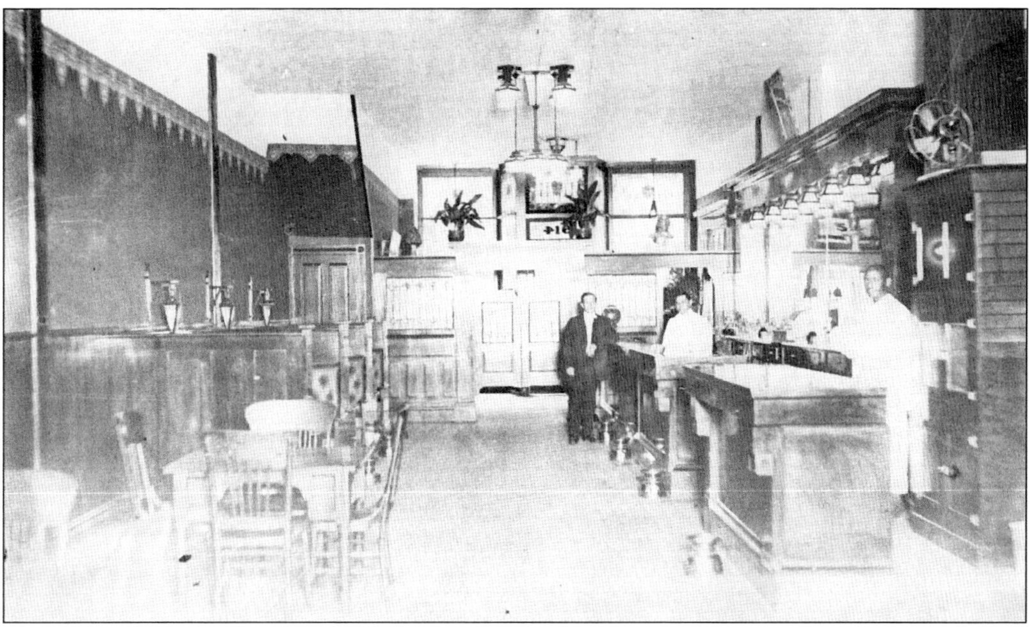

Prohibition was repealed in 1933, but many of the saloons were forced out of business during this time. Those that did manage to stay open called themselves "soft drink parlors"; after prohibition, they were called taverns. This picture of the Blue Ribbon Buffet and Saloon shows a typical saloon interior. Hiram Weber was proprietor.

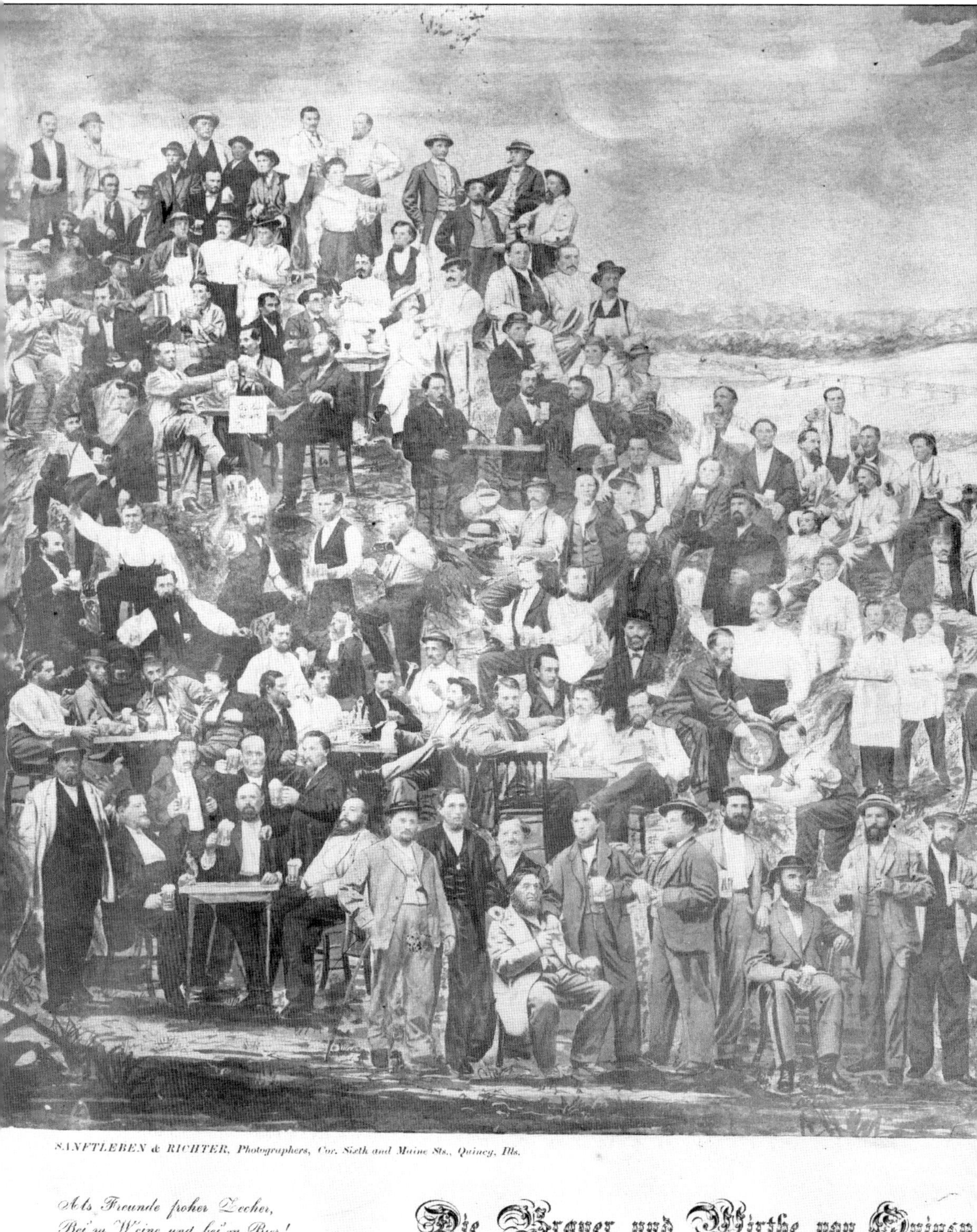
SANFTLEBEN & RICHTER, Photographers, Cor. Sixth and Maine Sts., Quincy, Ills.
Als Freunde froher Zecher,
Bei'm Weine und bei'm Bier!
Die Brauer und Wirthe von Quincy

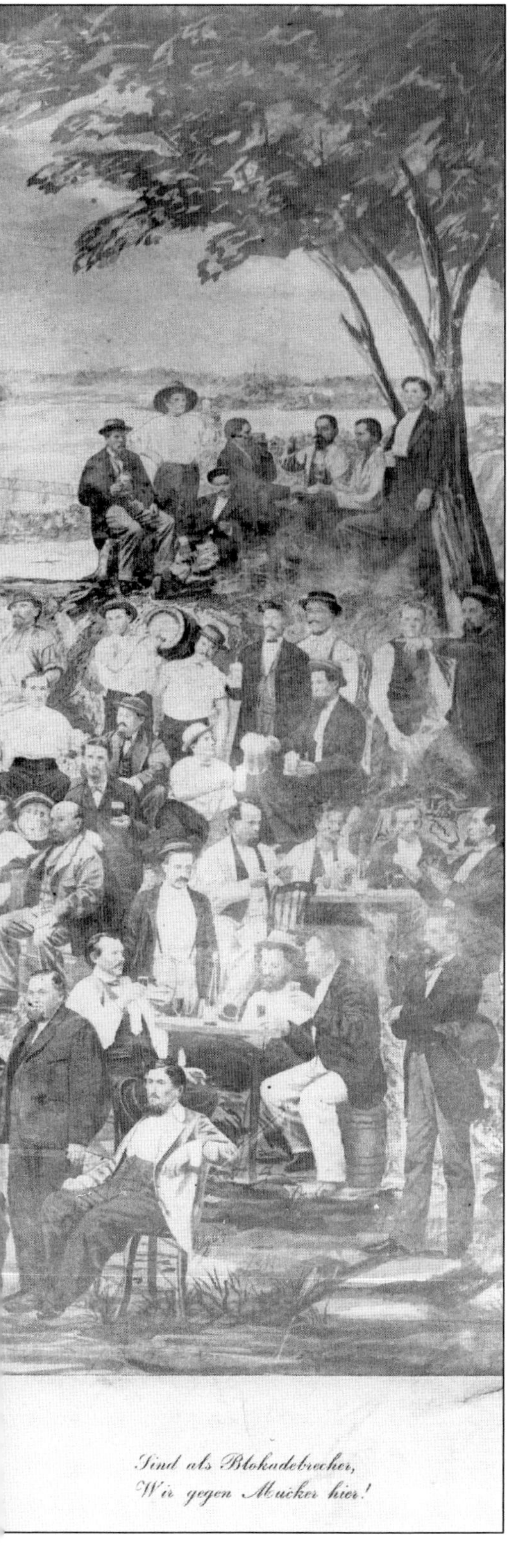

A montage of Die Brauer and Wirthe von Quincy, Illinois, shows the brewers and tavern-keepers of Quincy in 1870. The German culture has been felt in many areas of Quincy life. Many of the early German immigrants came to this country to escape military service and then wrote back to their relatives urging them and their neighbors to come to this country. Michael Mast has always been considered the first German immigrant in 1829, and the Anton Delabar family as the first German family in 1833. Delabar started the first brewery, and several others followed, including the Ruff Brewery, Wahl Brewery, Washington Brewery, Western Brewery, and, of course, the Dick Bros. Brewery. Outdoor beer gardens and many saloons opened. For years, only the German language was spoken in many homes and in church services, the latter of which gave way to one service in German and one in English. During World War I and World War II anti-German sentiment ran so high that much of the German culture was "covered over." Only in the last few years, with the establishment of the German Village Society, has Quincy really recognized the role Germans have played in the development of the city.

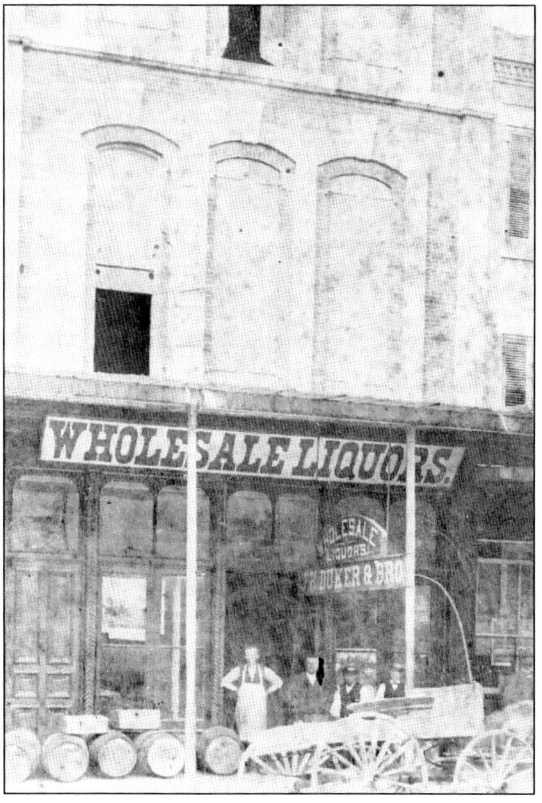

The J.H. Duker & Bros. Wholesale Liquors was typical of several Quincy wholesale liquor firms put out of business by prohibition. This photograph was taken in 1880, when they were located at 323 Hampshire Street.

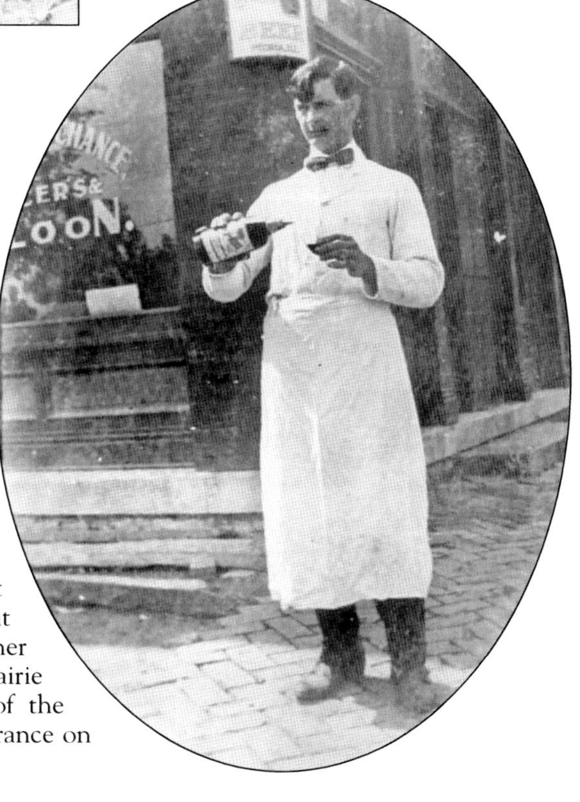

Bartender Henry Geise is shown in front of his tavern, the Last Chance Saloon, at 1141 Broadway in the 1880s. This corner had previously been the site of the Prairie House Saloon. Shortly after the turn of the century, Stroot Hardware made its appearance on this location.

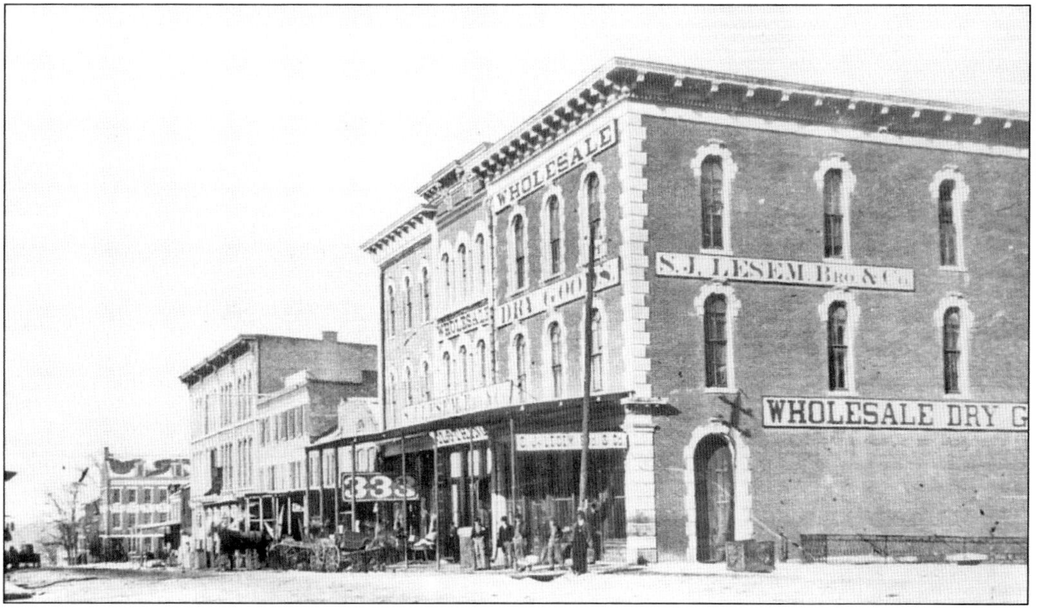

In 1856, Isaac and S.J. Lesem came to Quincy and established a dry goods business. As their business increased, they entered the wholesale field and moved into the new McFadon building, shown here, on the northwest corner of Fourth and Hampshire Streets. By 1871, they still needed more space, so they purchased the lot on the southwest corner of Third and Hampshire Streets and erected a large building that currently houses the Tiramisu Restaurant.

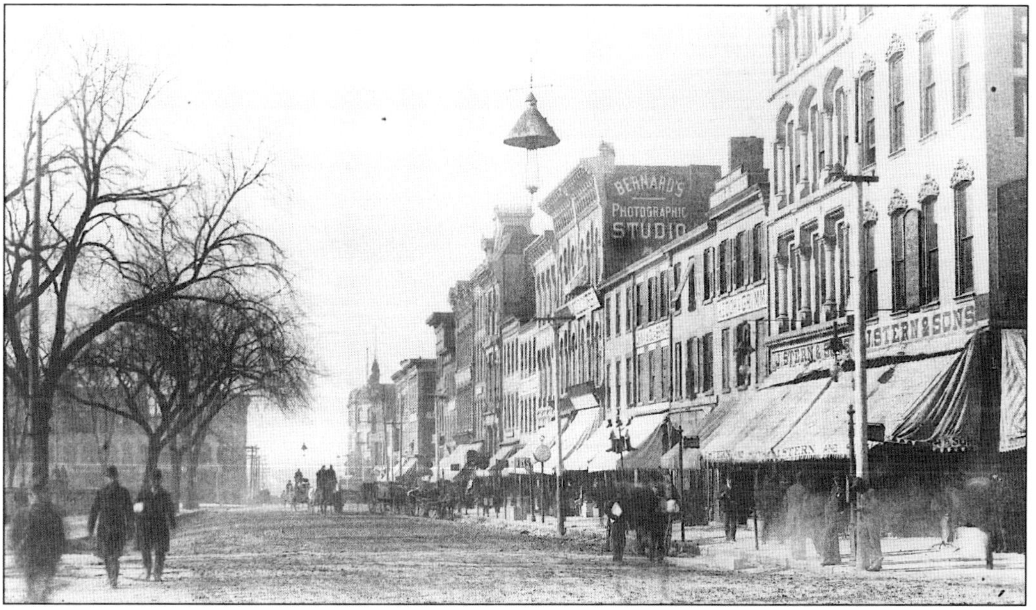

At one time Hampshire Street was a very busy commercial street. This photograph shows the north side of Hampshire Street across from Washington Park after the new arc lights were installed. J. Stern & Sons occupies the corner building. During their grand opening, they tossed 50 free overcoats from an upstairs window to the crowd in the street below.

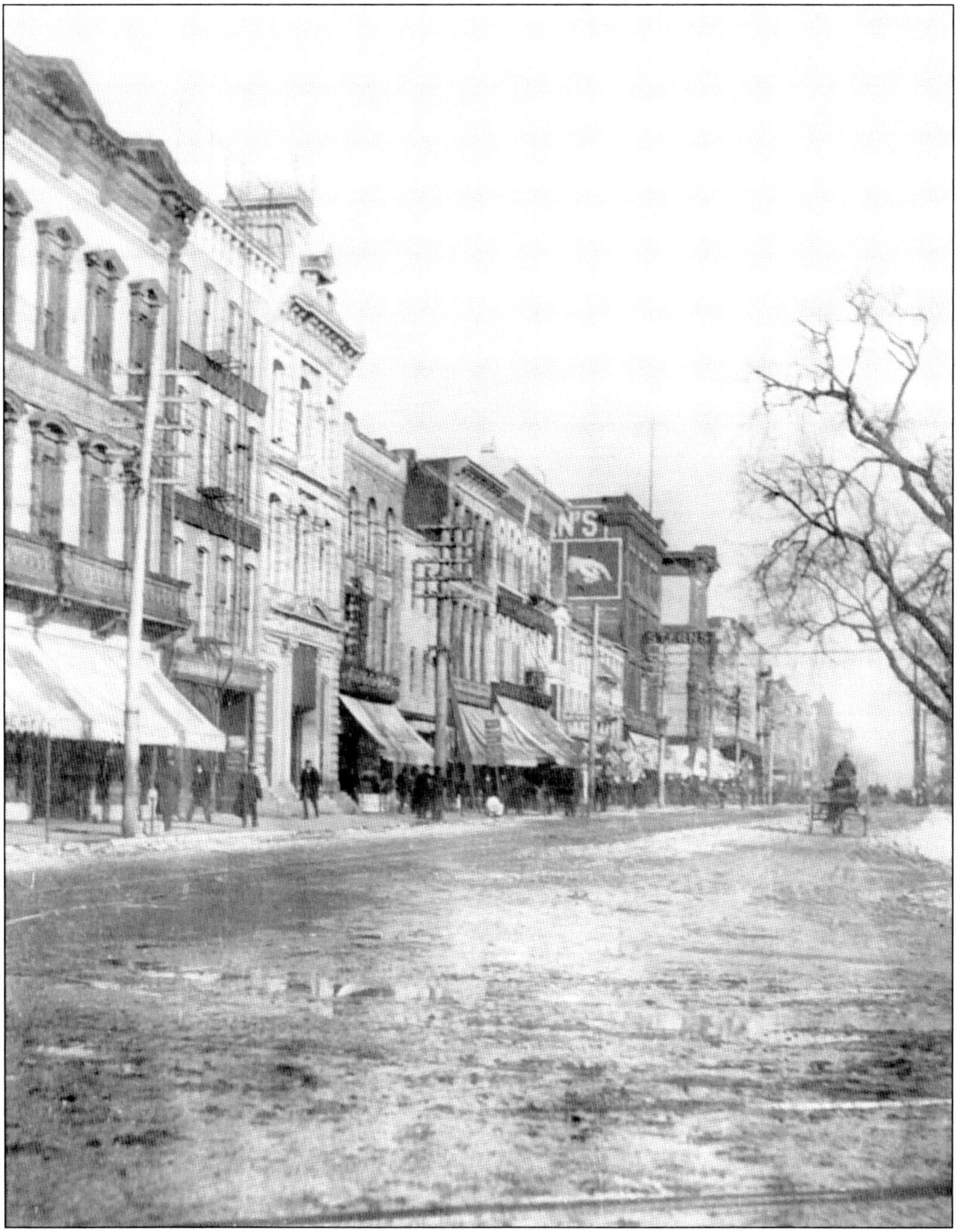

Looking east, this north side of Hampshire Street, between Fourth and Fifth Streets, shows the condition of the streets before they were paved. Ricker National Bank is in the large, three-story building, third from left. Henry F.J. Ricker conducted his first banking business at 508 Hampshire Street, but in 1876, he erected this modern bank building at 413 Hampshire Street. John McKean was the architect. Later, Harvey Chatten designed the addition, and the building size doubled to occupy 413-415 Hampshire Street.

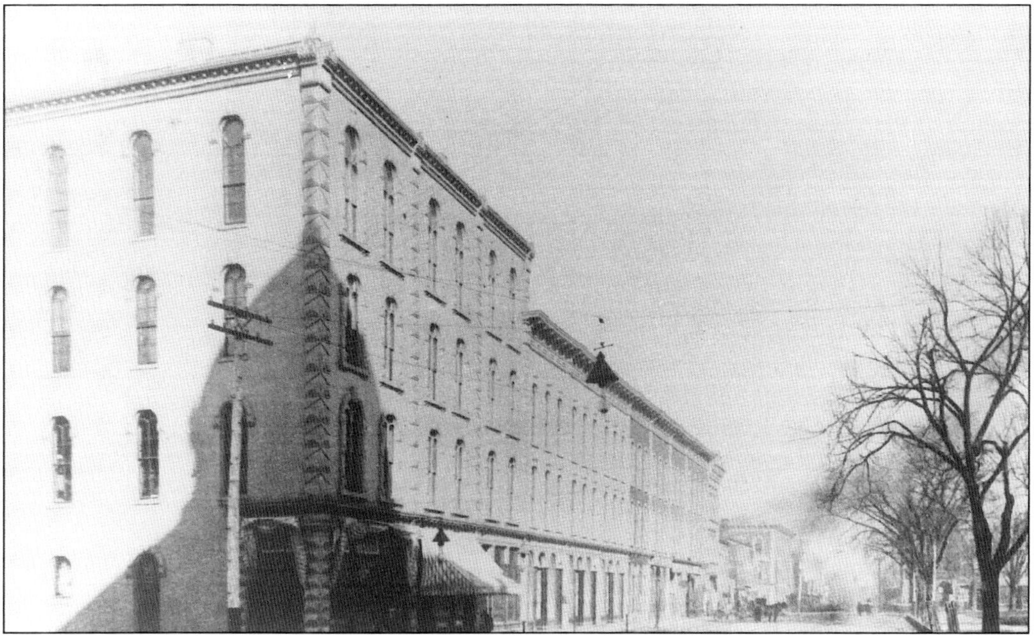

The Tillson building, on the left, was constructed by Robert Tillson in 1867 on the northwest corner of Fourth and Maine Streets. It was later renamed the Newcomb building for Richard F. Newcomb, who had invested in the structure. It had a large ballroom on the third floor and also housed the Union Business College, as well as telephone and telegraph offices at one time. It was razed in 1929 to make way for the Hotel Lincoln-Douglas, which also had a ballroom.

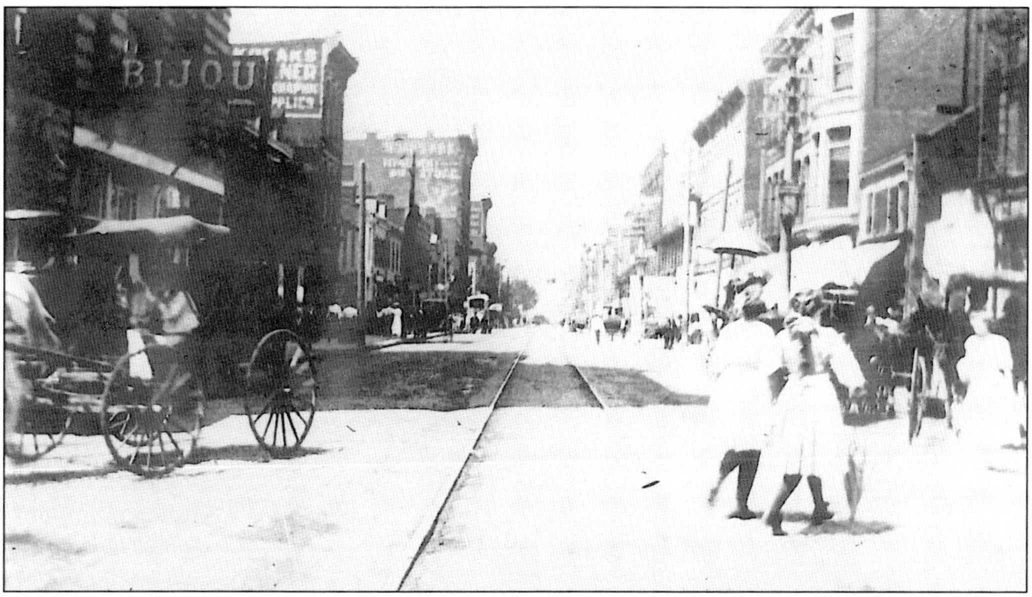

This view looks west on Hampshire Street between Seventh and Sixth Streets. The Bijou Theater, to the left behind the buggy, opened January 16, 1905. Many well-known vaudeville figures played here, including the four Marx Brothers, as well as local talent, such as Anna Mae Liebig Strauss, singer of illustrated song slides.

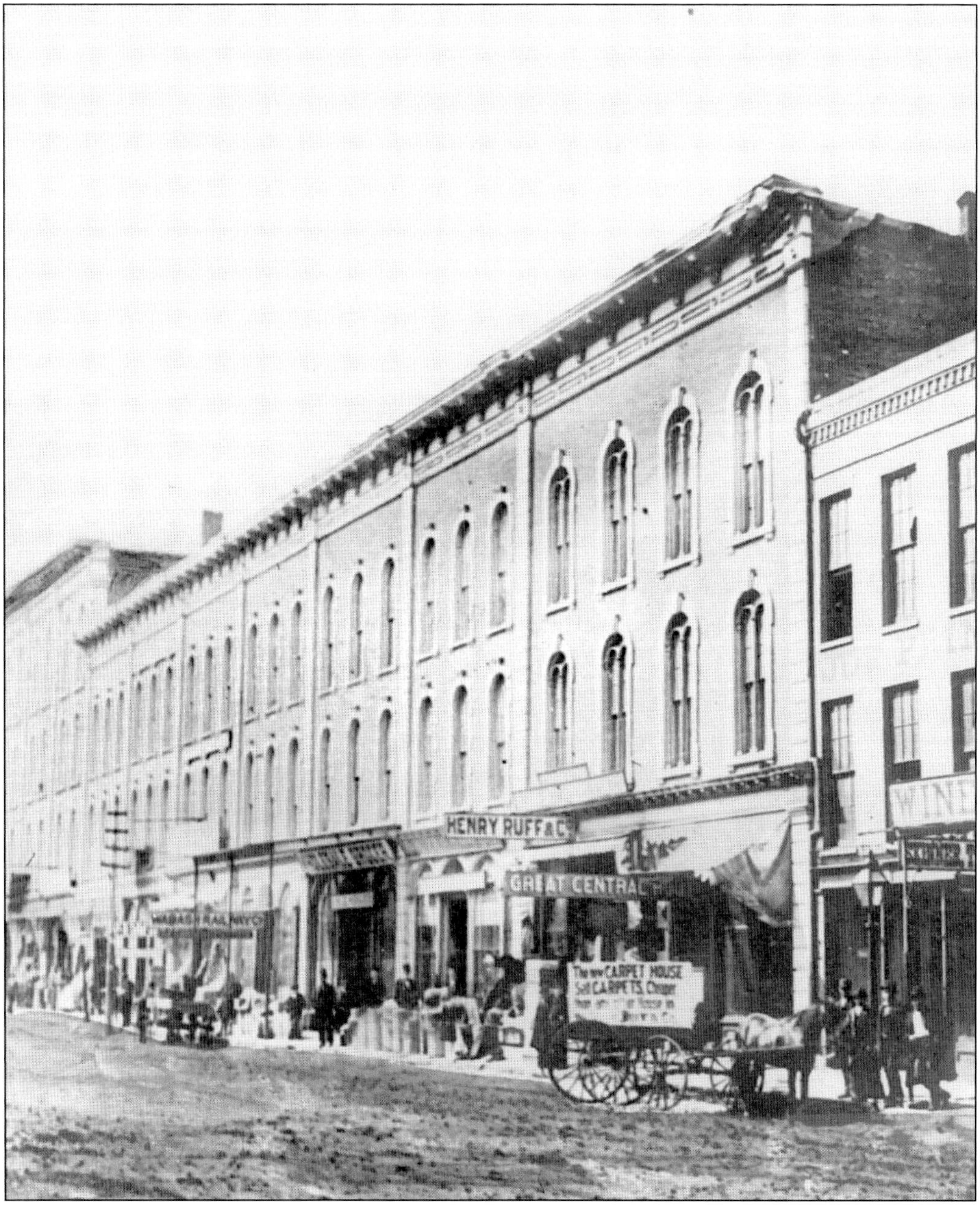

Again, note the condition of the streets in this view of Fourth Street between Maine and Hampshire Streets. The Henry Ruff & Co. store may be seen as well as their delivery wagon. Henry Ruff was the oldest son of Caspar Ruff, who owned the original Washington Brewery at the southeast corner of Sixth and State Streets in the 1840s, and later a brewery at Twelfth and Adams Streets. Henry assisted his father in the brewery until he opened a dry goods store at Sixth and Maine Streets, later moving to North Fourth Street, where he also sold carpets.

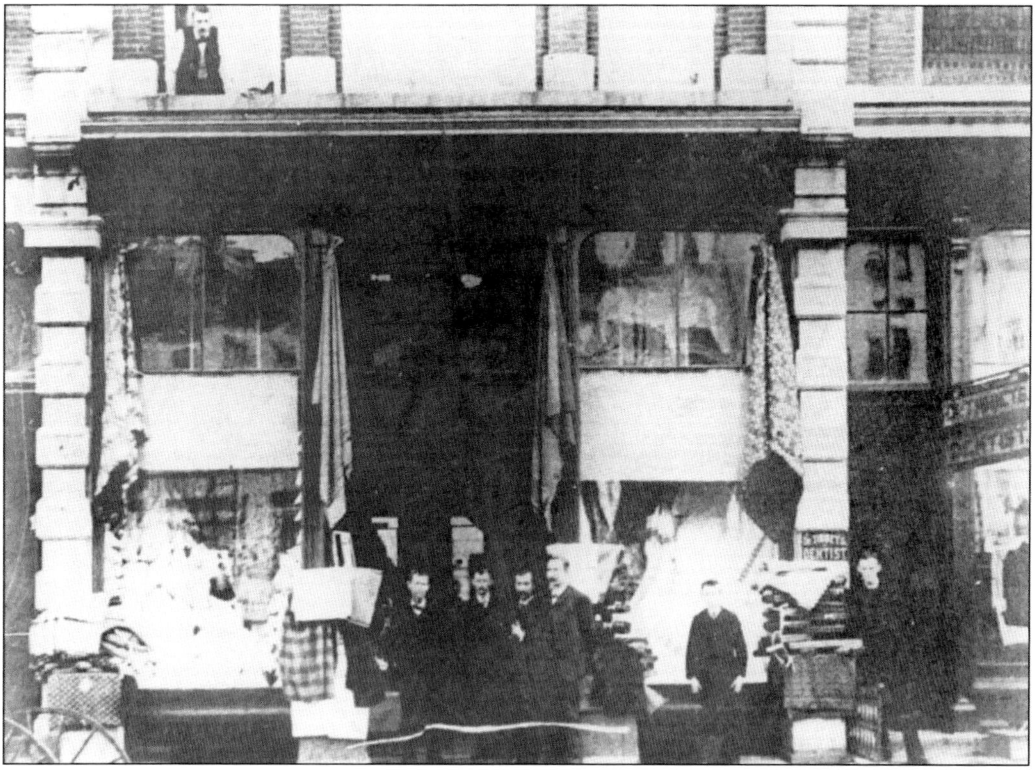

Employees are shown in front of the Halbach-Schroeder Store, located at 508 Maine, c. 1870s. Frederick Halbach and Henry Schroeder had purchased Julius Kespohl's dry goods business in 1871, when Kespohl went to Europe. They were first located at 508 Maine Street in the Benneson building and later enlarged to 510 Maine Street. Soon there were 14 employees, and by 1918, with larger quarters needed, a new store building was erected at 500 Maine Street. Known as the "Big White Store," the structure is still standing today.

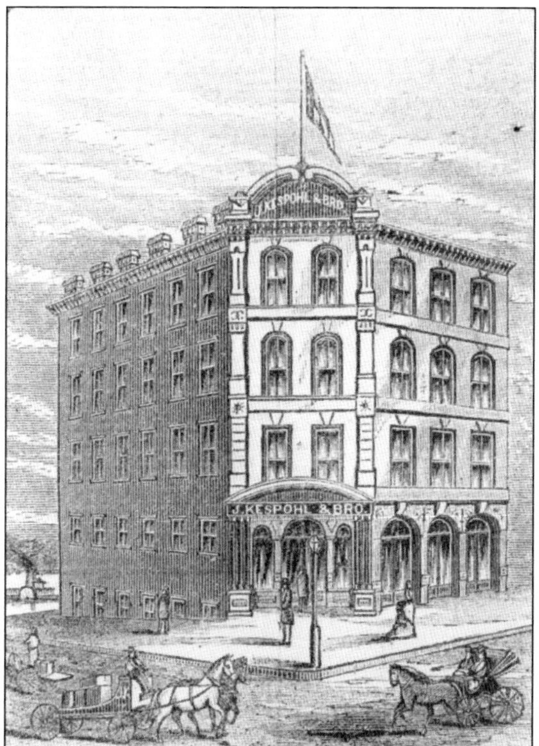

Upon returning to Quincy from a European trip, Julius Kespohl erected this large building on the northwest corner of Third and Hampshire Streets in 1875 for his dry goods business. Robert Bunce was the architect. For five years, J. Kespohl and Bros., Wholesale and Retail Dealers in Dry Goods, Fancy Goods, and Notions, carried on an immense business; however, in 1880, Kespohl sold out and moved to Lincoln, Nebraska.

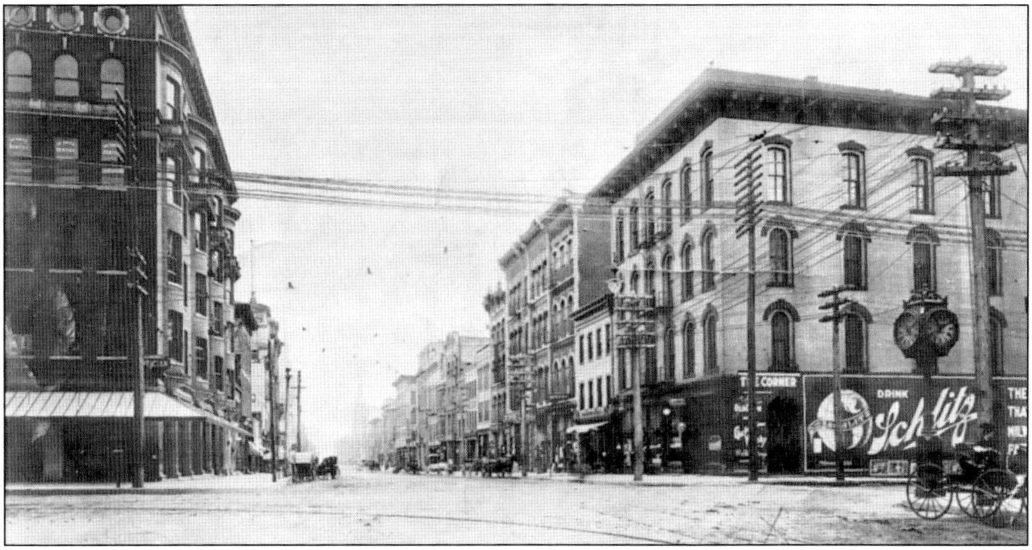

This view looks east from Fifth Street, *c.* 1898. Seen on Maine Street are the following: the Corner Saloon at 500, Miller & Arthur Drugs at 502, George Mersman at 504, Soebbing Bros. (hatters) at 506, Halbach-Schroeder at 508, Tenk Hardware at 512, Crooks & Cox (milliners) at 514, F.T. Hill (carpets) at 516, and August Basse, Jewelry, at 518.

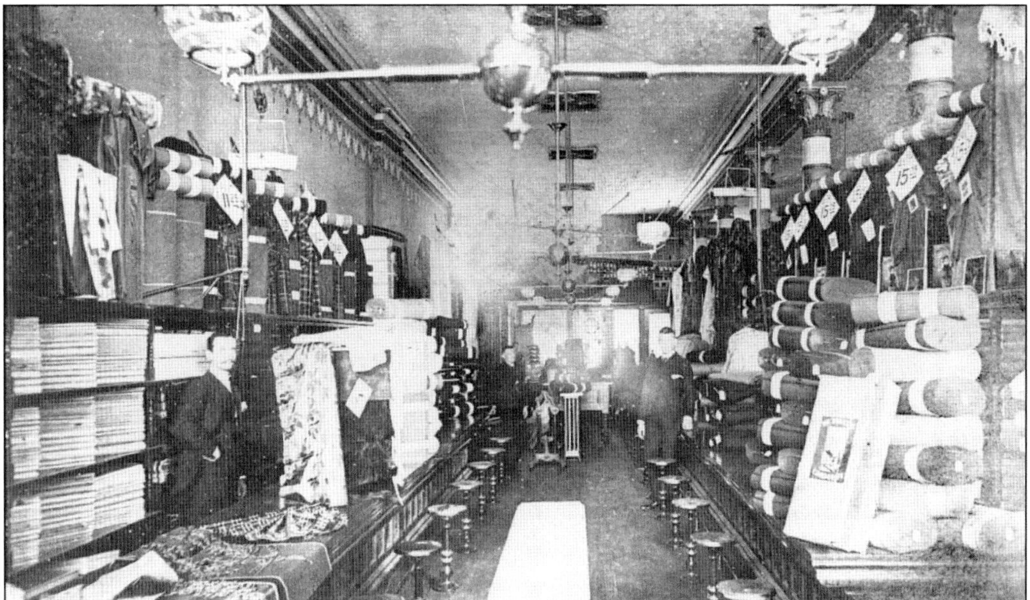

This view shows the interior of the Kespohl store at Third and Hampshire Streets. After Kespohl returned to Quincy from Nebraska, he again set up a store in the Tillson building, located at Fourth and Maine Streets. Then he moved to the Rogers building on the southeast corner of Sixth and Hampshire Streets in 1888. In 1899, he formed a partnership with his father-in-law, Otto Mohrenstecher. This firm, Kespohl-Mohrenstecher, would occupy the southeast corner of Sixth and Maine Streets for many years, until Block and Kuhl Company of Peoria came to that location in Quincy.

By 1896, the Jansen Furniture Co. was at 434 Maine Street. Frederick Jansen first started the business on Maine Street between Sixth and Seventh Streets, later moving to Sixth and Spring Streets. They later opened a store on North Fifth Street.

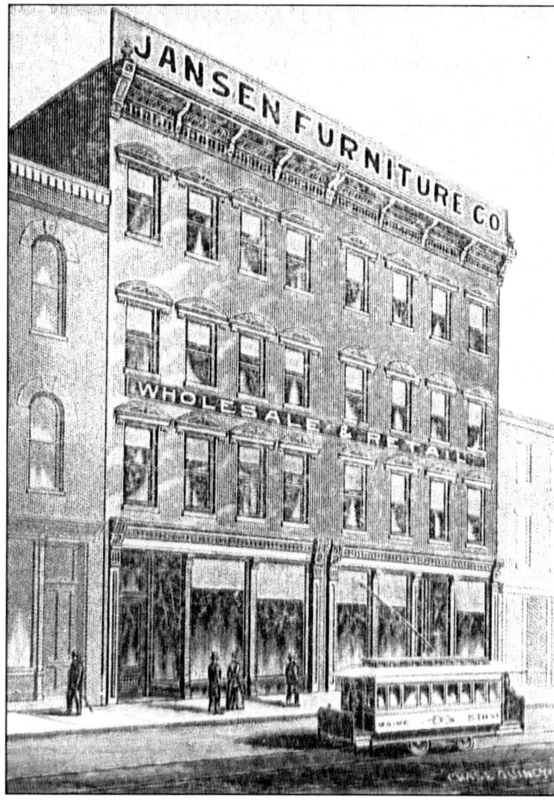

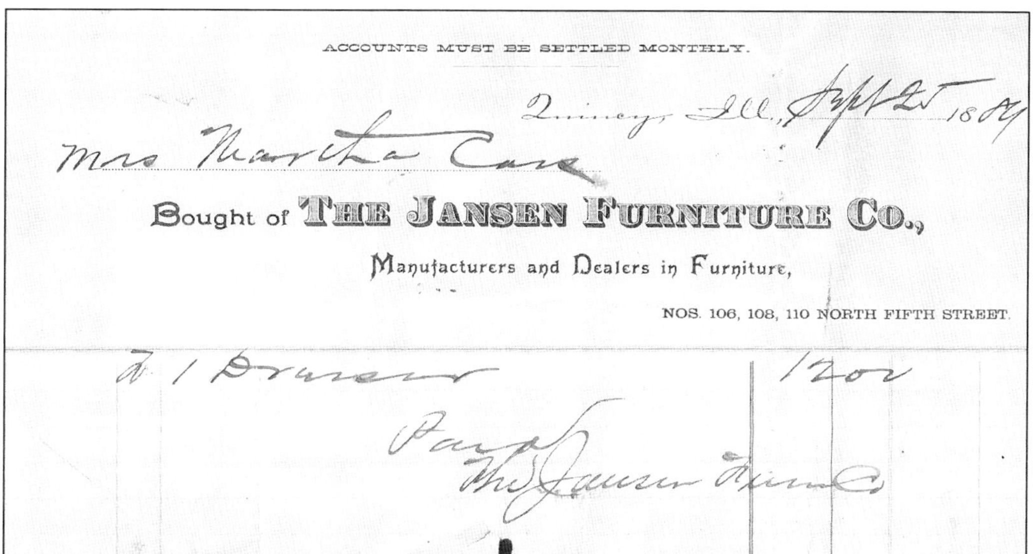

ACCOUNTS MUST BE SETTLED MONTHLY.

Quincy, Ill., Sept 25 1889

Mrs Martha Cass

Bought of THE JANSEN FURNITURE CO.,

Manufacturers and Dealers in Furniture,

NOS. 106, 108, 110 NORTH FIFTH STREET.

To 1 Dresser | 12.00

Paid
The Jansen Furn Co

Mrs. Martha Cass's receipt, dated September 25, 1889, indicates that she bought a dresser for $12 from the Jansen Furniture Co., which was located at 106-08-10 North Fifth Street. Upon the older Jansen's death, Frederick Jansen Jr. expanded the business, opened a new factory on South Front Street near Delaware, and moved the retail store to 434 Maine Street. Shortly after the turn of the century, Jansen Furniture was located at 521 Maine Street.

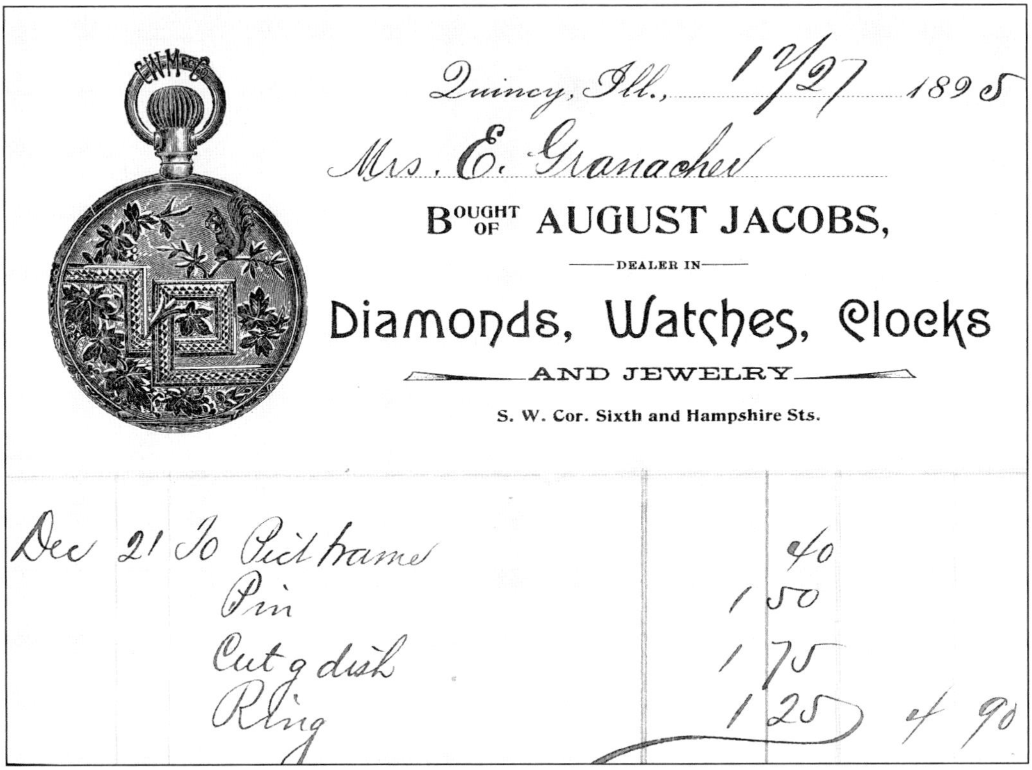

Quincy, Ill., 12/27 1895

Mrs. E. Granacher

Bought of AUGUST JACOBS,

DEALER IN

Diamonds, Watches, Clocks

AND JEWELRY

S. W. Cor. Sixth and Hampshire Sts.

Dec 21 To Pict frame	40	
Pin	1 50	
Cut g dish	1 75	
Ring	1 25	4 90

The Jacobs Jewelry Store was located on the southwest corner of Sixth and Hampshire Streets from the 1880s until c. 1960. On December 27, 1895, they sold Mrs. E. Granacher a picture frame, pin, cut glass dish, and ring, all for the sum of $4.90. There was no sales tax!

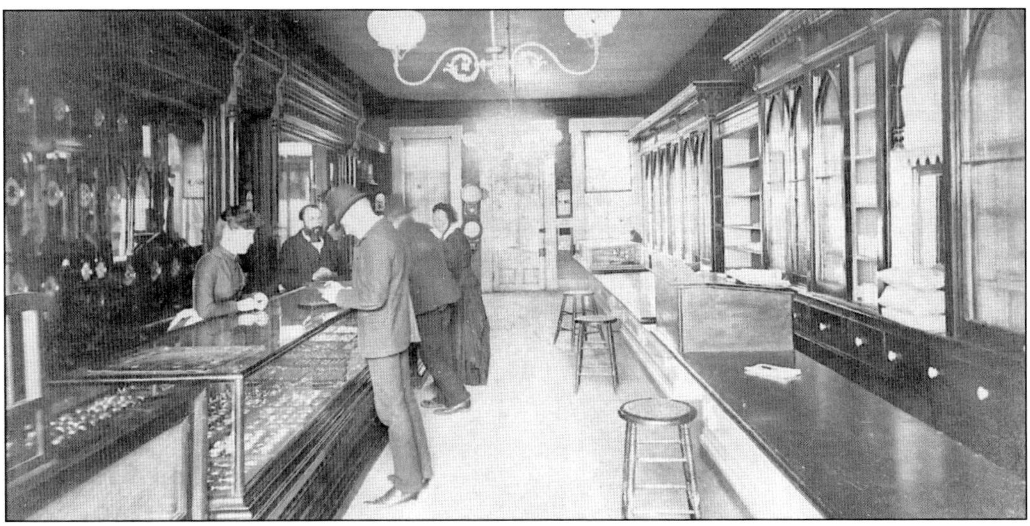

The identity of this jewelry store is unknown; however, as early as 1857, there were four jewelry stores in Quincy. One of the oldest was August Basse on Maine between Fifth and Sixth Streets. Other longtime jewelers have been Mathias Huffman; Trask and Plain; O'Dell's; Werner VonBurg; Hokamp-Keis; Likes; Sturhahns, Dame and Hurdle; and more recently Thomas Mating.

This image shows the chair factory of Herman Kalmer at 1252 Broadway. He made and repaired cane bottom chairs in the front part of the building. The family lived in the rear. At one time, he sold groceries and liquor in the front of the building as well. Although the numbering is not the same, it is believed that it is this building that houses the Dr. A.O. Mathew office today.

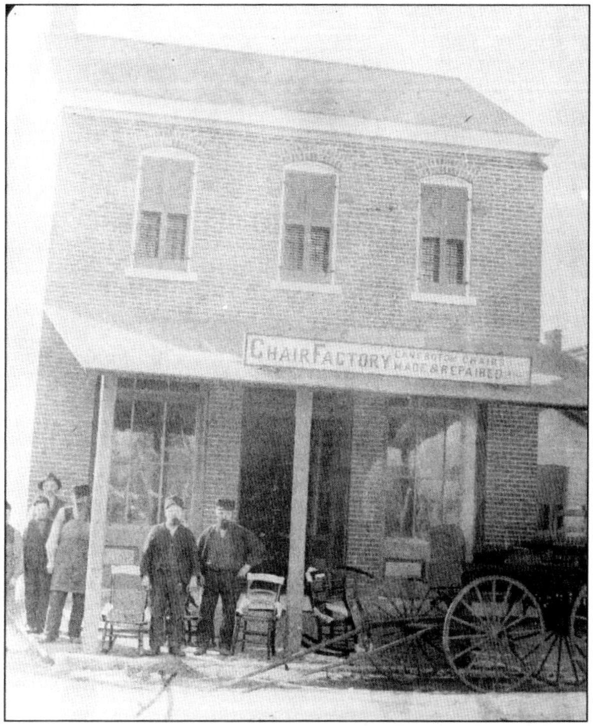

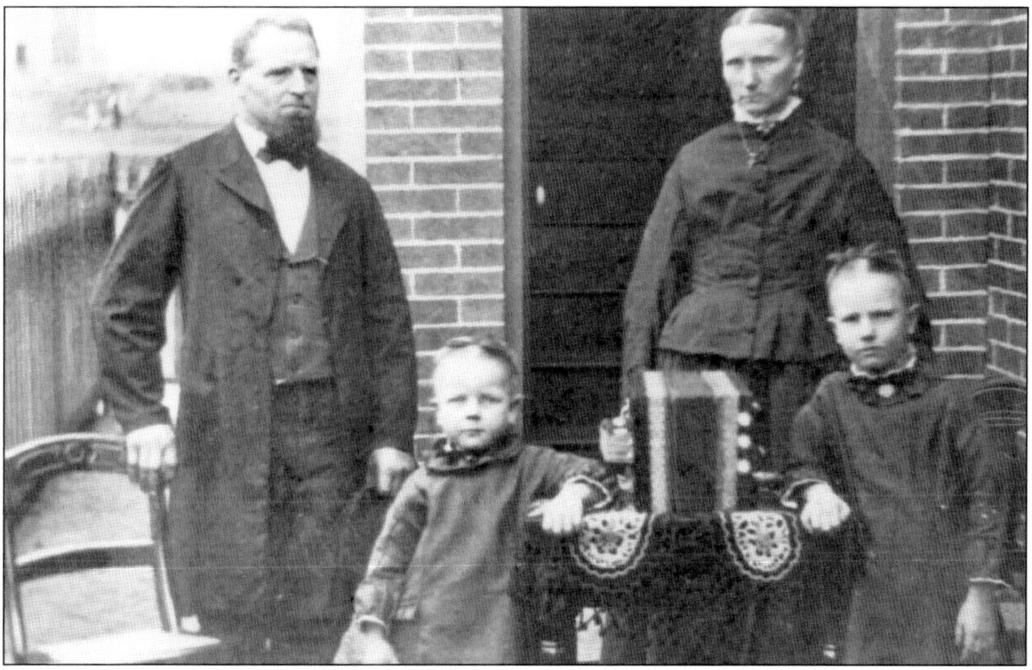

Herman Kalmer, born in Germany, came to the United States in 1864. He married Anna Lugering and had two children, Mary and Frances. The family were members of the Catholic Church, which was typical of many German-American citizens. As a newspaper article said of him, "he is most enterprising, possessed of energy, perseverance, good business ability, and generous liberality."

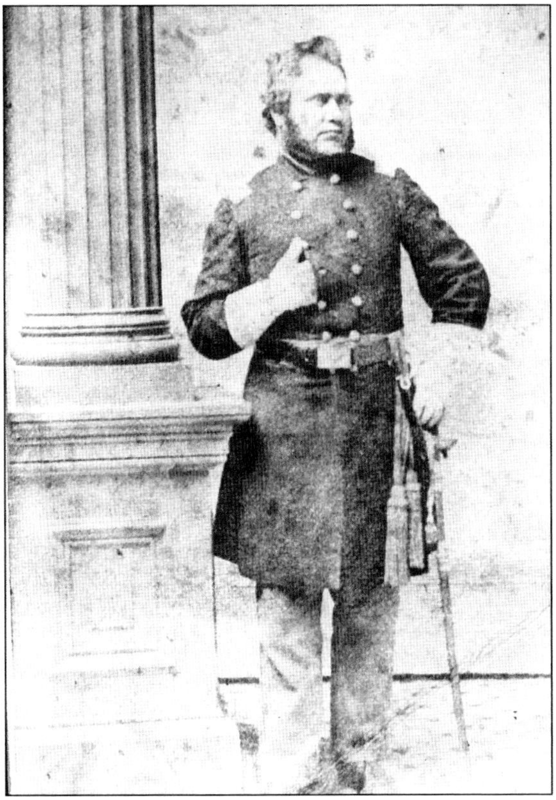

Col. Kiler K. Jones came to Quincy from Wisconsin in 1857. At one time, he was editor of the *Quincy Whig and Republican*. During the Civil War, he chose to enlist in a Wisconsin regiment and received a commission as lieutenant colonel in a Scandinavian brigade.

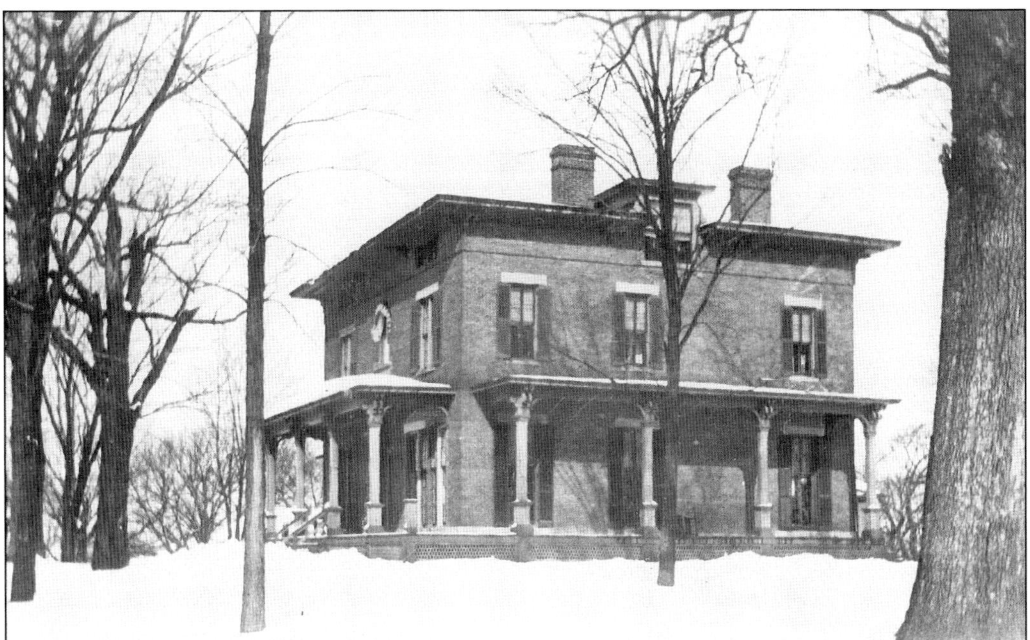

This home of Colonel Jones, located at 2335 North Twelfth Street, was known as the "Pines." The home later belonged to Al Hutmacher, as well as the Otto Langhanke family, whose daughter became the actress, Mary Astor.

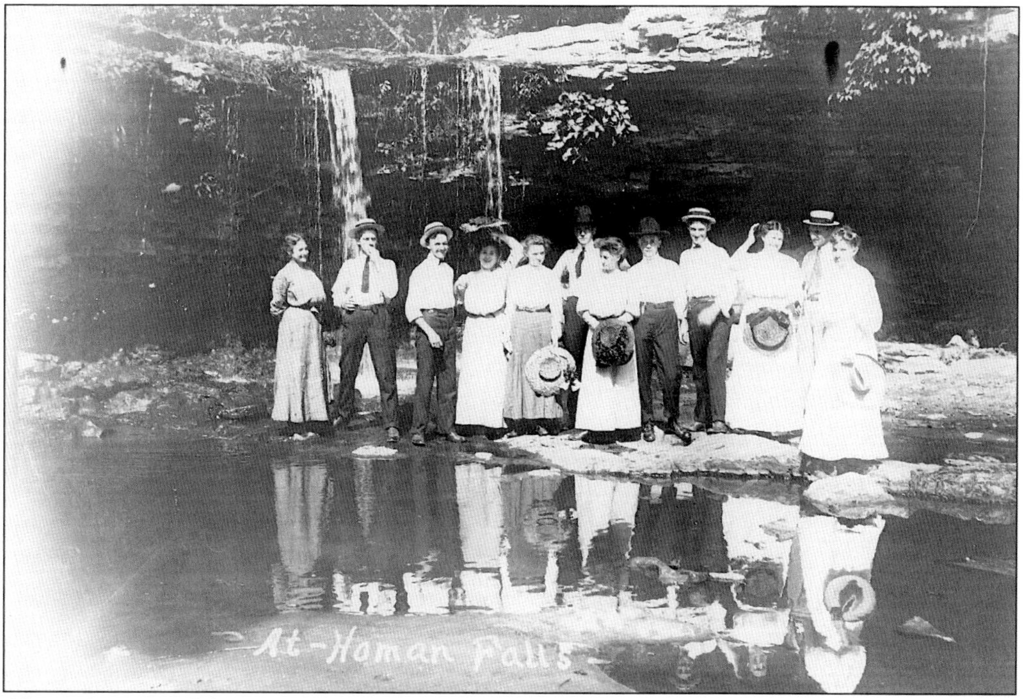

About the turn of the century, Homan Falls was a popular picnic area because of the beautiful scenery, which included trees, springs, and waterfalls. In 1916, a group of Quincy men purchased this area from Mrs. B.F. Homan. Today, it is a part of the Spring Lake Country Club. Additional land was purchased later, and the golf course was added in 1923.

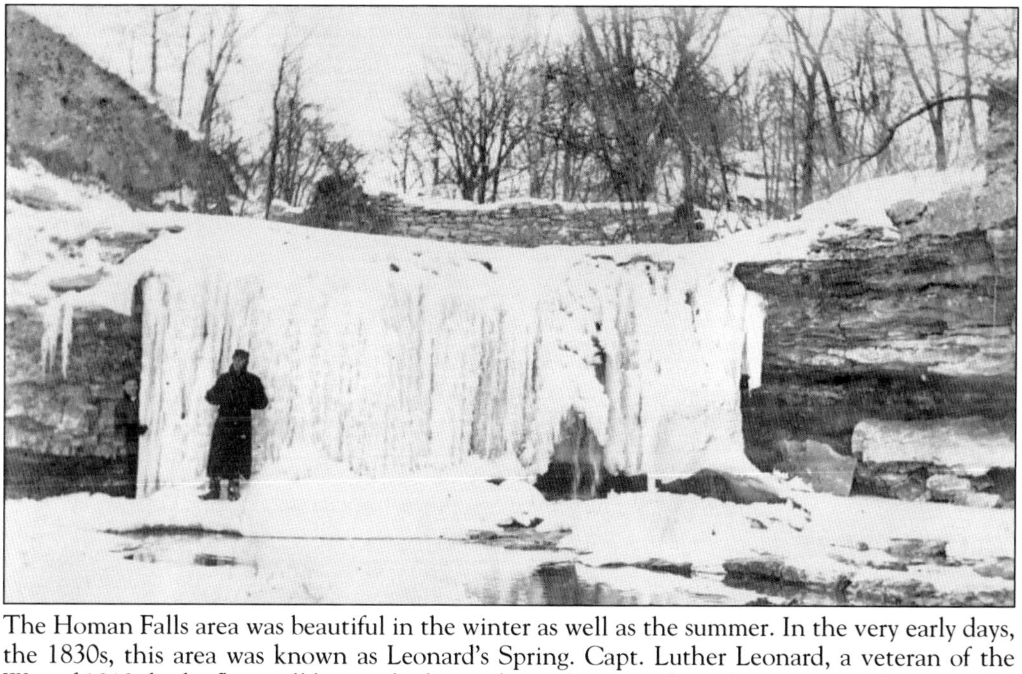

The Homan Falls area was beautiful in the winter as well as the summer. In the very early days, the 1830s, this area was known as Leonard's Spring. Capt. Luther Leonard, a veteran of the War of 1812, had a flourmill here, which was driven by water from the springs in the area. The property was sold to the Homans in 1840.

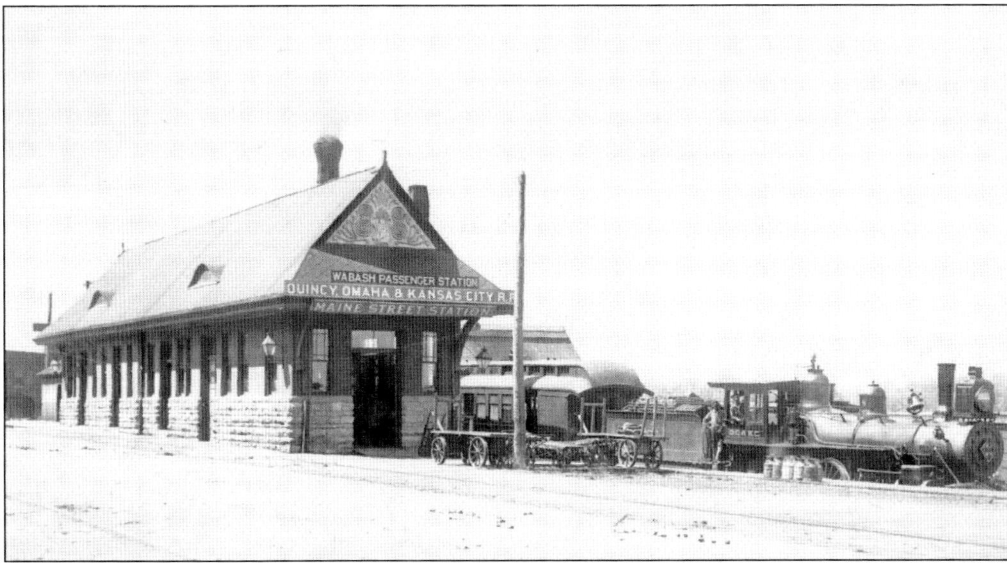

Several railroads have served Quincy over the years. The Quincy, Omaha, and Kansas City railroad station, seen here on Front Street between Maine and Jersey Streets, was built in 1888. It was razed in 1912. When the "O.K." closed its facilities, the Wabash took over. A passenger depot and freight office was built in 1903 on the southeast corner of Sixth and York Streets. It was abandoned in 1934.

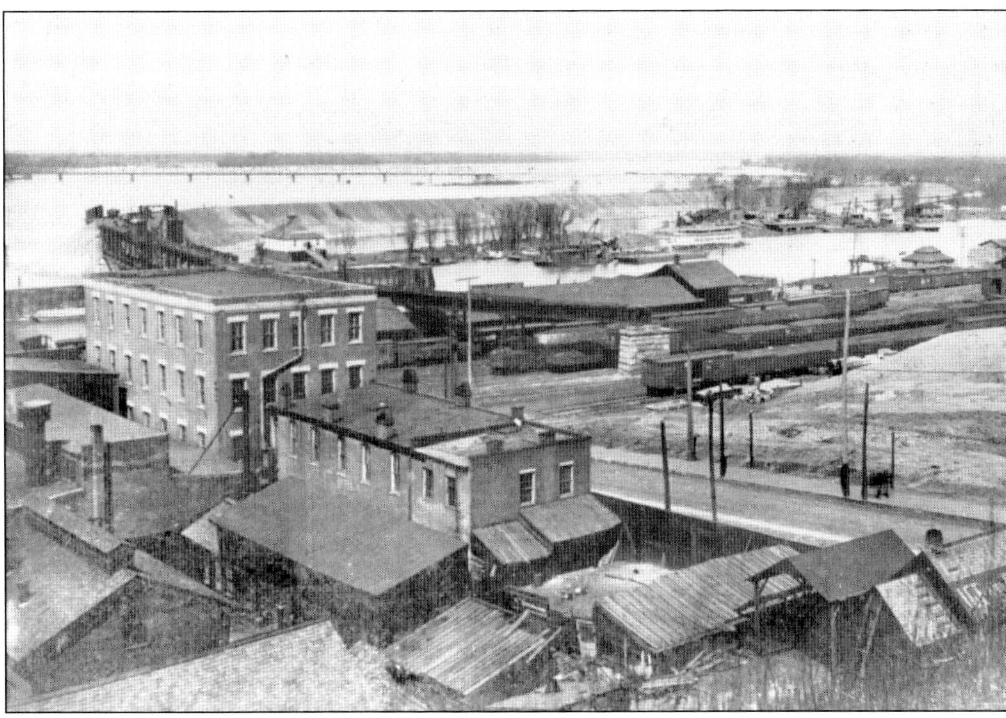

This picture shows the bridge across the bay and viaduct over Front Street, which was built to allow trains to come into Quincy from the west and go north to the CB&Q RR depot at Second and Oak Streets. Both the new bridge and new depot opened July 31, 1899. The large building on the left was the home of the Knittel Showcase Works, which manufactured store fixtures.

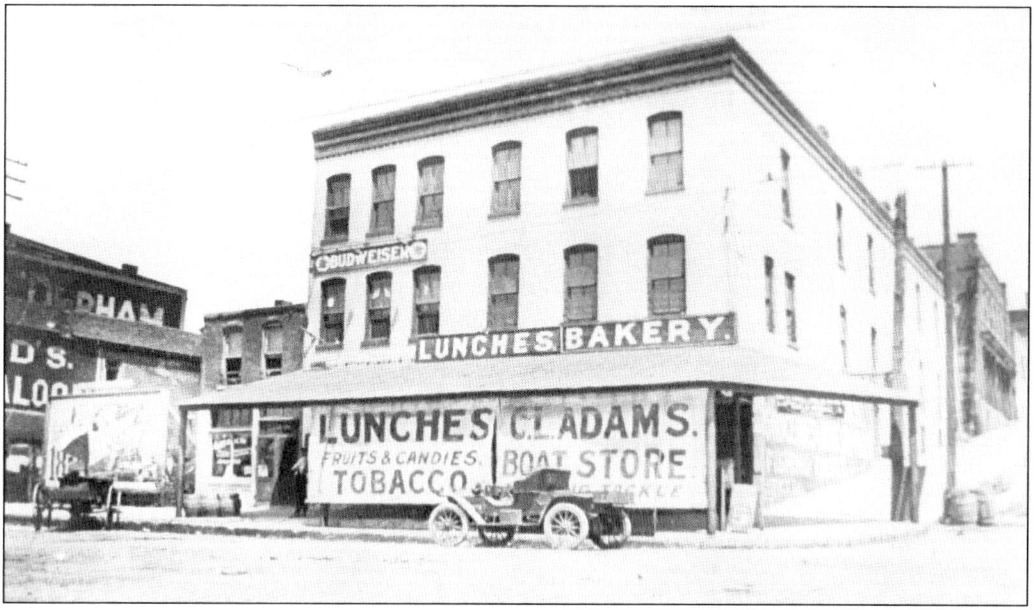

The CL "Clat" Adams Boat Store, located at the northeast corner of Front and Hampshire Streets, was a landmark on the levee (riverfront), or North Water Street, as Clat called it. A river man could buy boat supplies or a ham sandwich for 5¢ for many years. Clat Adams was the dean of rivermen, known by pilots, engineers, fishermen, and sportsmen, up and down the river, from St. Paul to New Orleans.

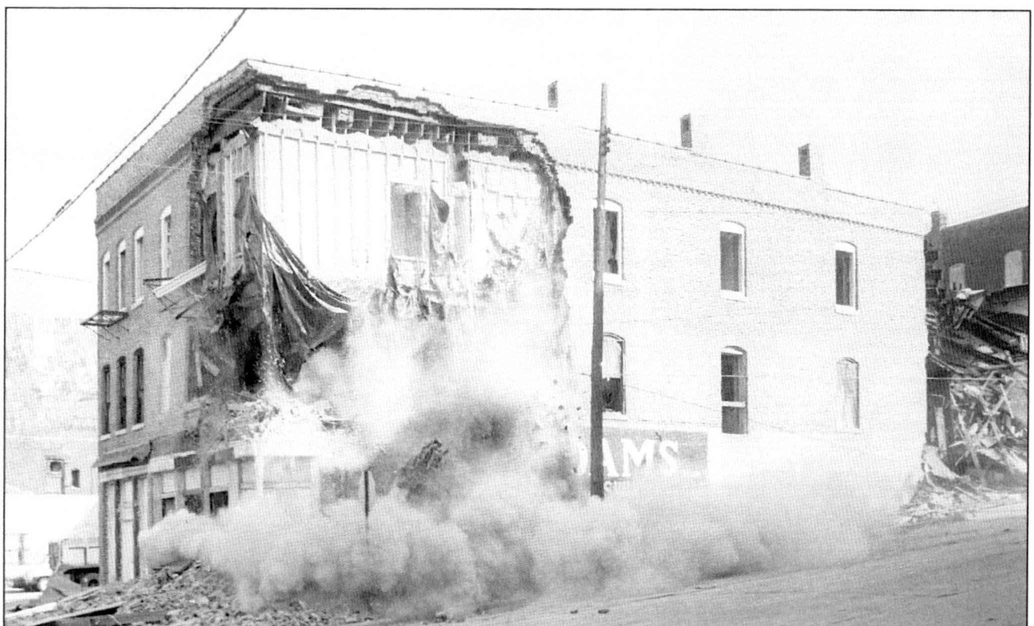

The Clat Adams store terminated business with a closeout sale in late summer of 1950. Clatworthy "Clat" Adams had died in November 1949. Thus ended an era when the St. Louis and St. Paul packets, and later the Streckfus excursion steamers, would tie up at the Diamond Jo boathouse as the rivermen would visit the store. By November 1978, the building had been deemed unsafe, and the landmark was demolished.

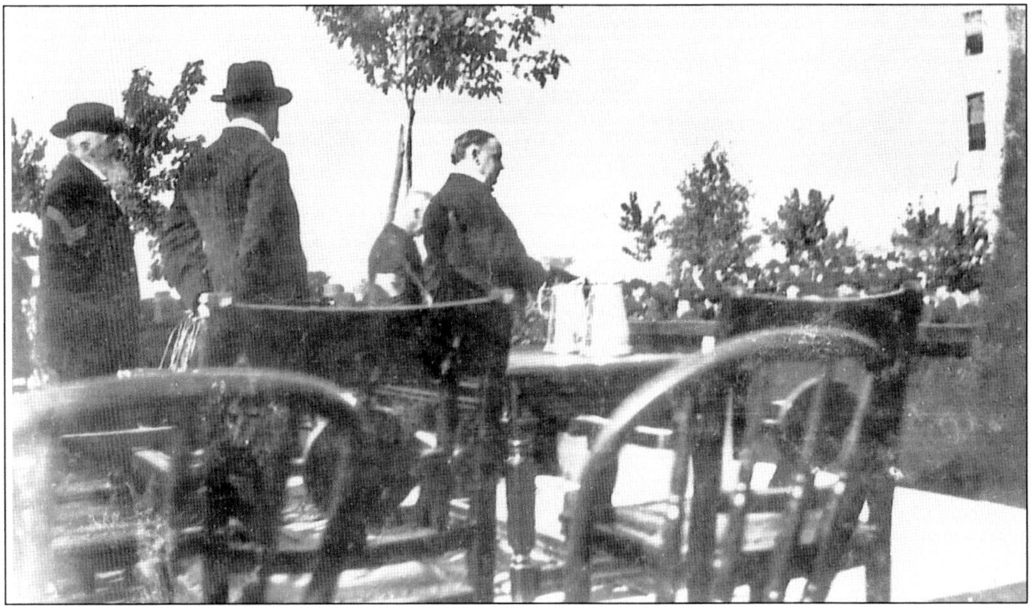

President William McKinley was a guest of the city on October 6, 1899. The Presidential Special pulled into the railway station at the Soldiers and Sailors Home at 7:59 a.m. There was a procession through the grounds to the reviewing stand, with the cannon at the home sounding out its presidential salute of 21 guns. Over 1,500 veterans passed in review before the President.

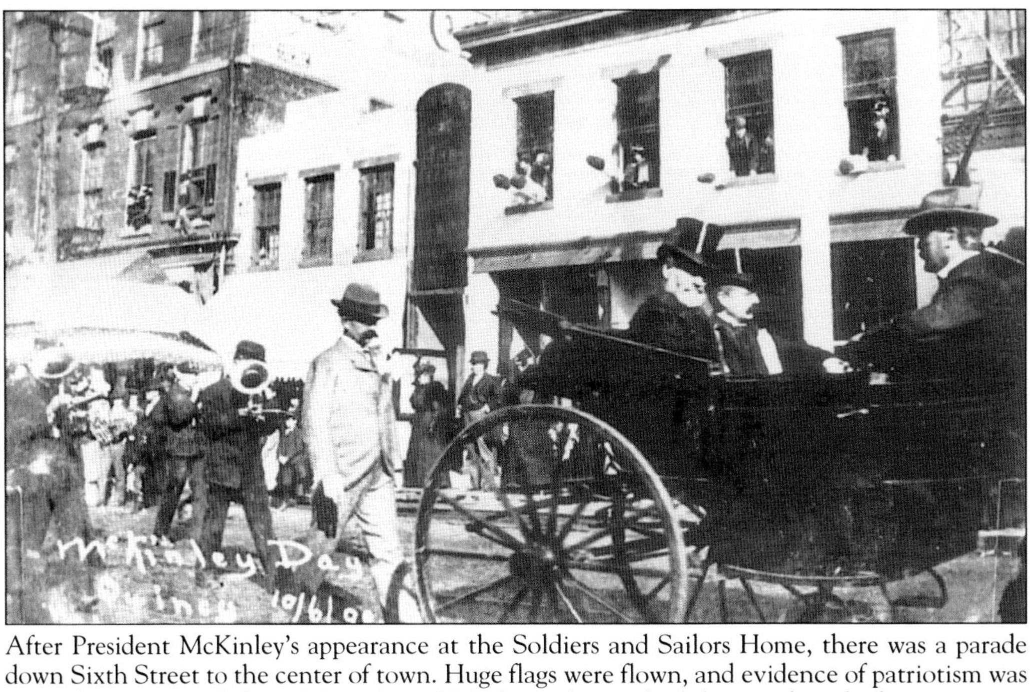

After President McKinley's appearance at the Soldiers and Sailors Home, there was a parade down Sixth Street to the center of town. Huge flags were flown, and evidence of patriotism was in profusion. It was believed that about 20,000 people watched the parade or had some part in it. Several bands escorted the President, who was seated in an open barouche.

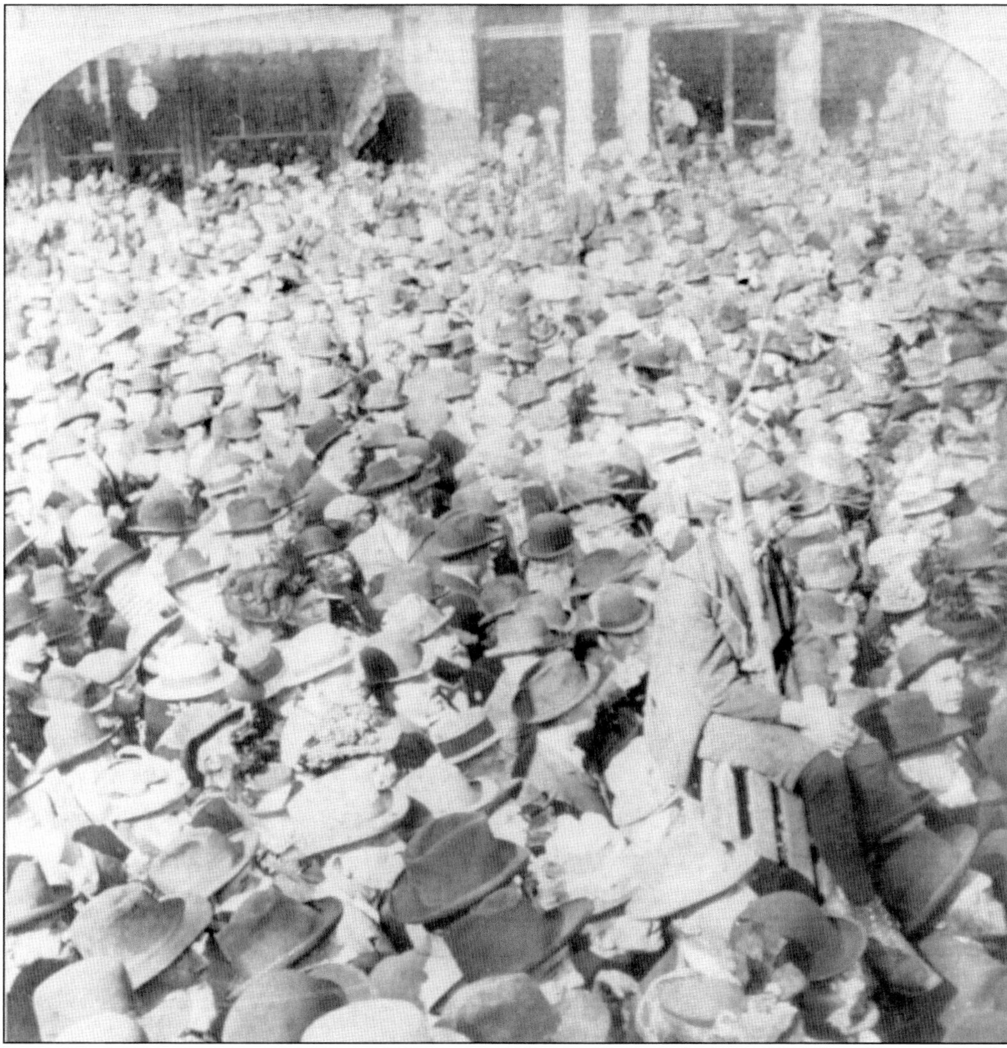

President McKinley faced this vast throng in Washington Park. After short speeches by several dignitaries, including Secretary of State Hay and Secretary of War Root, McKinley spoke for 3 minutes. Note the boy in the foreground. He has a good vantage point, even though it may have been a bit uncomfortable sitting atop the protective fencing around the tree.

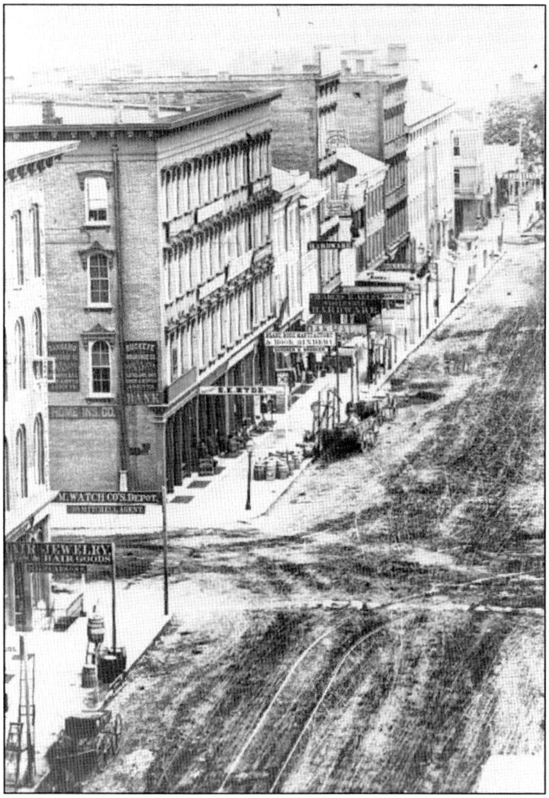

This view shows Fifth and Maine Streets, c. 1869. The Merchants and Farmers National Bank was located at 436 Maine Street. Lorenzo Bull was president and C.H. Bull was cashier. The Charles Allen Hardware Store was at 424 Maine Street. Nathan G. Pearsons, longtime manufacturer and dealer in human hair goods, hair jewelry, wigs, switches, curls, and hairdressing, was located at 500 Maine Street.

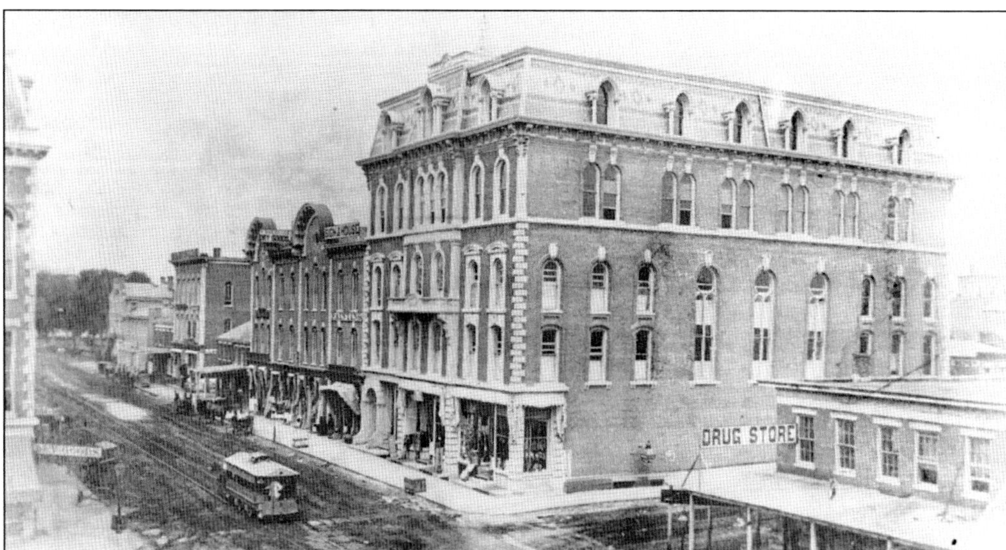

For many years, the building on the northeast corner of Sixth and Maine Streets housed a drugstore. The first drugstore in this building was owned and operated by Charles Haxel. It later became Thienemann and Haxel. After the drugstore occupancy, it housed saloons for several years until December of 1927, when Walgreen Drug Store opened on this corner. They continued in this location until 1962, when they moved across the street to 600 Maine. The opera house building is on the northwest corner of the intersection.

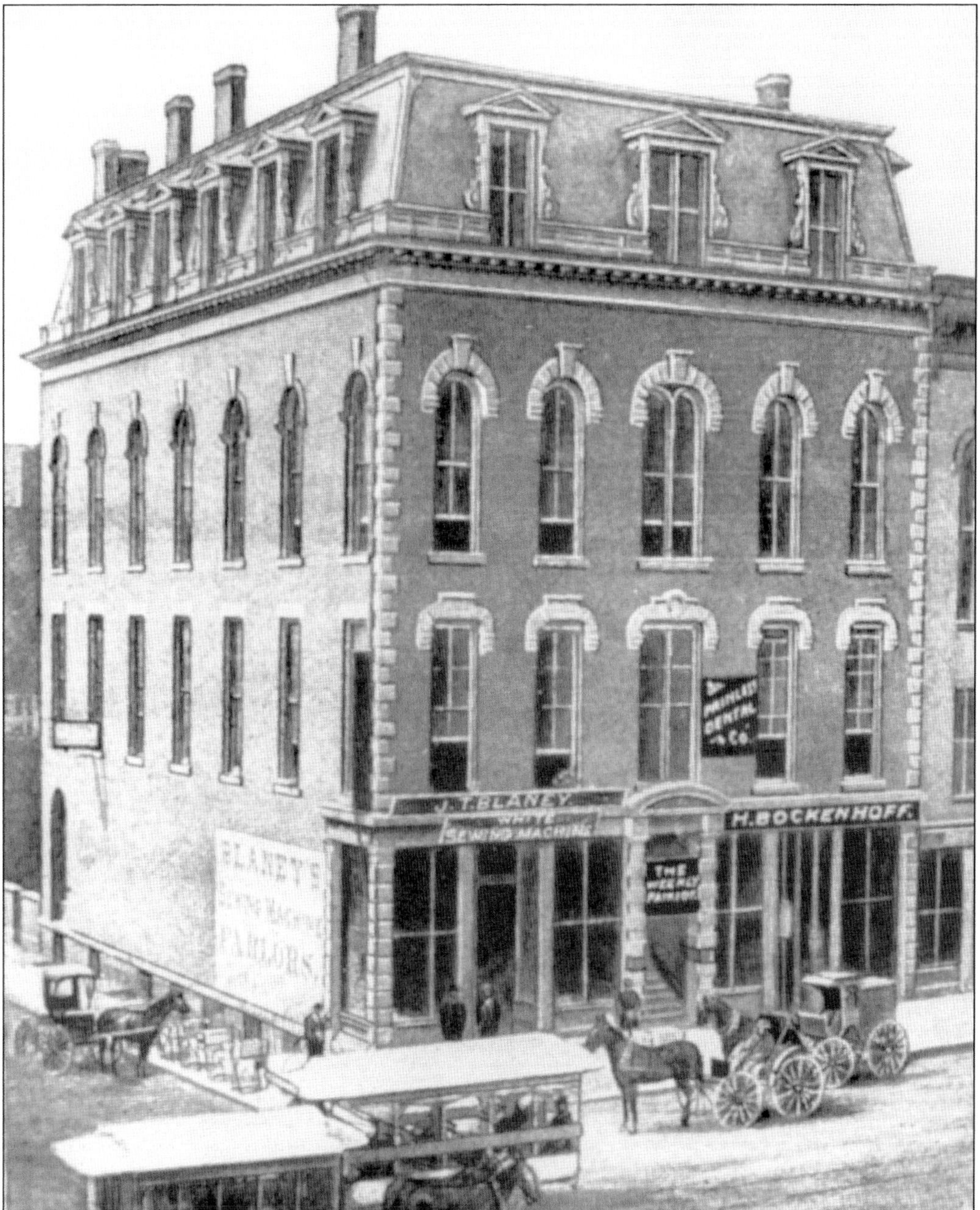

In 1850, Orrin Kendall erected a three-story brick building on the southwest corner of Sixth and Maine Streets. He had a cracker and confectionery business on the first floor. Kendall Hall was on the second floor. Many political meetings were held in Kendall Hall. Abraham Lincoln spoke here in 1854, when he was still a young lawyer. In 1867, a fire started in the National Hall to the west, causing severe damage to both buildings. This large brick building was built to replace the Kendall building. It resembled the Opera House in architecture and was known as the Kingsbaker building when Samuel and Moses Kingsbaker bought it. In November 1916, S.S. Kresge Co. bought the building and later erected its own building.

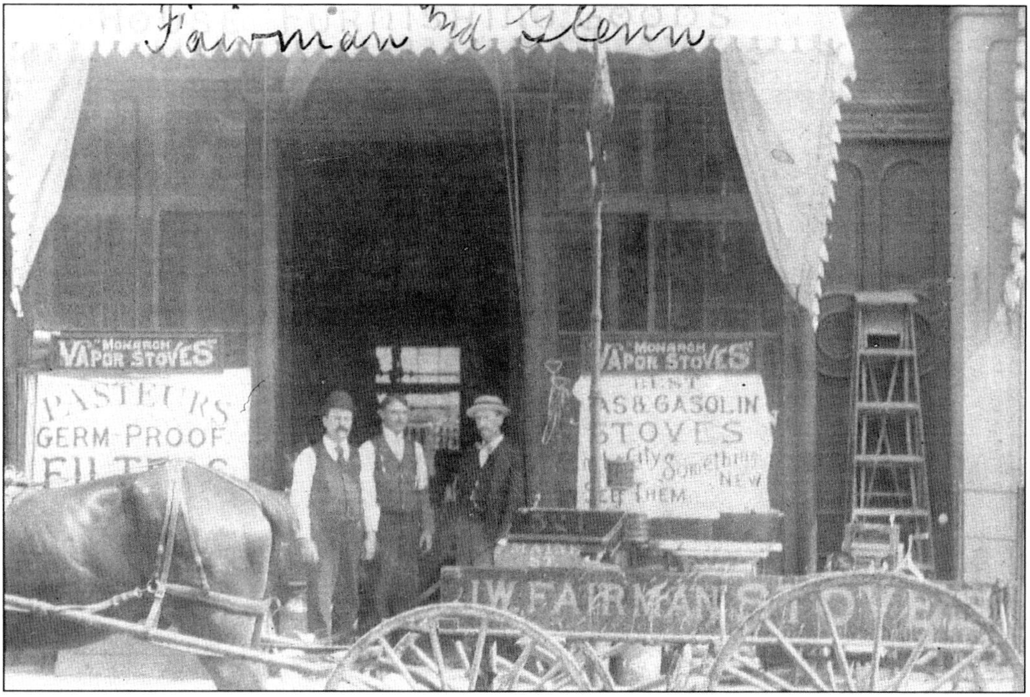

Just before the turn of the century, Quincy had five stove manufacturing companies and about 20 retail outlets. This picture shows the J.W. Fairman Stove retail store at 521 Maine in 1892, which sold Monarch vapor stoves and Pasteurs germ-proof filters.

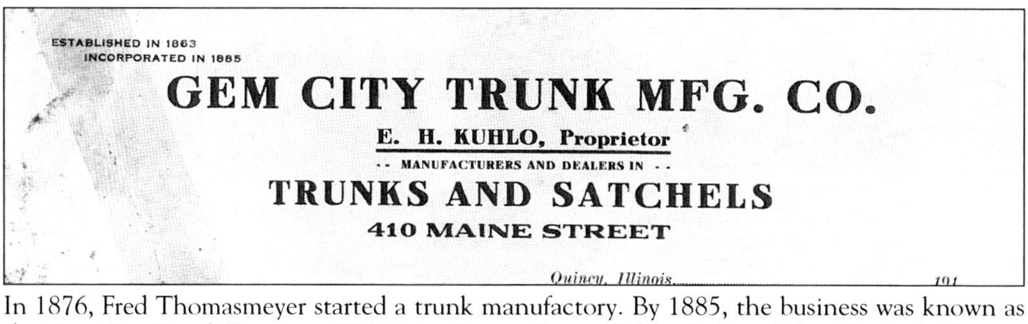

In 1876, Fred Thomasmeyer started a trunk manufactory. By 1885, the business was known as the Gem City Trunk Factory at 634 Maine Street. Ernest Kuhlo, father of Mrs. Elizabeth Hunter, worked for Thomasmeyer to earn money to go to medical school. Upon Thomasmeyer's death, his widow and three girls asked Kuhlo to stay on and run the factory. He eventually bought it and moved the business to 410 Maine Street.

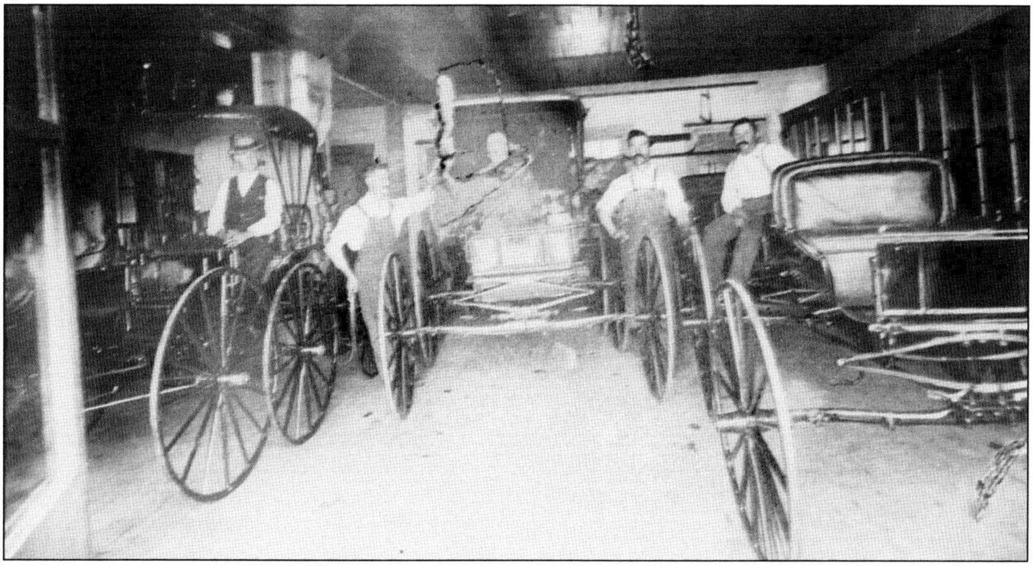

The E.M. Miller Company was established in Quincy before the Civil War as a carriage making business on the west side of Sixth Street between Maine and Jersey Streets. Additional buildings were added as the business grew. The firm made buggies, wagons, landaus, broughams, omnibuses, auto hearses, and even circus wagons.

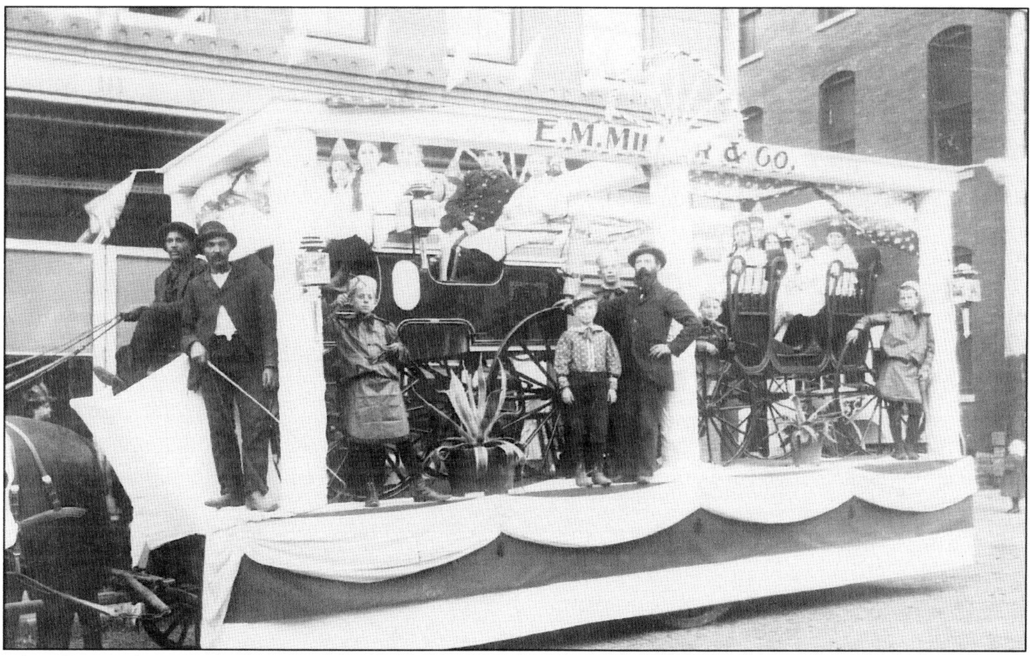

This float, showing two of the vehicles made by E.M. Miller & Co., took first prize during the Fall Festival in the Merchants and Manufacturers Parade held October 21, 1897. At its peak, E.M. Miller employed 140 men. Its largest order was for 75 horse-drawn omnibuses for use in New York City. They also built 12-passenger buses for the Columbian Exposition in Chicago, which were later used as stagecoaches in the west.

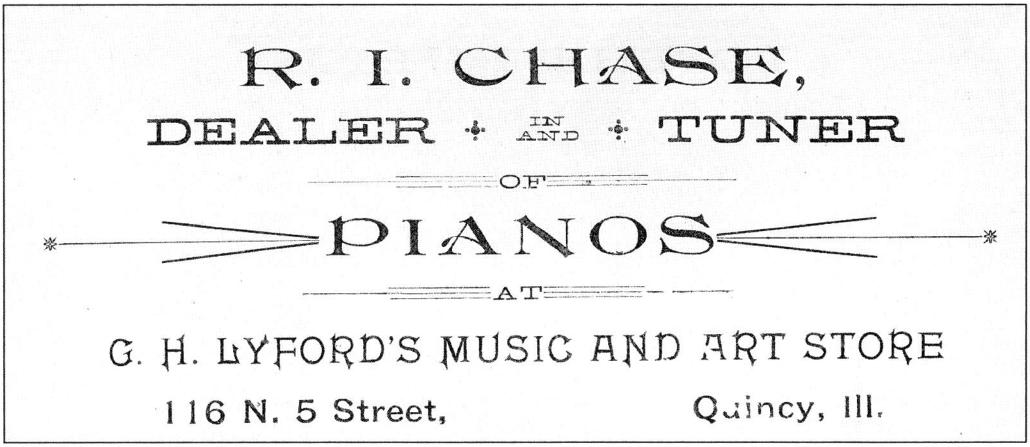

In 1847, the first music store, B.F. Wiggins, came to Quincy.It was located on Hampshire Street between Fifth and Sixth Streets. By 1850, B.F. Wiggins advertised the new popular song, "Quincy Waltz." Over the years, there have been many other stores, including G.H. Lyford's Music and Art Store at 116 North Fifth Street. This card, advertising R.I. Chase, states on the reverse side that Mr. Chase is a piano tuner from New York, "late from Steinway & Sons."

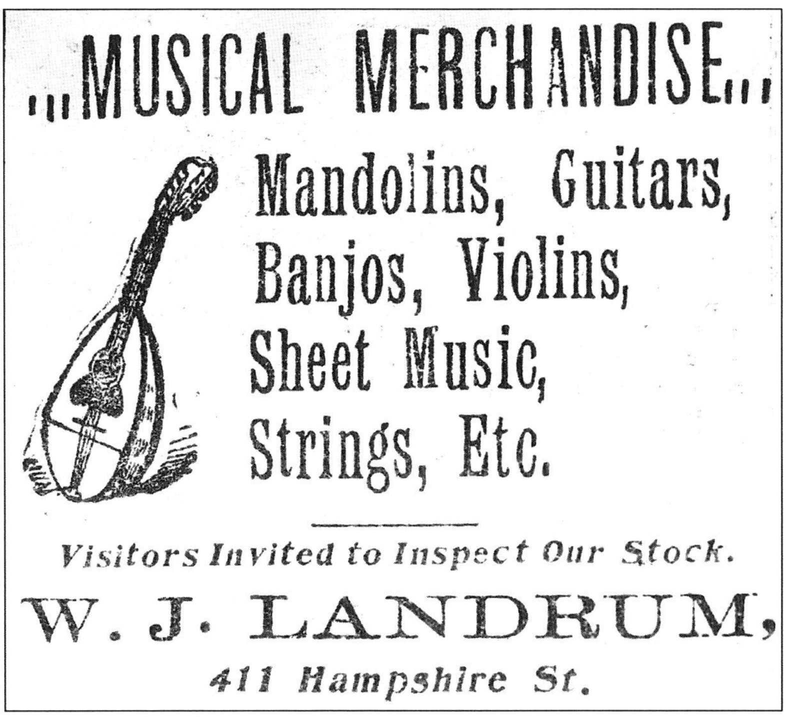

In the 1880s, John W. Everett opened a music store at 524 Maine Street before moving to 412 Maine Street. In 1892, the author's father, W.J. Landrum, went to work as a clerk in the Everett Music Store. After the death of Mr. Everett, Mrs. Everett continued to operate the store for a short time and then sold out to Mr. Landrum, who moved the store to 411 Hampshire Street.

In 1899, two Weiler brothers, Joseph and Charles, purchased Mr. Landrum's music store at 411 Hampshire Street. About 1902, the Weilers moved their music store to 128 North Fifth Street, where they remained until 1915, when they moved to 122 North Fifth Street. At one time, son-in-law Glen Thompson managed the store. Mrs. Lenore Weiler Thompson handled sheet music, and Mrs. Roy Havens, mother of Quincy's outstanding trombonist, Bob Havens, was in charge of records.

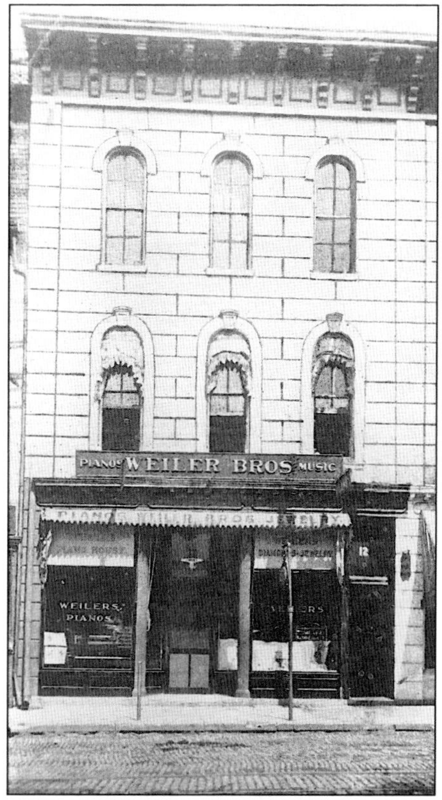

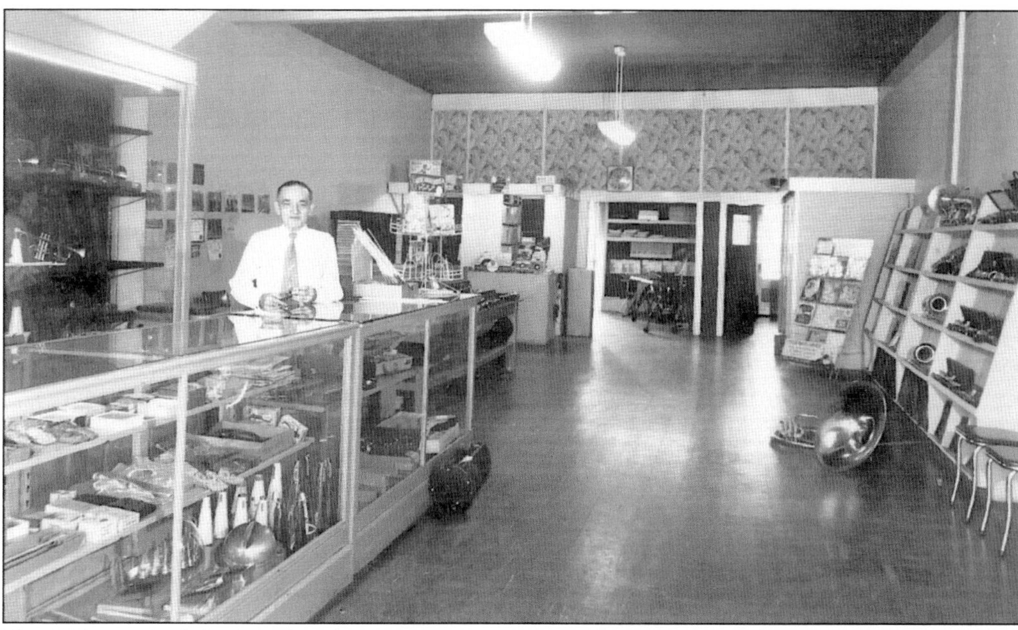

Floyd Hamm had the band and orchestra instruments department in the Weiler store. He later opened his own store shown here at 828 Maine Street. The author later purchased this music store and operated it until 1990. Other music stores, no longer in business include the following: Andrew Musholt, Killams, Delabars, Tanners, and Spurriers.

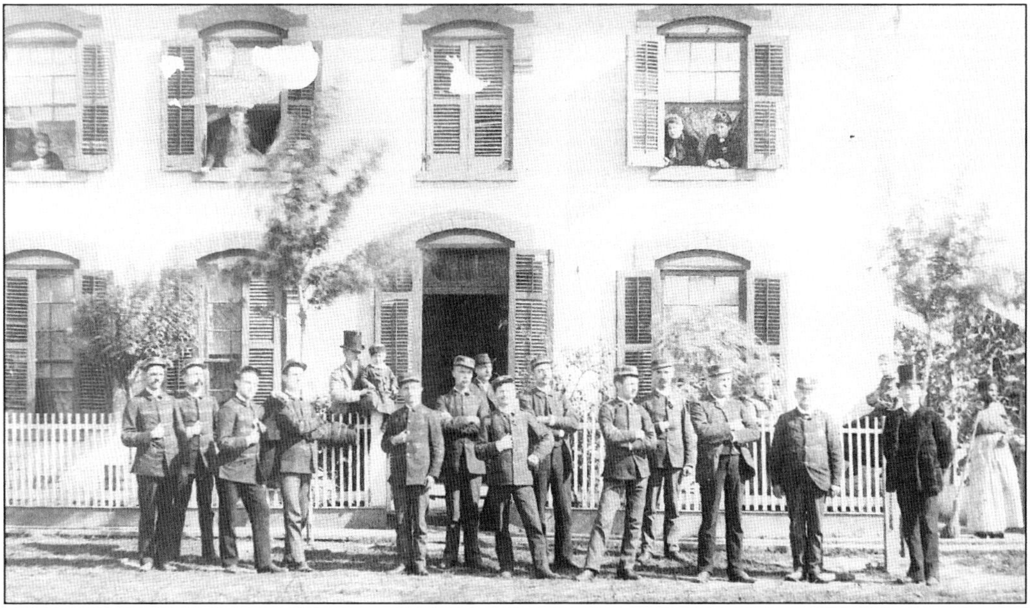

Before the turn of the century, there were many family bands or groups available to entertain at picnics, dances, etc. One of those was the Olker Band. Pierre Olker came to Quincy in 1885 with his three sons. All were musicians. This picture was taken in Palmyra, in 1889, with the following players: Robert Broemmer, Barney Damhorst, unidentified, Albert Olker, Albert Schilling, Pat Lenane, Oscar Schilling, William Holtschlag, Louis Olker, Pierre Olker, Valentine Schilling, and Andrew Rosenbusch.

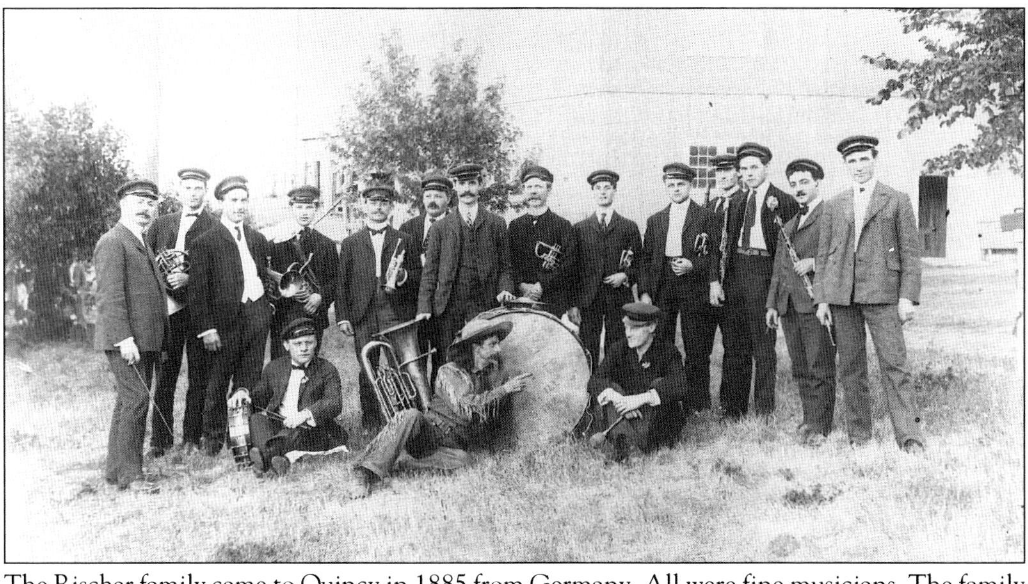

The Rischar family came to Quincy in 1885 from Germany. All were fine musicians. The family orchestra consisted of Louis Rischar, Max Rischar, Jacob Omlar, Eduard Rischar, and the father, Nicholas Rischar. At one time, Louis Rischar directed the Empire Theatre Orchestra. In the summer, the Rischars made the Chautauqua circuit in Colorado, where this picture was taken at Boulder.

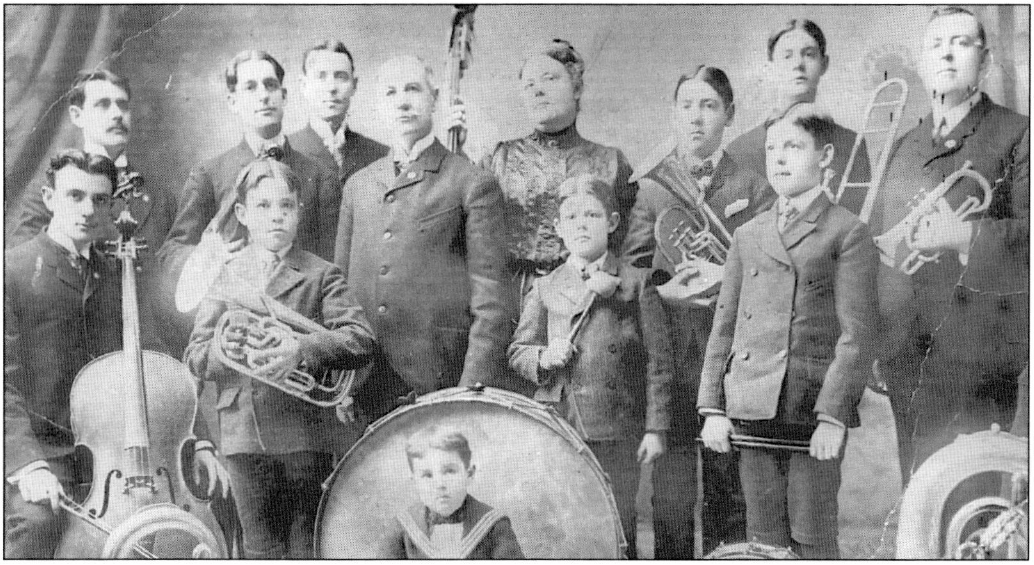

The Markee family came to Quincy in 1896 from Columbus, Ohio; five members of the family played musical instruments. As each of the 11 sons became old enough to play an instrument, he became a member of the group. This picture, taken in Quincy, shows father Robert, mother Lucille, and 11 sons.

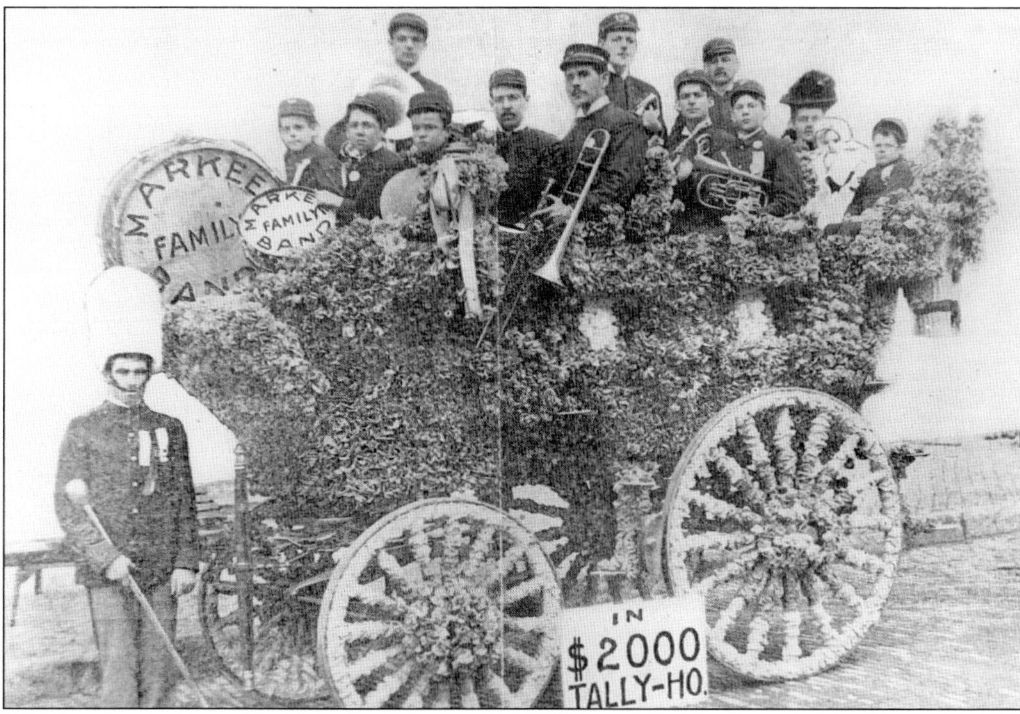

This picture, taken in 1899 after another son had been added to the family, shows them apparently ready for a parade. The Markee Band advertised that they played for the following engagements: Chautauquas, camp meetings, conventions, Grand Army of the Republic reunions, log rollings, street fairs, county fairs, picnics, excursions, parades, receptions, parties, and balls.

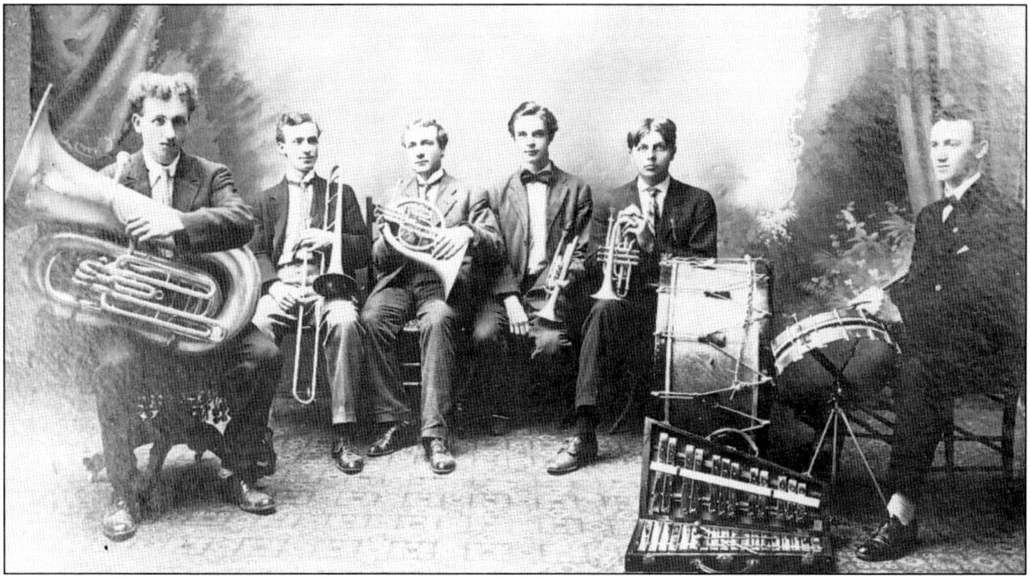

Harry Mayhall came to Quincy with his older sister and brothers, c. 1908. He became a member of the old 5th Infantry Band and played in theater pit orchestras. He soon started his own band, shown here, which included, from left to right, George "Babe" Mayhall, tuba; Leslie Mayhall, trombone; Harry Mayhall, alto; Allen Deege, cornet; John Steinbach, cornet; and William Judson, drums.

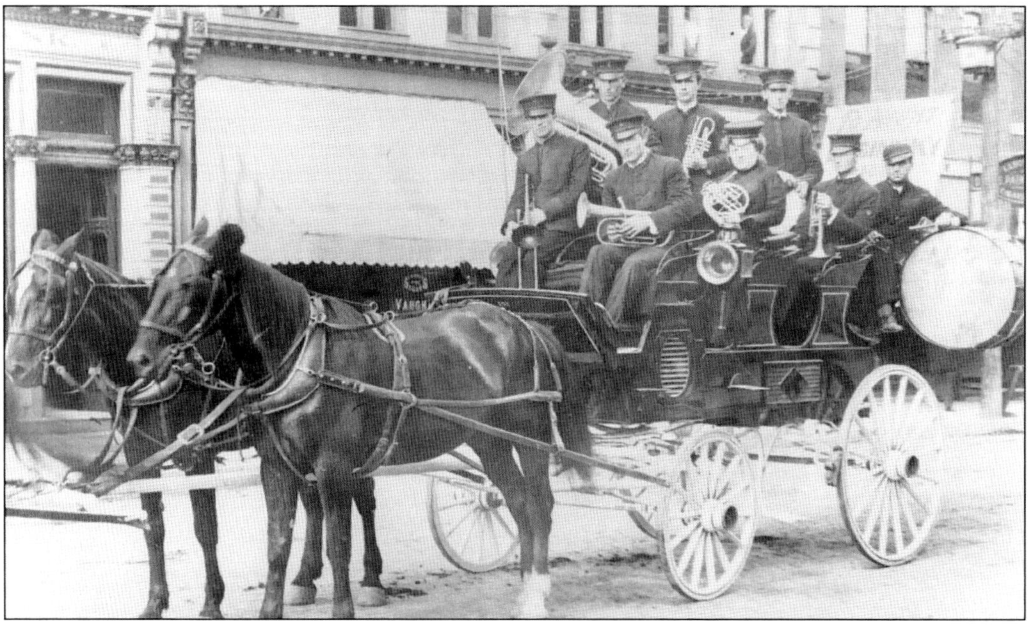

Later the Mayhall Band played on excursion boats, at the Empire Theatre, and at the Orpheum Theatre. When the Dubinsky Stock Company came to Quincy, the Mayhalls joined up. This picture was taken in Lexington, Missouri, in 1909 with the Dubinsky show. Shown here, from left to right, are as follows: (front row) Les Mayhall, Harry Mayhall, Esther Mayhall, and Clarence Warner; (back row) George Mayhall, Allen Deege, and William Judson. The bass drummer was a member of Dubinsky show.

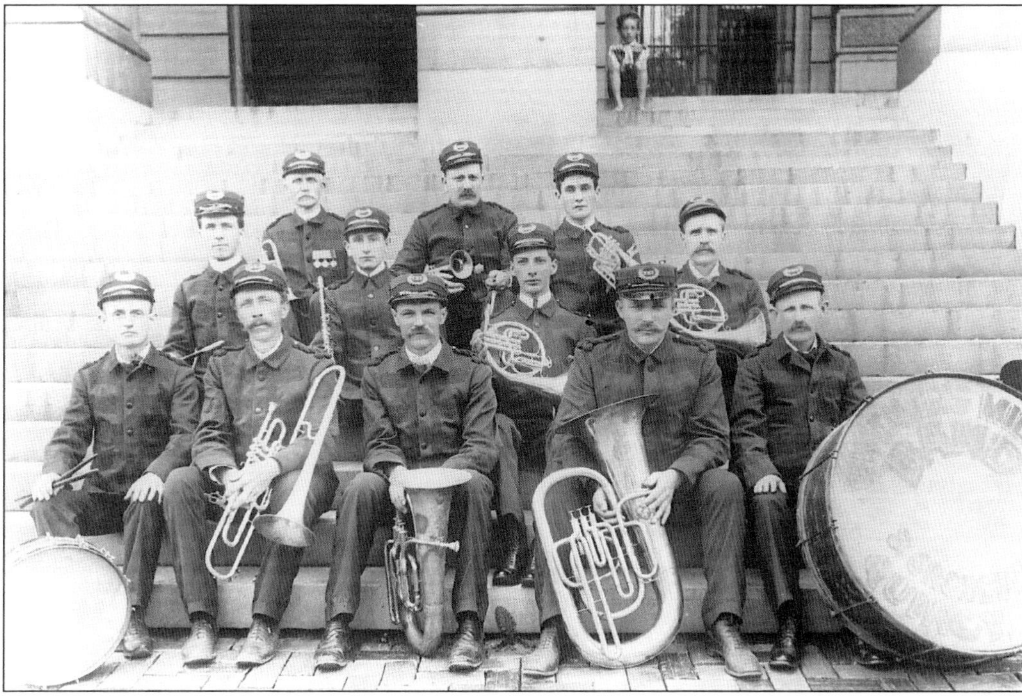

In addition to running a music store, Joseph and Charles Weiler took over the Carl Gardner Military Band when Gardner left Quincy in 1900. This 1904 picture shows the following people, from left to right: (front row) Oscar Schilling, William Holtschlag, Robert Broemmer, William Fessler, and Albert Schilling; (second row) Joseph Weiler, Louis J. Keis, Albert Gardner, and Barney McCoy; (back row) Bernard Krebber, William Edward Gillespie (manager), and George Fenwick. Those not present include Charles Weiler, Frank Holtschlag, and Bernard Damhorst.

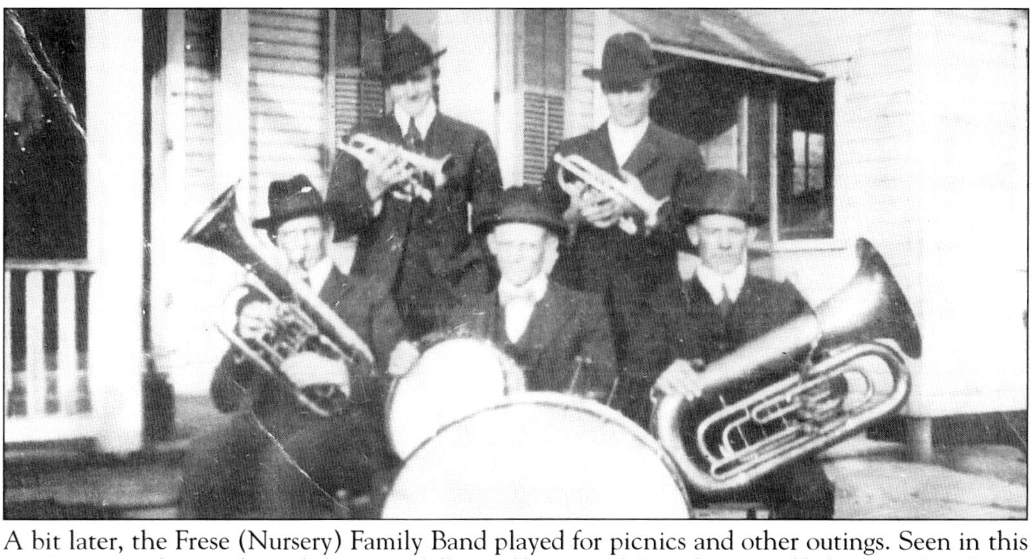

A bit later, the Frese (Nursery) Family Band played for picnics and other outings. Seen in this 1926 picture, from right to left, are as follows: (front row) Joseph, Louis (father), and William; (back row) Louis and Edward. Frank Speckhart and George Hagerbaumer also played at various times for the band during its period of operation from 1900 to 1935.

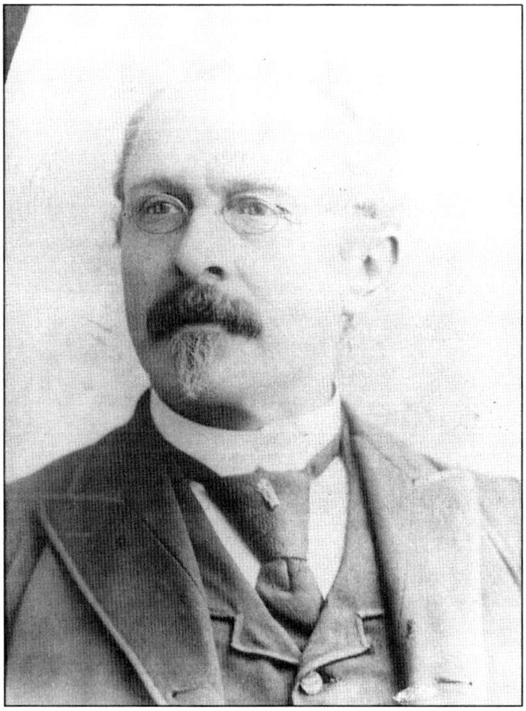

Louis Kuehn was leader of the Kuehn Band in Quincy from 1869 to 1881. He played cornet, violin, and piano. Four sons played in the band, as well as John Schwab, George Schaefer, and Barney Krebber. Kuehn's Band played a concert in Washington Park July 4, 1872, which included several original numbers written by Kuehn.

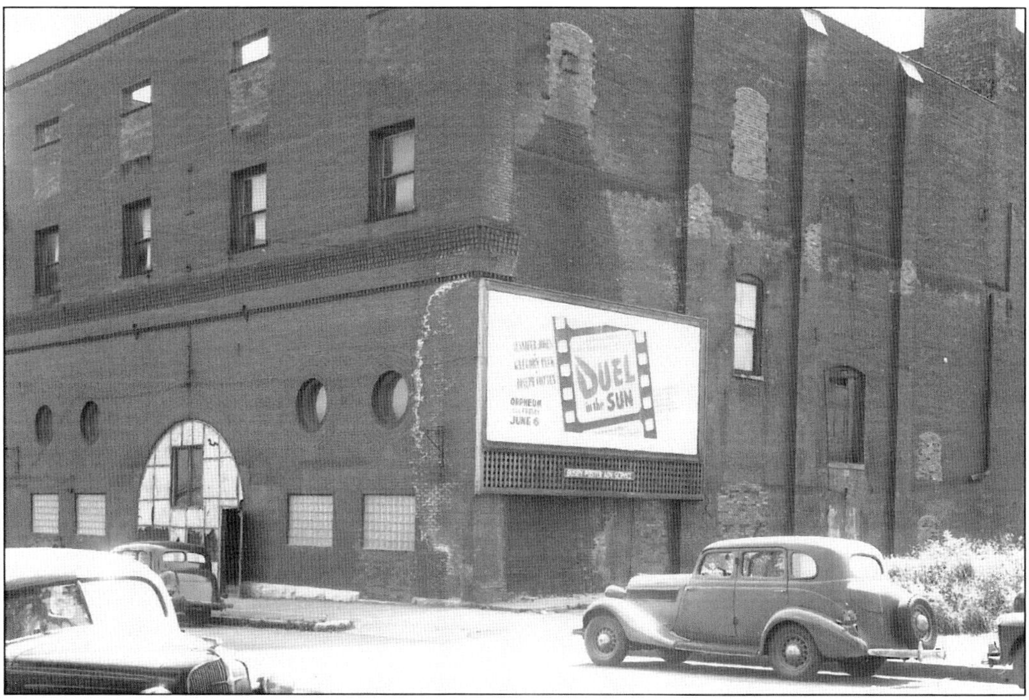

The Empire Theater, located at 115 North Eighth Street, opened to the public for the first time on December 21, 1893. Many of the family bands played the Empire at some time. The Empire had local groups, traveling groups, and vaudeville groups for many years before closing in 1926. This picture was taken after it had been remodeled into apartments.

Four

1900–1916

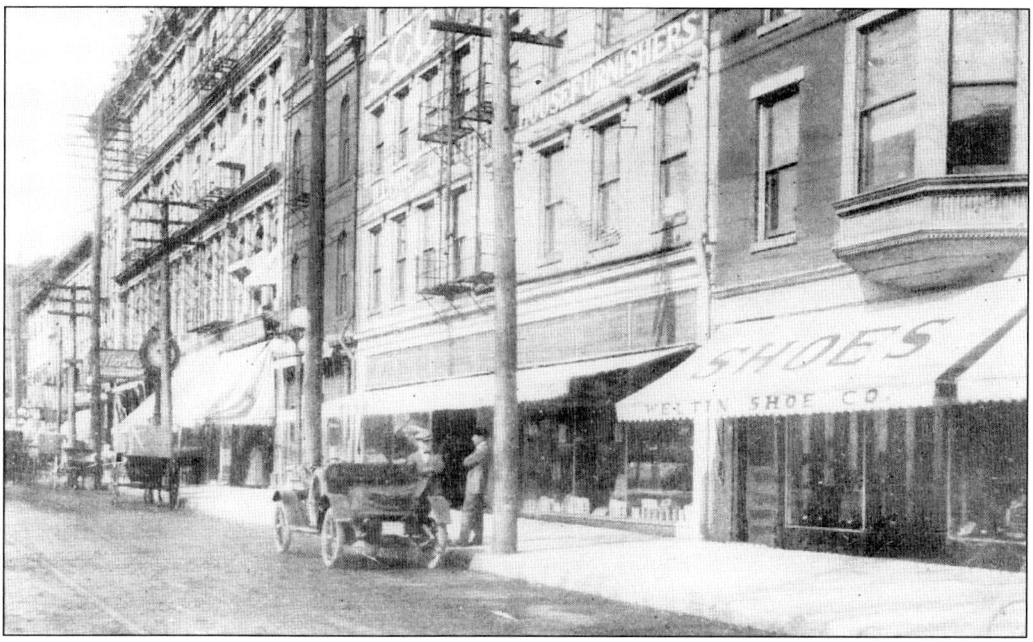

In 1912, Weltin's Daylight Shoe Store, located at 104 North Fifth Street, was managed by William H. Hellhake. The Scovill Co., located to the north at 106-110 North Fifth Street, provided house furnishings and was managed by C.H. Ott. Farther north, one can see the Model Clothing Co. store, which was organized by four Stern's Clothing Co. salesmen in 1909. These four salesmen were John A. Ohnemus, Fred Tiemann, Herman Jochem, and J. Henry Meyer.

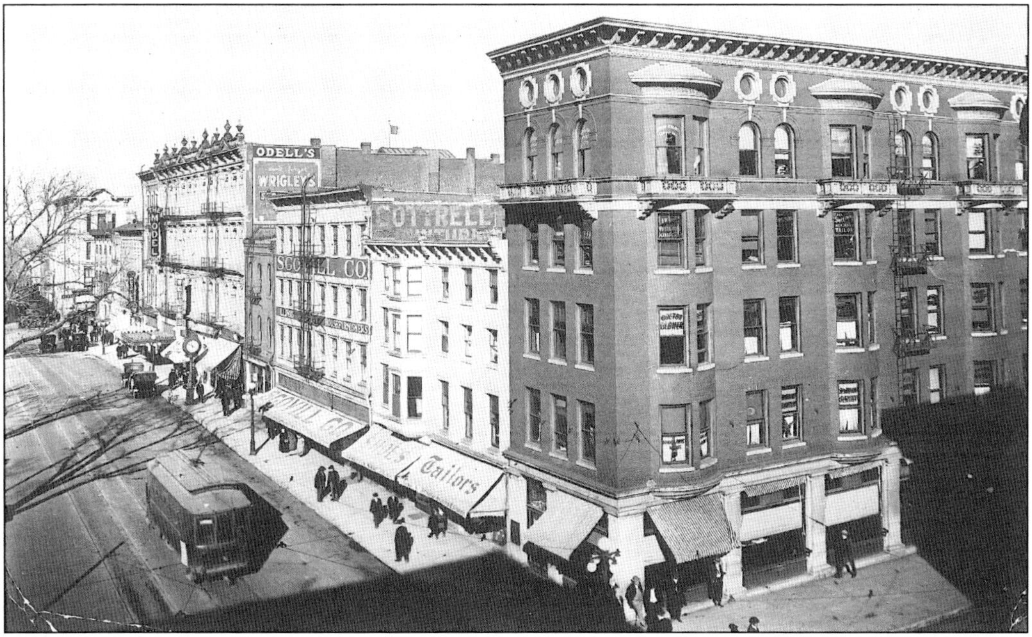

The large five-story building shown here on the northeast corner of Fifth and Maine Streets was completed in December 1897. A drugstore and an optical firm occupied the first floor. The Mercantile Trust and Savings Bank was organized in 1906 and the building was then remodeled for the bank in 1908. The main entrance to the bank at that time was on Maine Street.

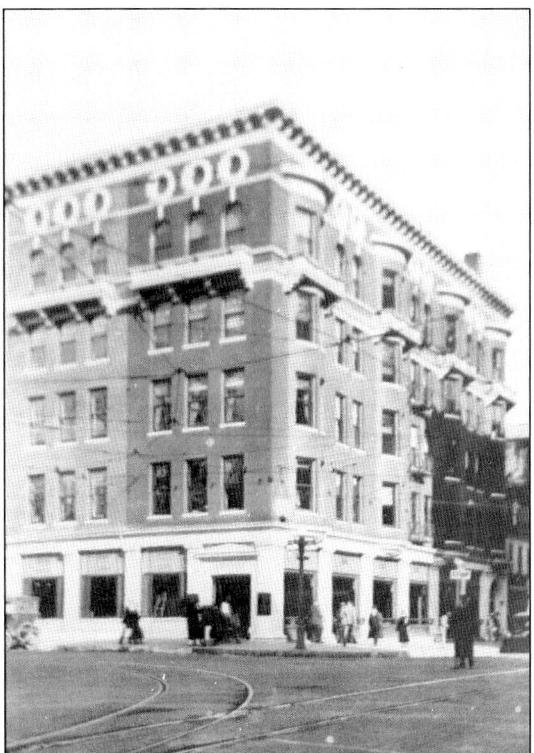

On November 10, 1922, the bank building sustained a fire. It was then decided to remodel the building and to add a five-story matching building on the north. The main entrance was then changed to Fifth Street. Ernest Wood was the architect for the first building as well as the addition. The Mercantile Bank remained in this location until they moved to their new building on the southwest corner of Fifth and Maine Streets in 1960.

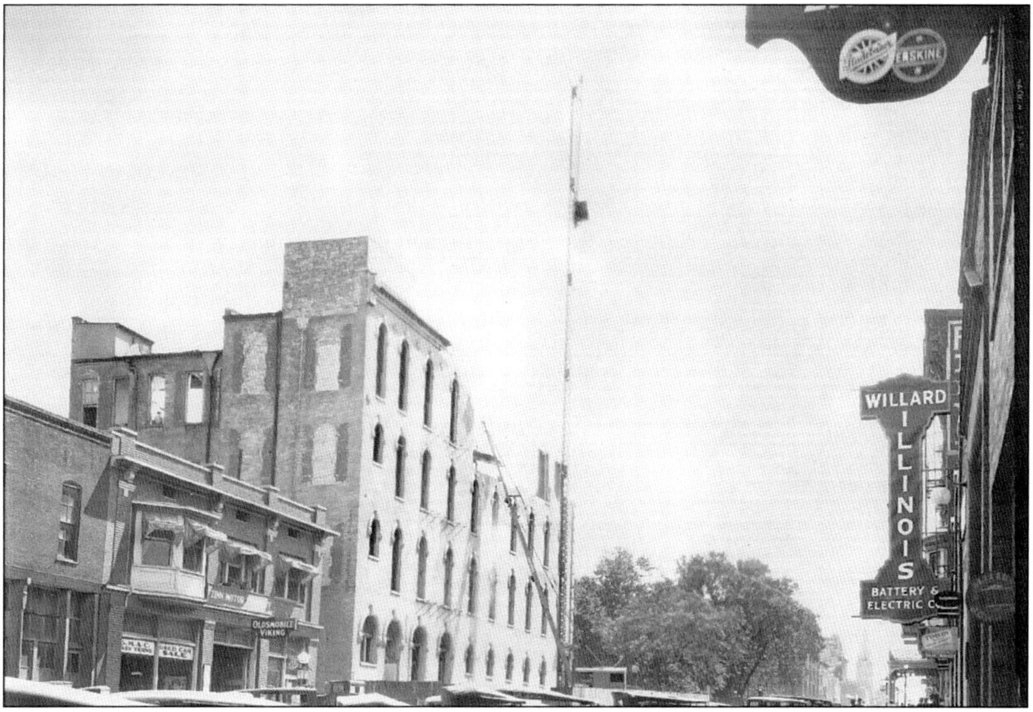

The year 1930 saw many changes on Maine Street between Third and Fourth. This shows the Tillson building, on the northwest corner of Fourth and Maine, being demolished to make way for the Hotel Lincoln-Douglas in 1930. Zinn Motor Company is to the left. Later Jefferson-Johnston Motors would occupy this location.

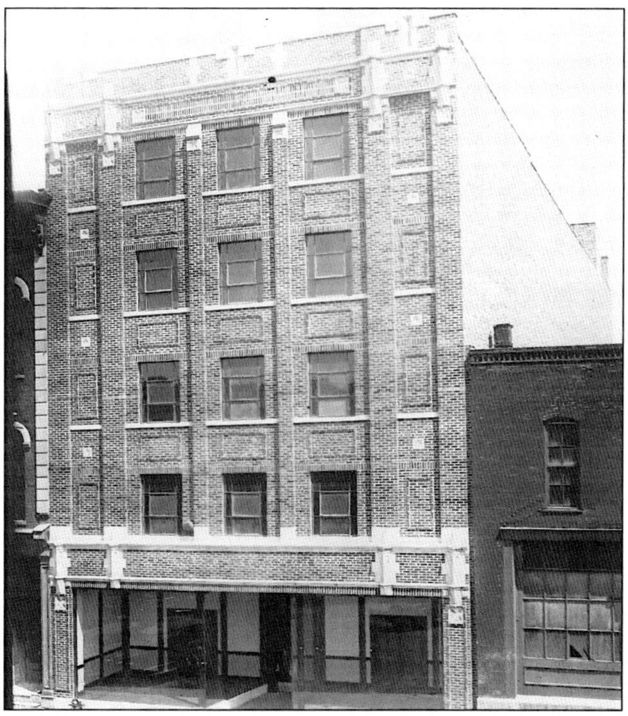

The Roy Bennett Furniture Store opened in their new building, located at 311-313 Maine Street, with a grand opening celebration from August 7-9, 1930. They are still in business at the same location today. Bennetts had previously been at 303 Maine Street.

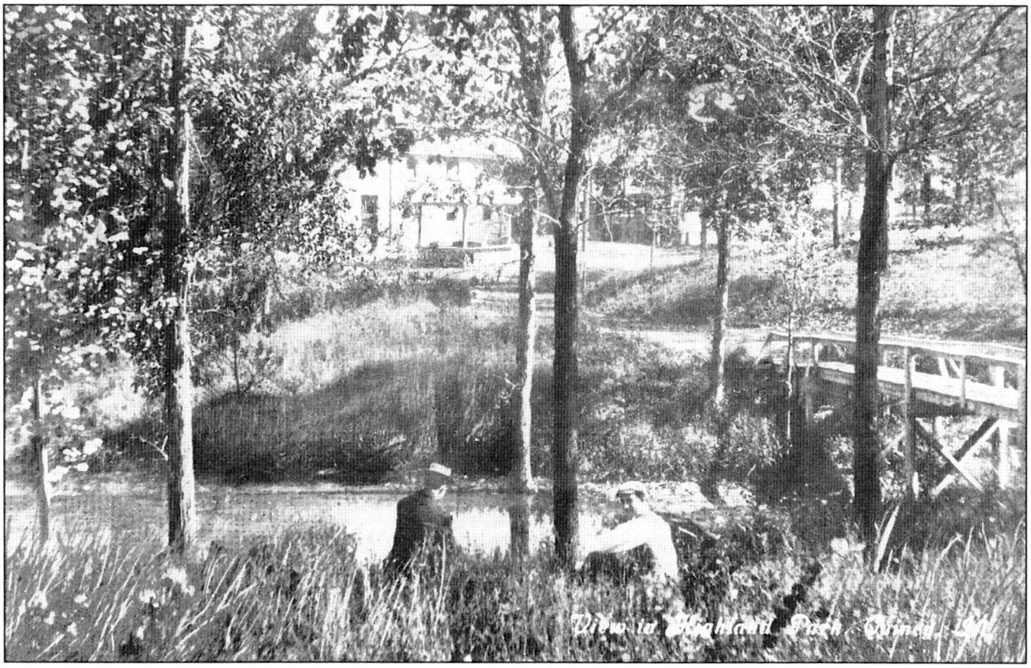

The original tract of land that comprised Highland Park was first known as Moore's Mound for the owner Francis Moore. On July 28, 1871, Moore sold the tract to Lorenzo Bull, Charles Bull, Orville Browning, Nehemiah Bushnell, and E.K. Stone, who made up the Quincy Horse Railway & Carrying Co. The 80 acres of land had a grove of trees in the northwest corner. This grove became Highland Park, located from Eighteenth to Twentieth Streets, between Cherry and Spruce Streets.

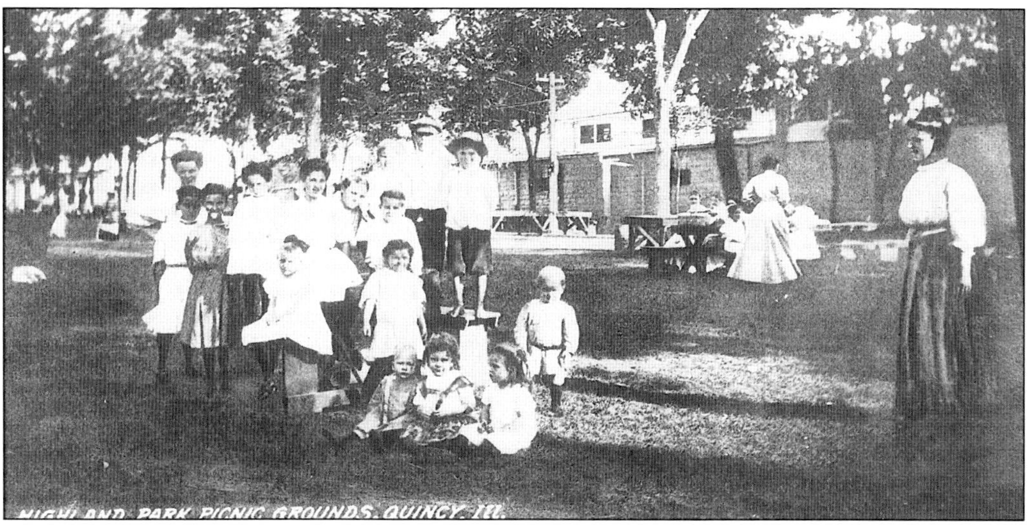

The Quincy Horse Railway and Carrying Co. soon extended its lines to Highland Park, making it a popular place for picnics. The large German element in Quincy had the habit of gathering for family picnics and outings at the many beer gardens. It was much more strict at Highland Park; beer and light wine were sold, but the bar was not conspicuous.

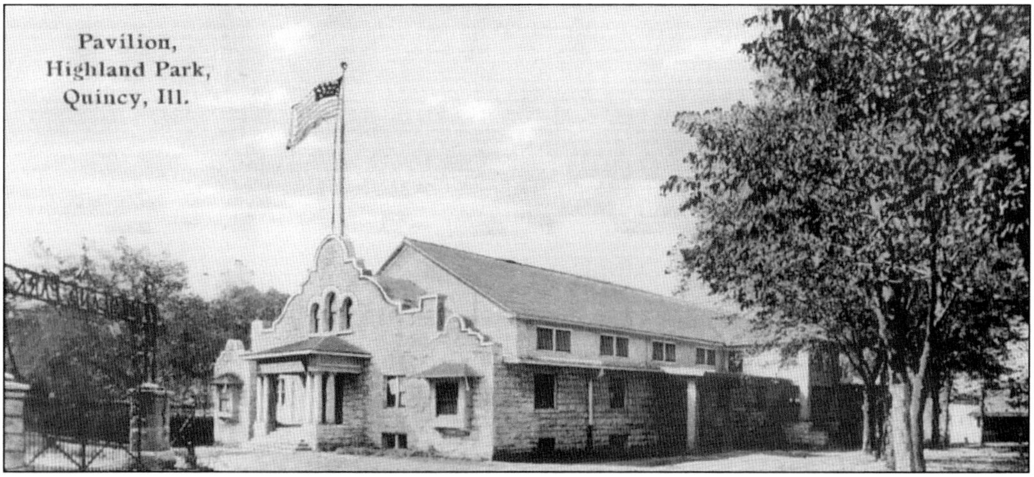

About 1900, Henry Gredell became manager of the park after A.C. Bickhaus. On November 6, 1906, Gredell announced that architect Martin Geise had been engaged to draw plans for a stone pavilion that would replace the old frame pavilion at a cost of $10,000. The park was fenced in, and attractions included a zoological garden, a roller coaster, and a swimming pool. In 1910, management passed to Harry Hofer and Oscar Shannon.

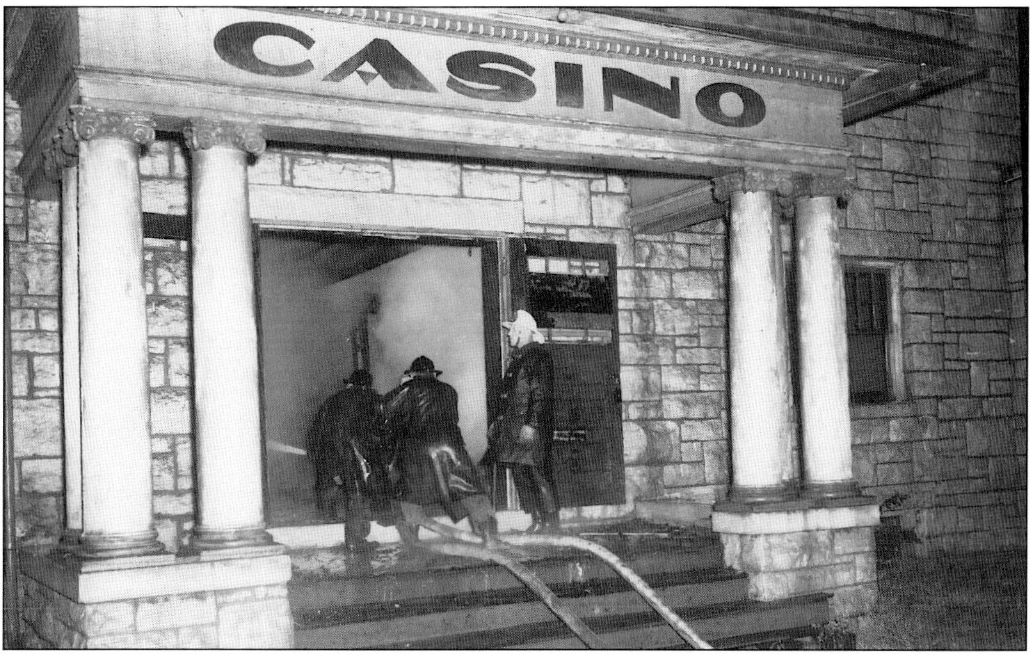

In 1935, Robert "Bob" Christ took over management of the stone building at Highland Park, calling it the Casino. In October 1947, the Casino burned. After being rebuilt, the "new Casino" opened April 1949, with bowling alleys on the lower level and the ballroom upstairs. Name bands appearing at the Casino included Art Kassel and His Kassels in the Air; Jan Garber, the Idol of the Air Lanes; Herbie Kay; Ted Weems with Perry Como; Lawrence Welk's six-piece group, the "Hotsy-Totsy Boys"; the Dorsey brothers (Tommy and Jimmy); Wayne King; Harry James; and Guy Lombardo's Royal Canadians.

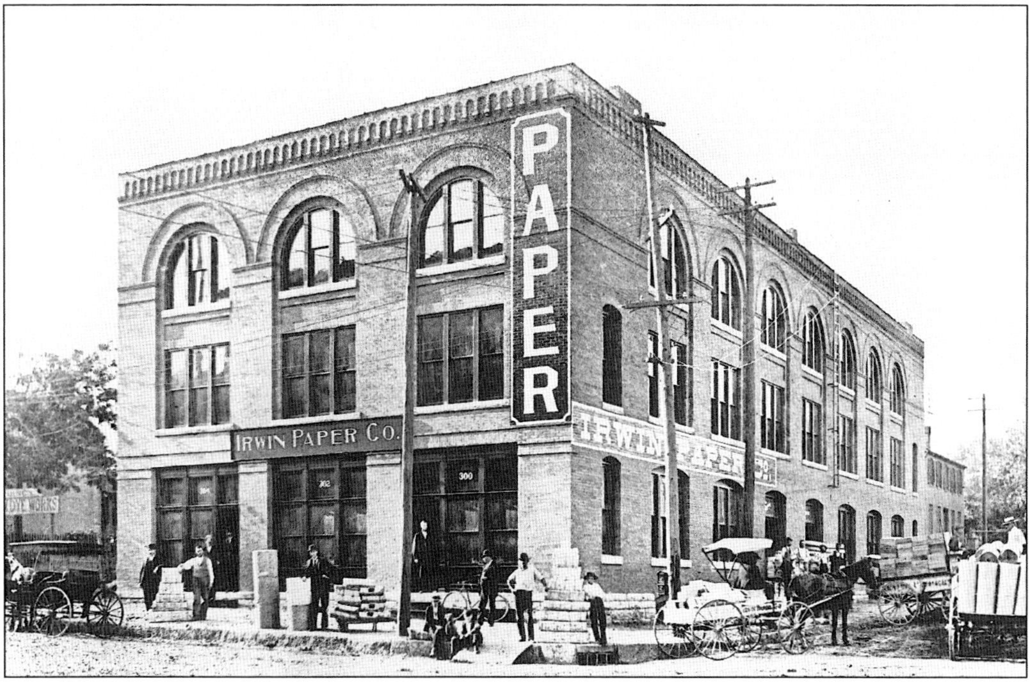

On October 14, 1887, Leaton Irwin purchased stock in the Lyon Paper Co. and was elected president. In September 1890, the name was changed to Irwin Paper Co. The company was first located on North Sixth Street between Hampshire and Vermont Streets, then on South Fifth Street, and then on Hampshire Street between Third and Fourth Streets. When John H. Best's sons erected this building on the southeast corner of Third and Maine Streets as a memorial to their father in 1896, the building's first and only occupant was the Irwin Paper Co.

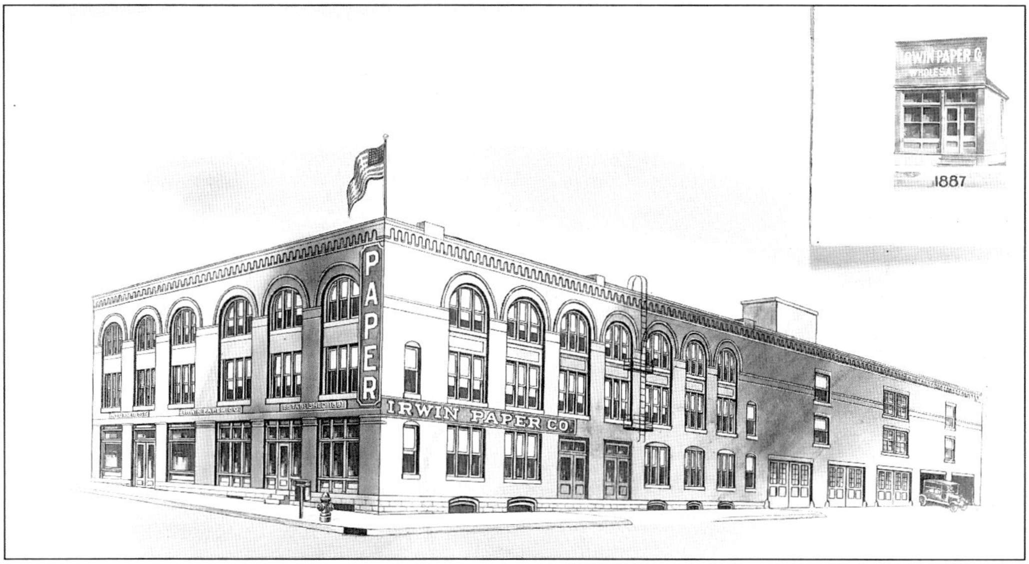

The building was purchased by Leaton Irwin on March 30, 1905, and later transferred to the Irwin Paper Co. At that time, an addition was constructed on the east matching the original structure. Leaton Irwin's son Mac and grandson George continued in the business for many years. In 1987, Irwin Paper relocated to larger quarters, and this building was razed in 1988.

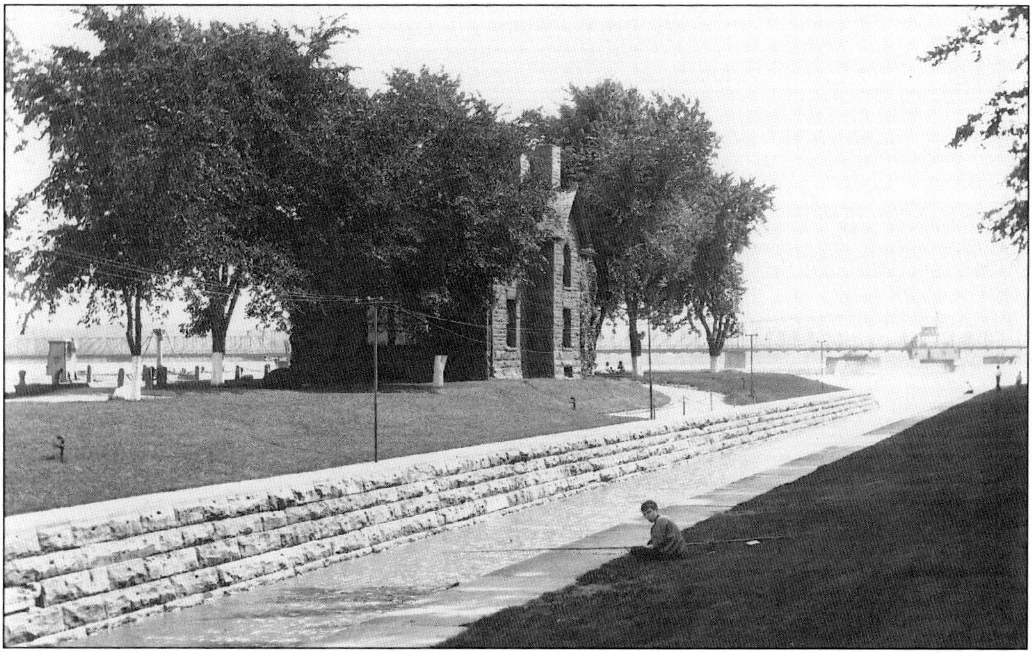

This picture shows the old lock and canal at Keokuk before the construction of the new lock, dam, and hydroelectric plant that was built in 1911 and 1912. The new lock was put into operation on June 12, 1913. The formal celebration of the completion of the work was held August 26, 1913.

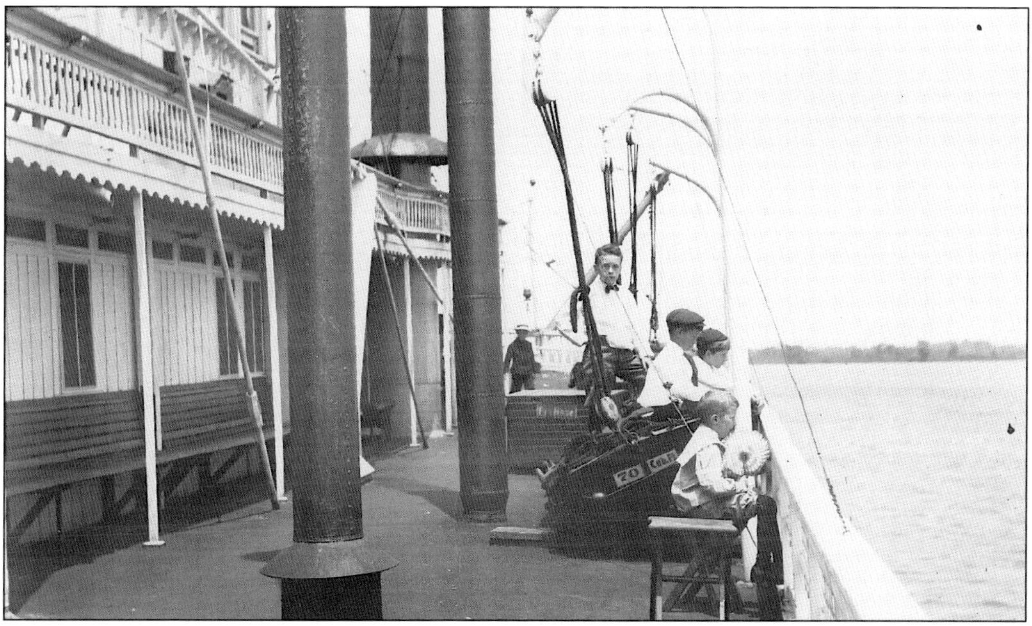

For many years Quincyans enjoyed steamboat outings on the river. This picture shows a group of boys on a Congregational Church excursion in 1907. When the new dam was about three-fourths completed, Quincyans were invited to Keokuk to see the progress. On August 23, 1912, the excursion steamer G.W. *Hill* made the all-day trip, with 1,000 passengers. This trip continued to be a popular excursion trip for many years.

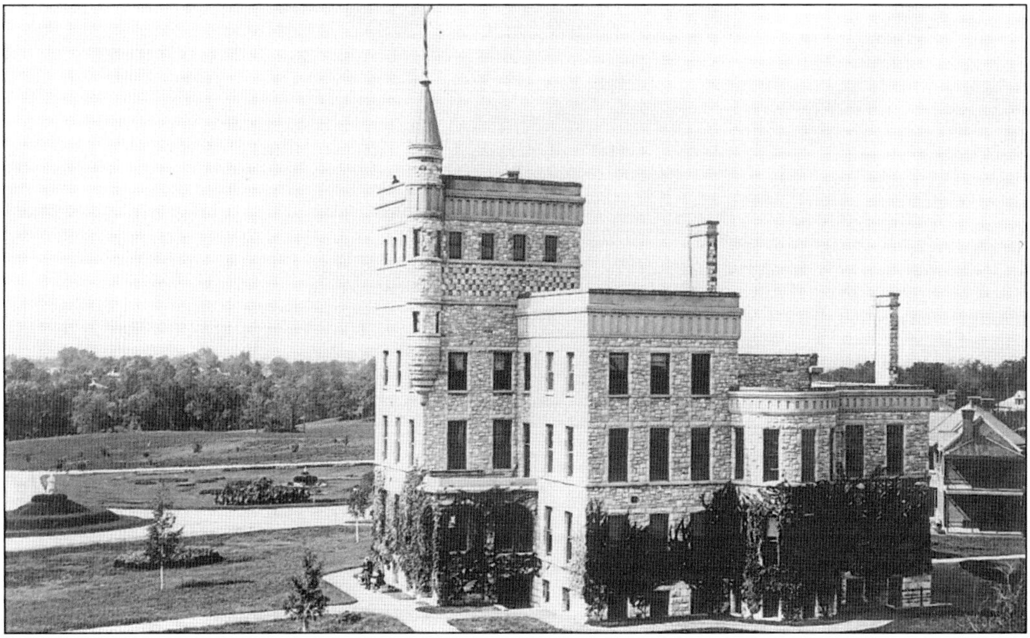

The administration, or headquarters, building of the Illinois Soldiers and Sailors Home was one of the first erected. The Home was opened in 1886 at the north edge of Quincy. On July 1, 1885, legislation had been passed appropriating $200,000 for a home for the aged soldiers and sailors of the State of Illinois. Commissioners from various cities were appointed to select a site, and a number of cities offered locations. On December 2, 1885, the locating commissioners selected Quincy in Adams County.

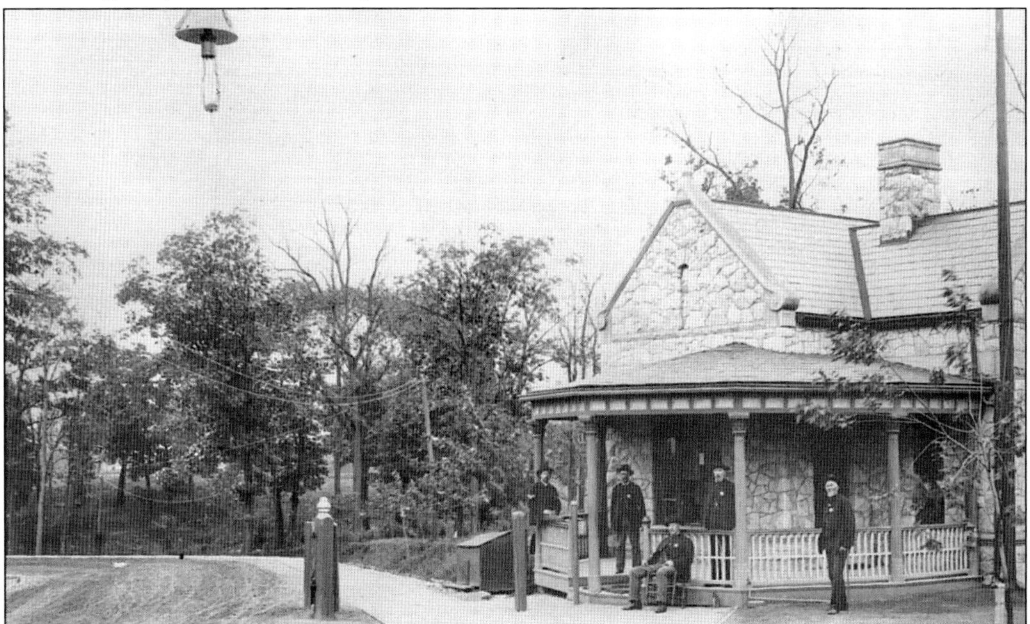

Pictured here is the "guard house" at the entrance to the Illinois Soldiers and Sailors Home, Eighth and Locust, shortly after the home opened in 1886. In 1912, iron gates were installed, as well as an overhead name sign. Later another entrance was added off of Twelfth Street.

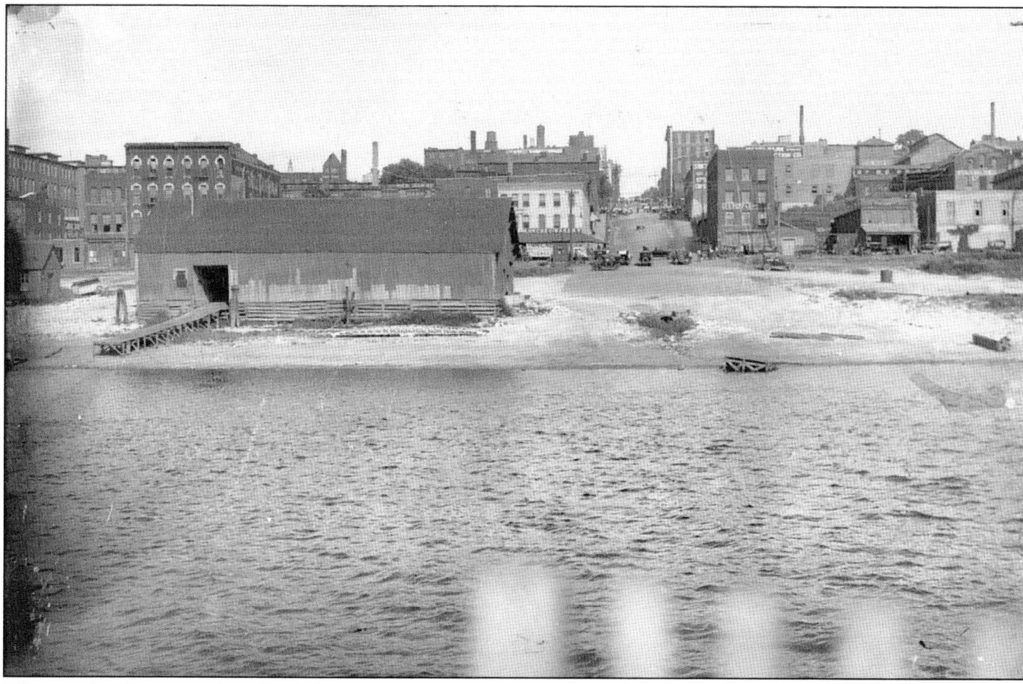

This is the Diamond Jo boat house, at the foot of Hampshire Street, Quincy, where boats could tie up and passengers could board for trips on the river.

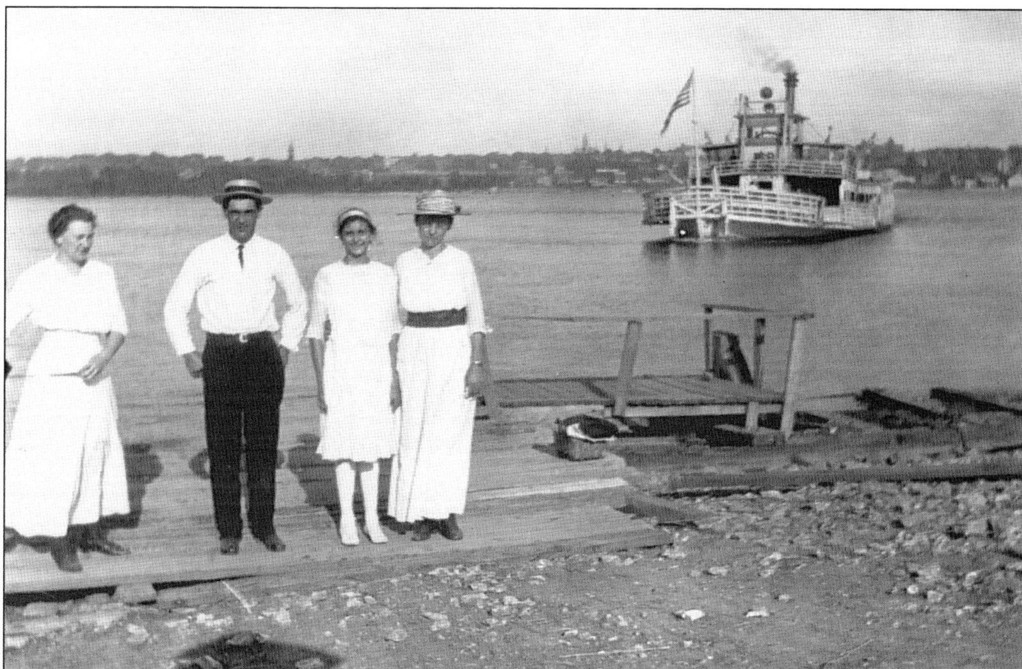

Shortly after the turn of the century, Sherman Park, West Quincy, was a popular area. Dances were held, high-diving exhibitions were given, and several balloon ascensions were made here. The Ferry *B.B.*, owned by Clat Adams, is shown approaching Sherman Park, carrying passengers from Quincy.

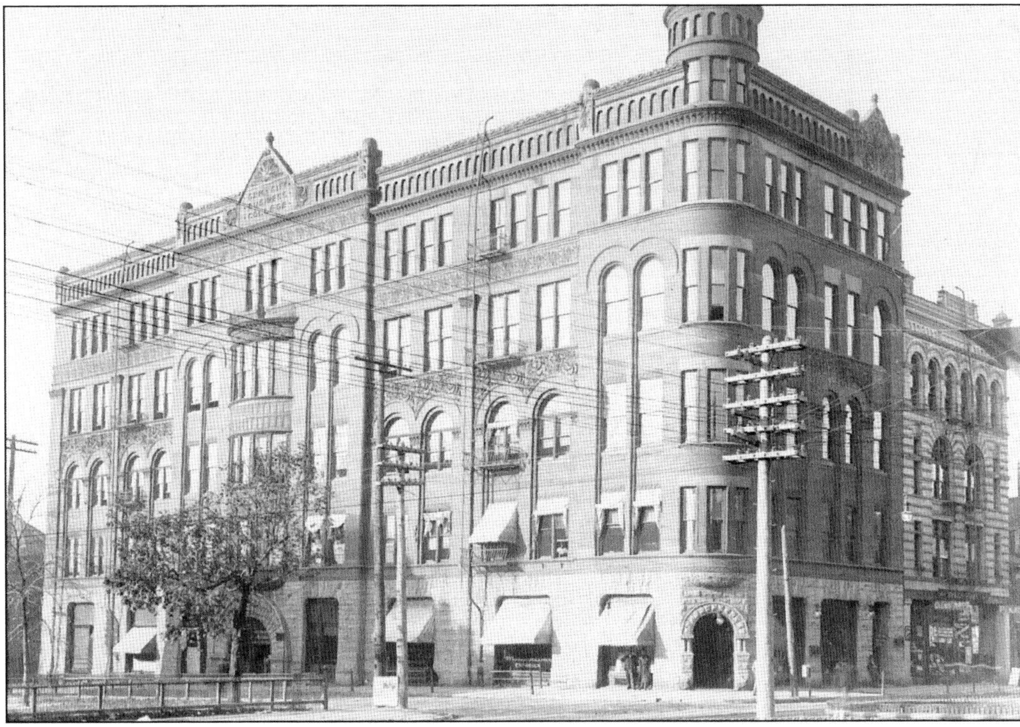

The Gem City Business College, also known as the Musselman building, was built in 1892 at a cost of $100,000 on the southwest corner of Seventh and Hampshire Streets. It first started as the Quincy Commercial College in the Benneson building at 510 Maine Street, with D.L. Musselman as one of the teachers and owners. By 1871, the name was changed to Gem City Business College.

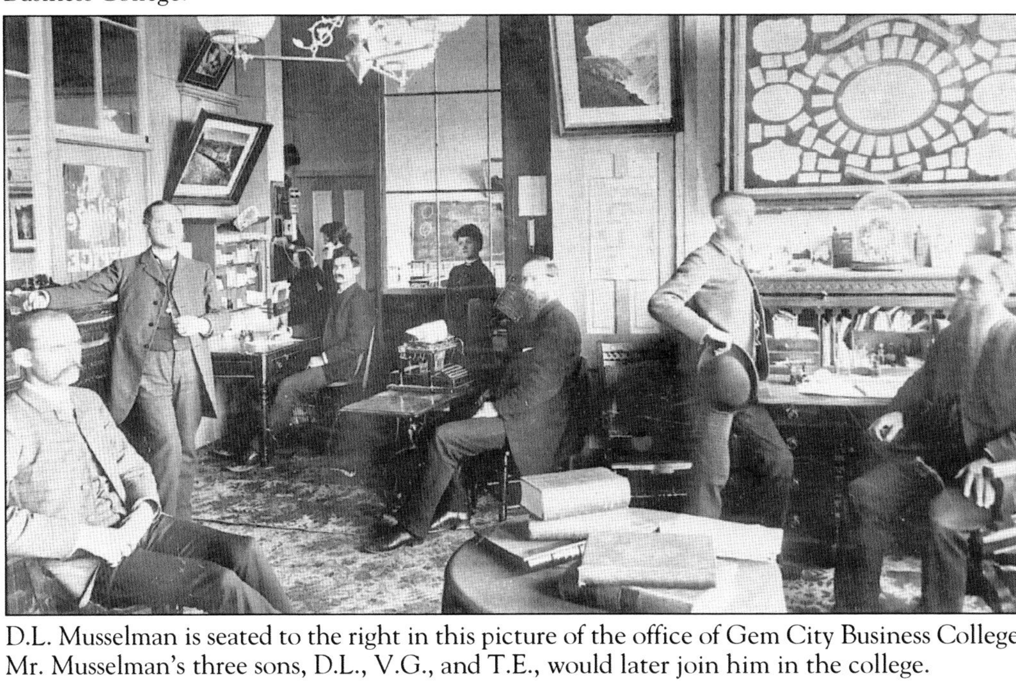

D.L. Musselman is seated to the right in this picture of the office of Gem City Business College. Mr. Musselman's three sons, D.L., V.G., and T.E., would later join him in the college.

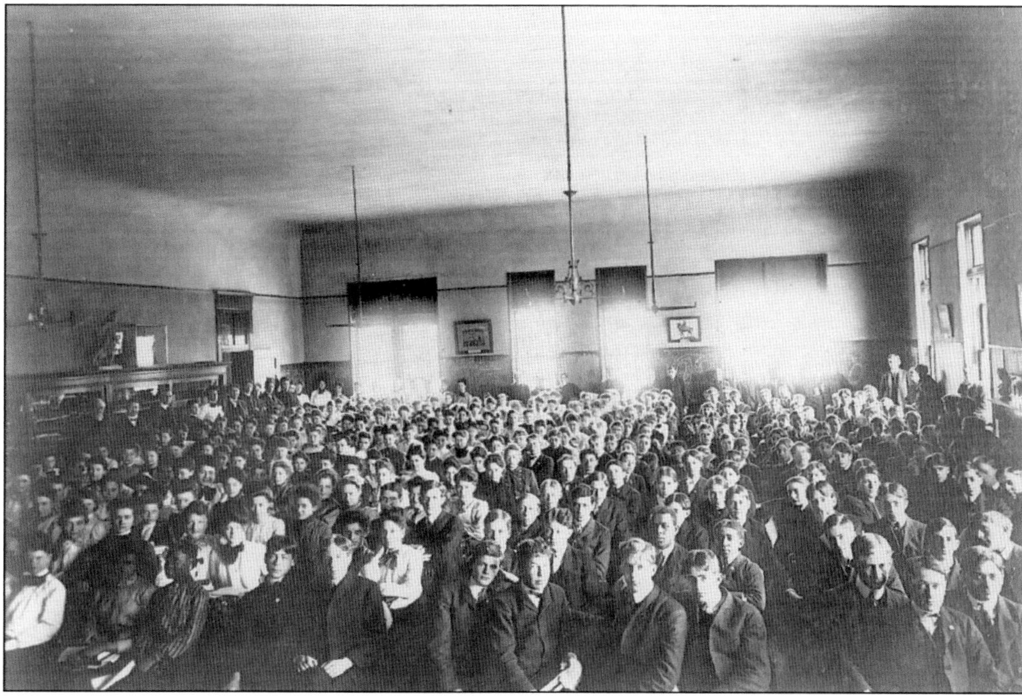

Gem City Business College was highly recognized and attracted students from all over the country. These students of the college were photographed shortly after the turn of the century.

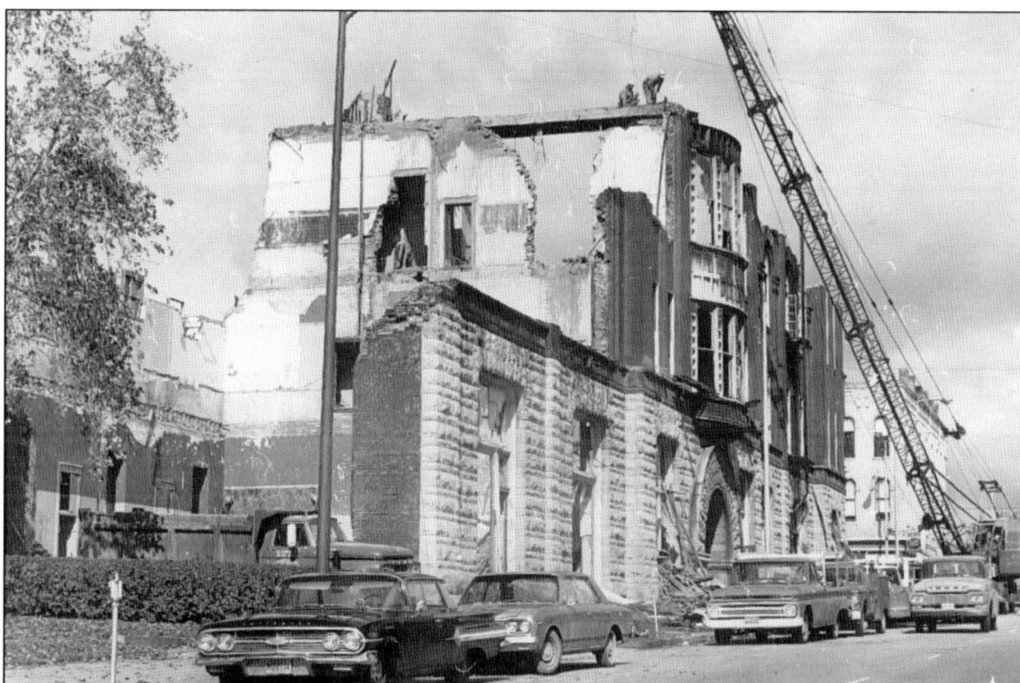

The name was changed to Gem City College in 1963 and the school moved to Seventh and State Streets. Gem City Savings and Loan purchased the building in 1963 and it was razed.

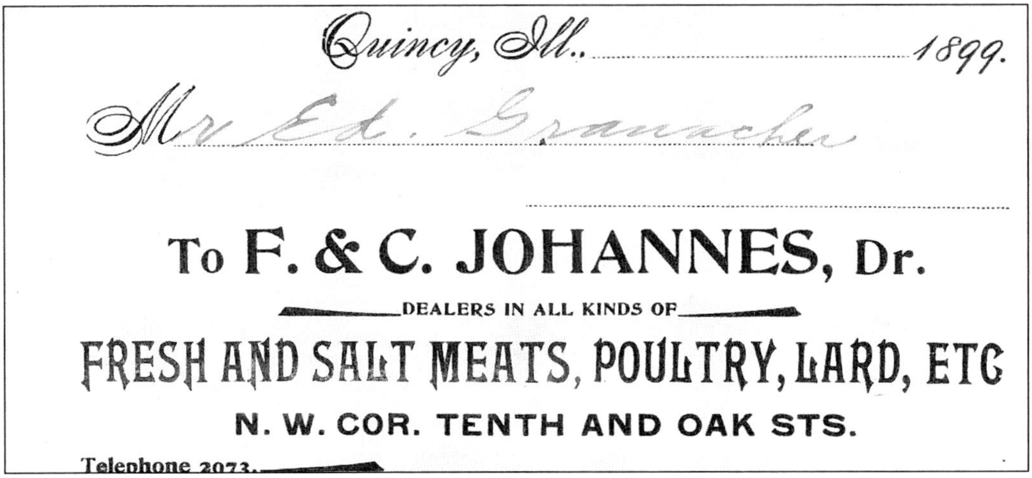
Quincy, Ill.. 1899.

Mr Ed. Grauacher

To F. & C. JOHANNES, Dr.

DEALERS IN ALL KINDS OF

FRESH AND SALT MEATS, POULTRY, LARD, ETC

N. W. COR. TENTH AND OAK STS.

Telephone 2073.

For many years, a meat market was on the northwest corner of Tenth and Oak Streets. In 1887, Frederick Bangert had a meat market there; by 1898, F.&C. Johannes, Dealers in all kinds of fresh and salt meats, poultry, lard, etc. was there. Johannes remained in this location until the building was purchased by Blessing Hospital. The building was razed only recently.

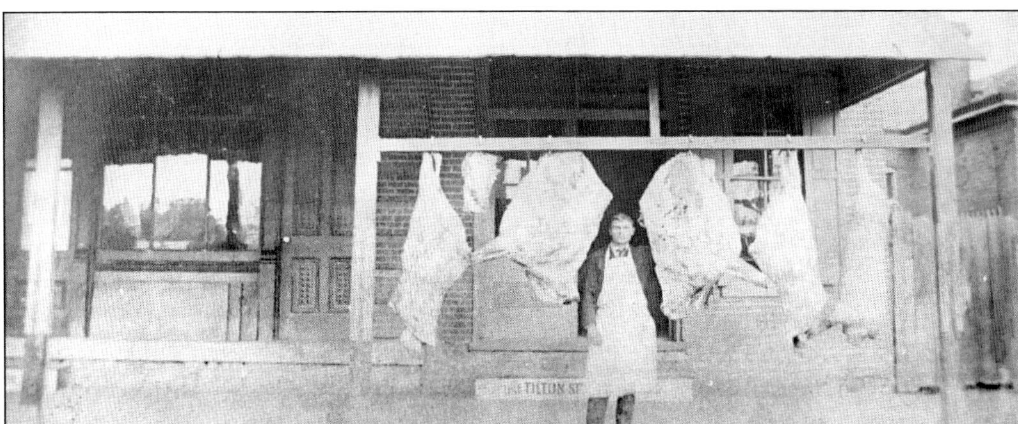

The corner grocery was a part of the housewife's life before refrigeration. Many times, daily trips would be taken to the store for meat, and many charged their purchases until the end of the month. One long-time grocery was the Altmix Store, located at 1138 North Tenth Street; fresh meat may be seen hanging out in front of the store.

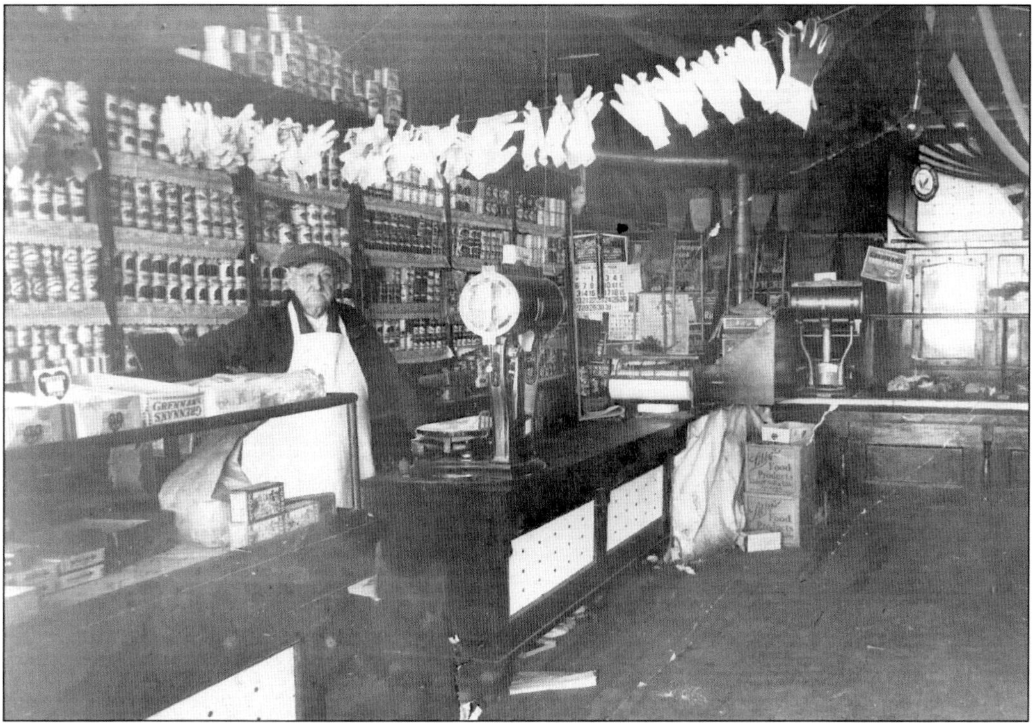

Located at 1800 College Street, John H. Geers Meats and Grocery Store was the first store opened in the 1890s. This picture was taken in 1924; the family lived upstairs. Other Geers stores would follow, but this particular store was sold in 1937.

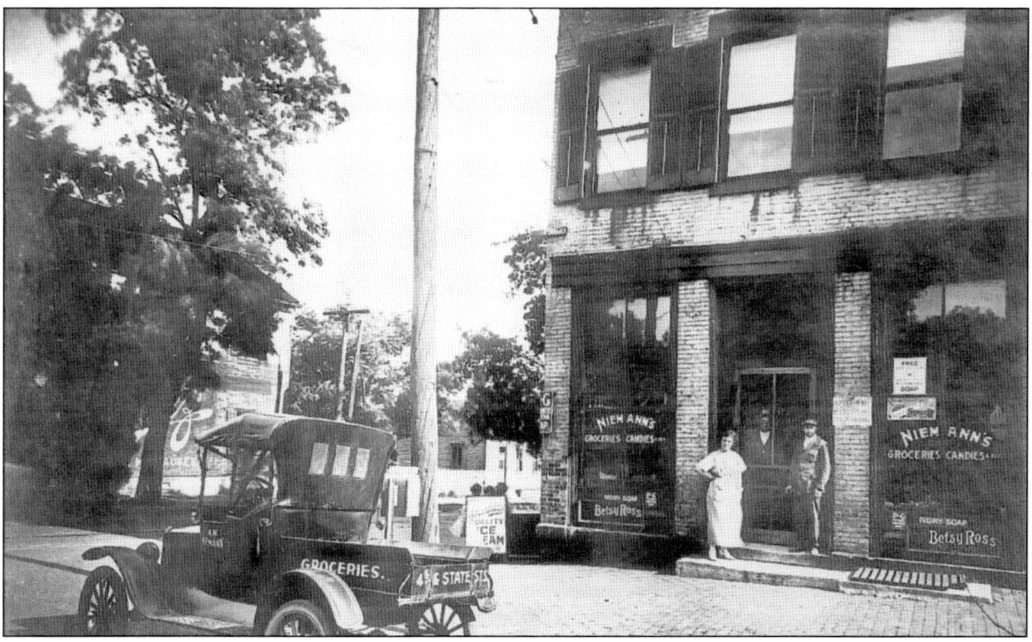

Although many customers would "walk-in" to the early corner grocery stores, some businesses had delivery service also. One of those was Niemann's on the southwest corner of Fourth and State Streets, which was run by A.W. and Ollie Niemann.

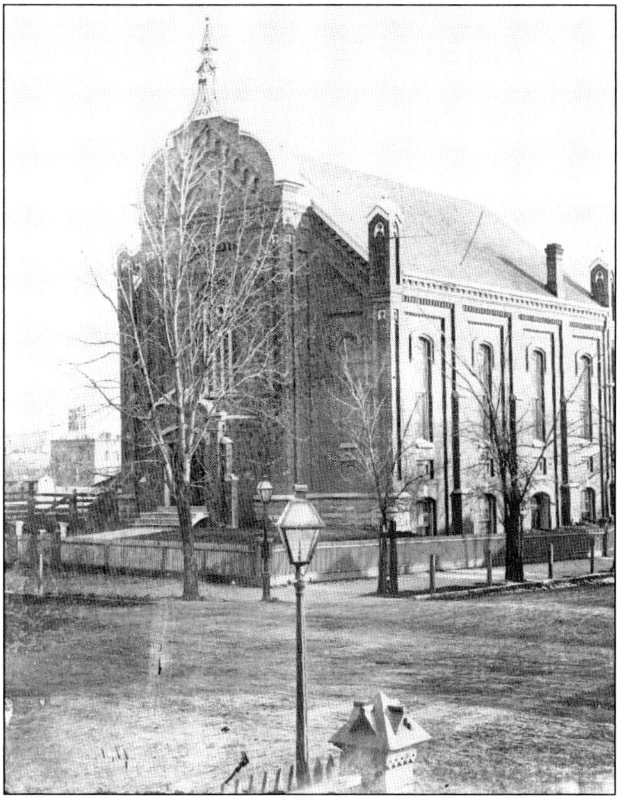

This is the First Christian Church building on the southeast corner of Ninth and Broadway Streets, c. 1870s. The congregation remained here until 1928, when they moved to a new building at 1415 Maine Street.

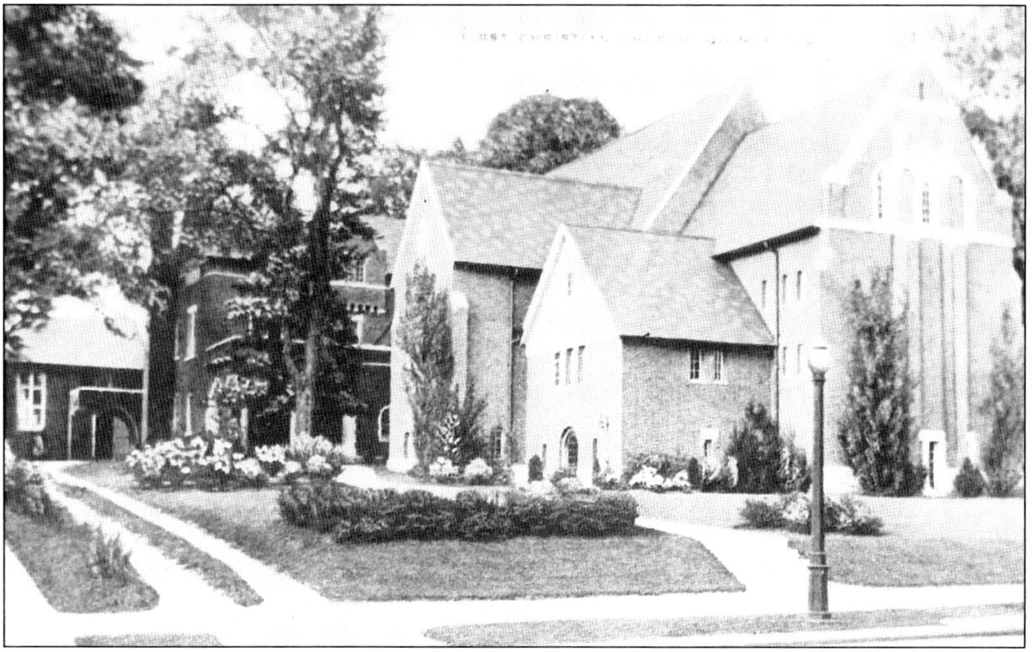

The new First Christian Church at 1415 Maine Street cost $112,000. The structure was built on the front of the old John Seaman house. They used the house for part of their educational building.

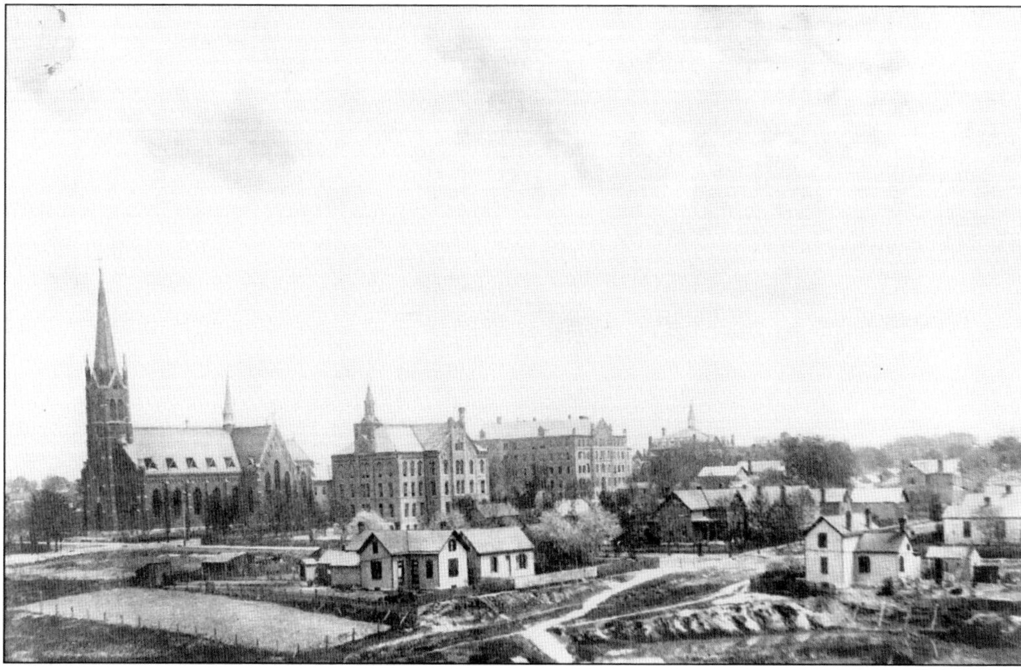

This view shows the St. Francis Church and vicinity at Seventeenth and Eighteenth Streets, and Vine (later renamed College) Street, *c.* 1896. Construction of the church started in 1884 and cost about $62,000.

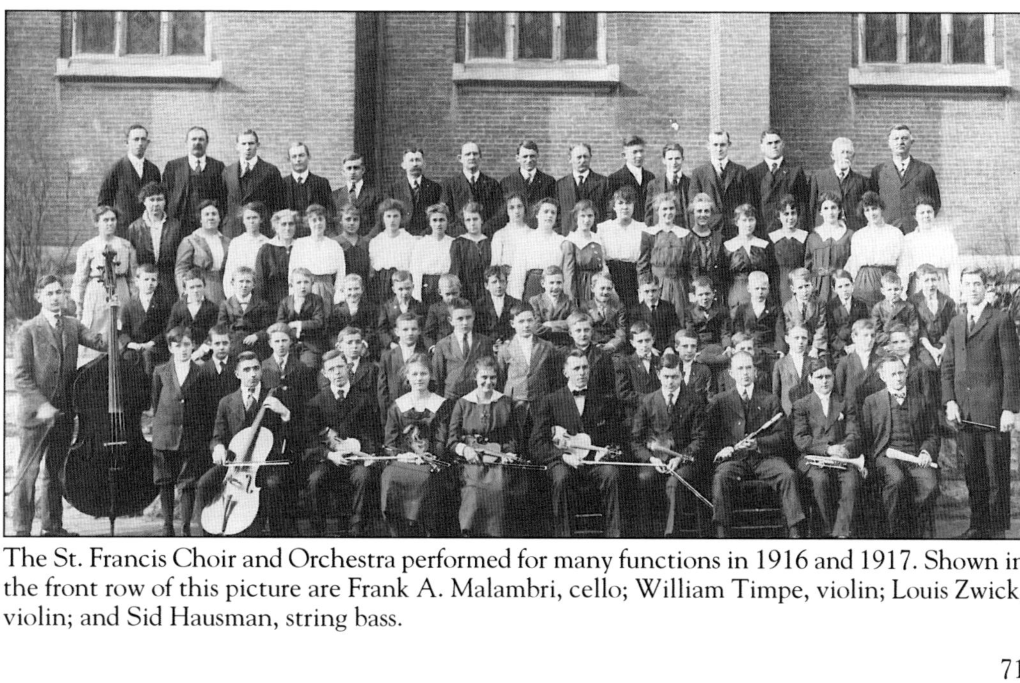

The St. Francis Choir and Orchestra performed for many functions in 1916 and 1917. Shown in the front row of this picture are Frank A. Malambri, cello; William Timpe, violin; Louis Zwick, violin; and Sid Hausman, string bass.

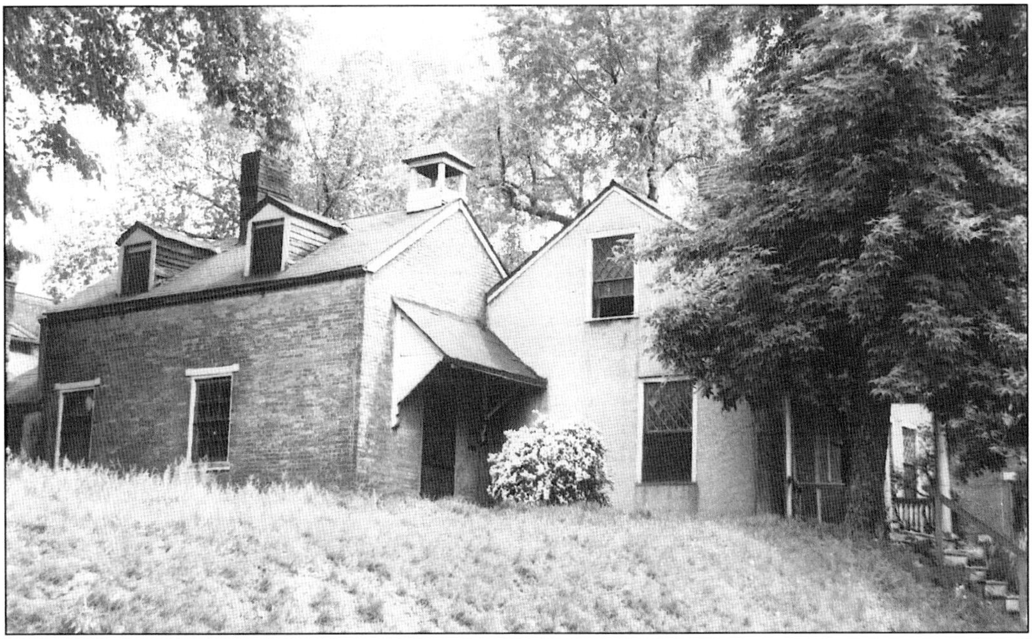

For many years, the house on the southeast corner of Fourth and Vermont Streets was considered the oldest structure in Quincy, having been erected before 1834. Mrs. Elizabeth Lindsay, a member of the Episcopal Church of St. John, was living in the frame-brick house when she died. She willed all of her property to the church, with the stipulation that the house should be used for the poor persons of the Protestant Episcopal Church of Quincy.

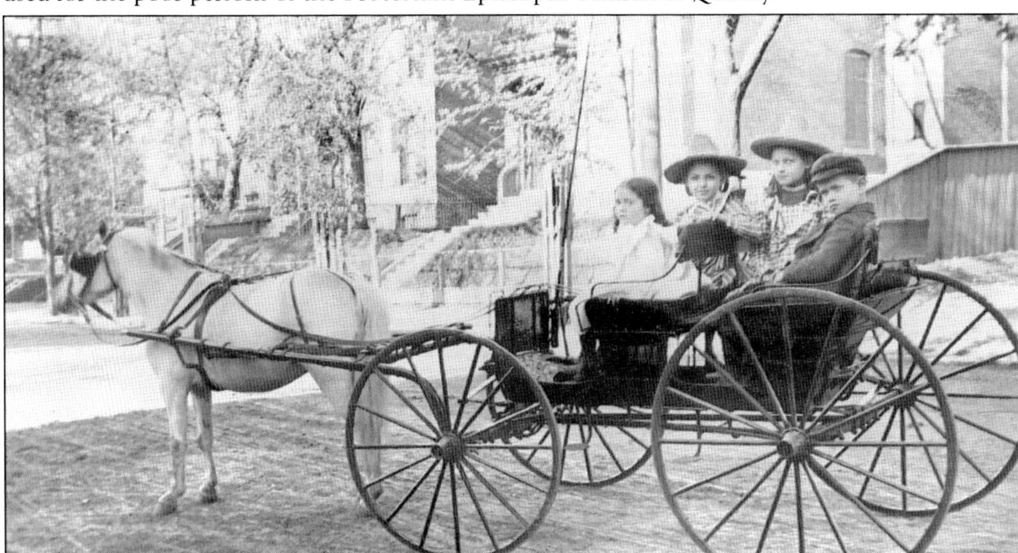

Ben Porter, sisters Louise and Harriet, and Frances Eldred are in front of the Porter home at 214 South Third Street. Ben Porter's father, B. Frank Porter, was manager of Quincy Transfer Co. Miss Eldred married Paul Morrison, Harriet Porter married Dr. E.L. Caddick, and Louise Porter married George Pennoyer. Paul Morrison was supervisor of music in the Quincy Public Schools and Mrs. Morrison was a piano teacher. The family home was located at 1454 Hampshire Street.

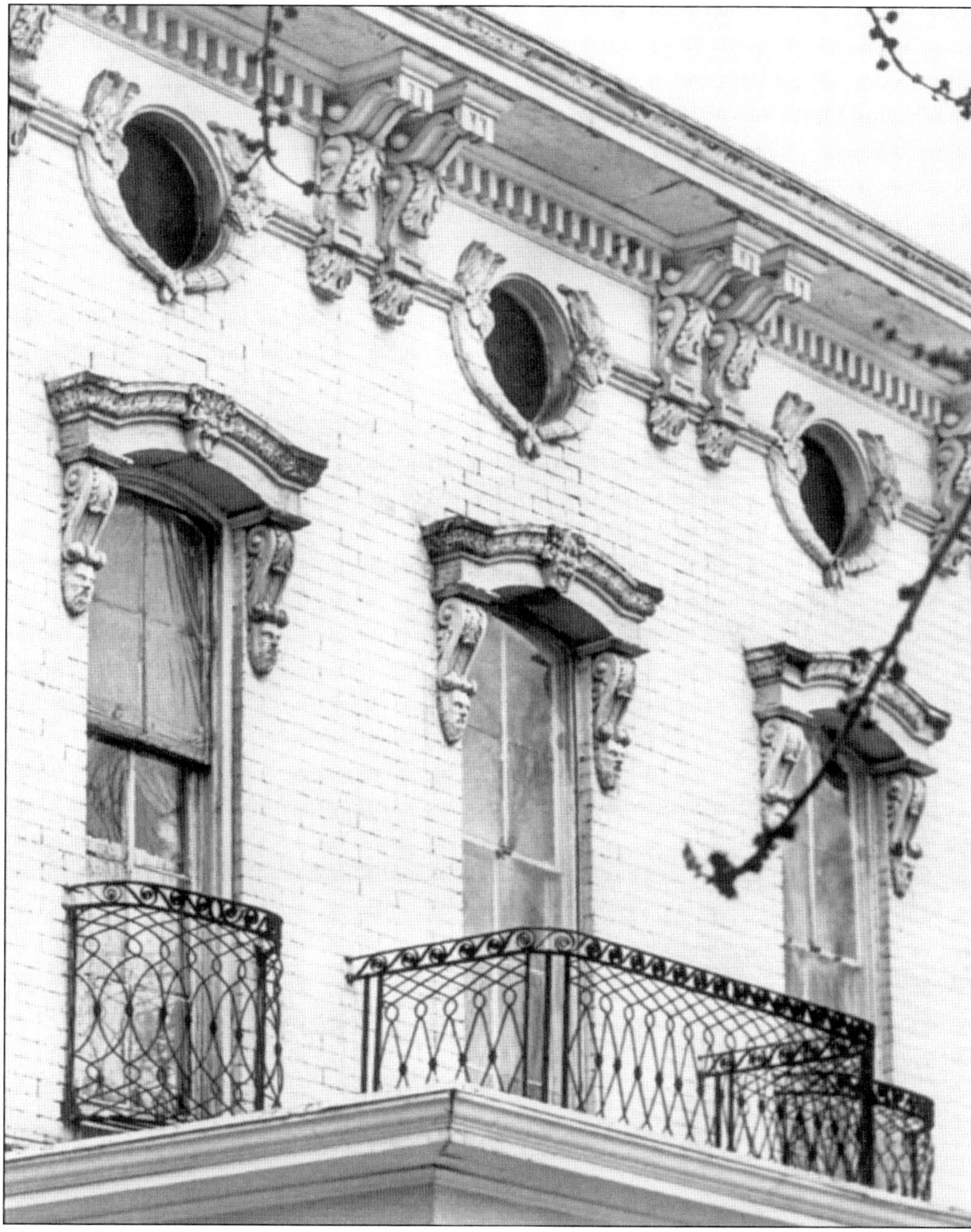

This home of chemist and sculptor John Hobrecker, located at 415 York Street, had very unusual detail. Above the front windows and front door were heads, which many persons claimed were meant to represent the Twelve Apostles and Satan. The heads of two apostles support each ornamental lintel or pediment. Centering each pediment was a leering, horned Satan. The ornamental work about the round windows represented "horns of plenty."

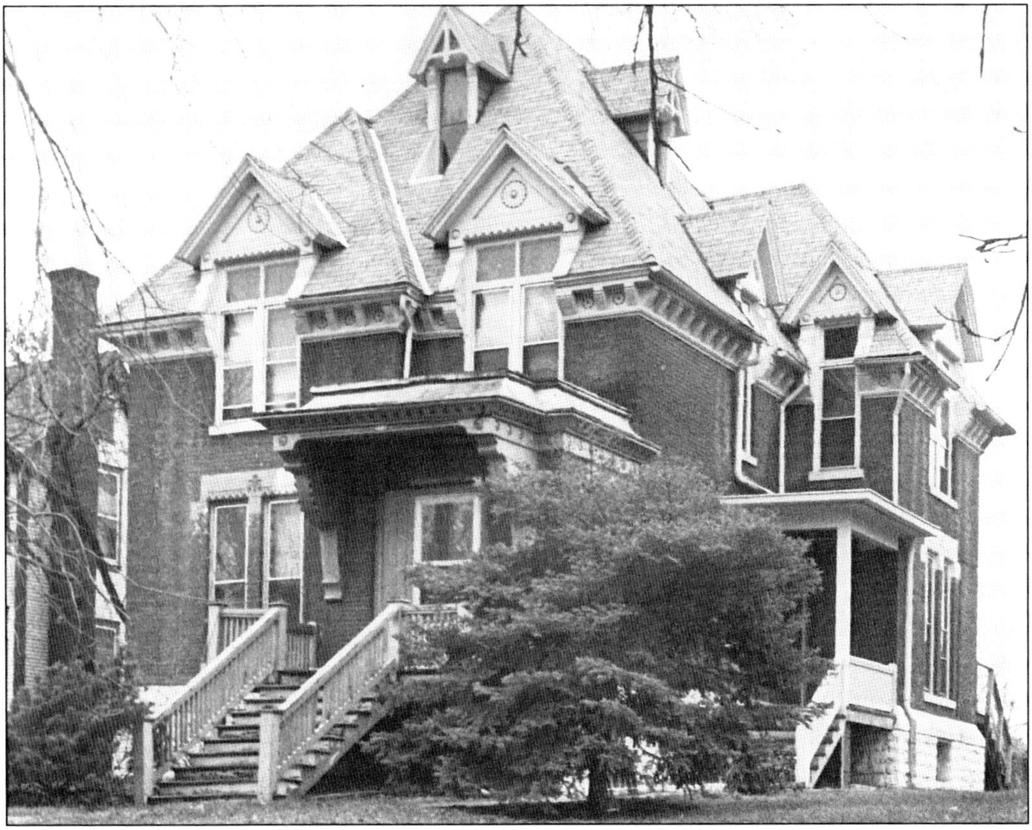

For many years, the "House of Seven Gables," located at 819 North Fifth Street, was the residence and office of Dr. William A. Millen.

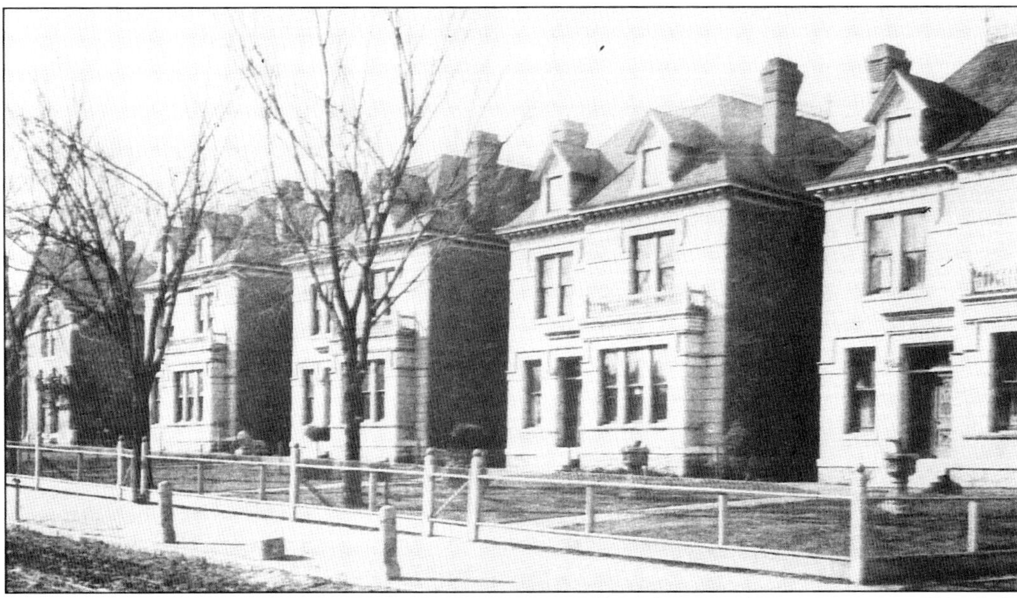

These five houses on South Twelfth Street between York and Kentucky Streets were all built by Menke Stone and Lime Co. They were brick, with stone fronts.

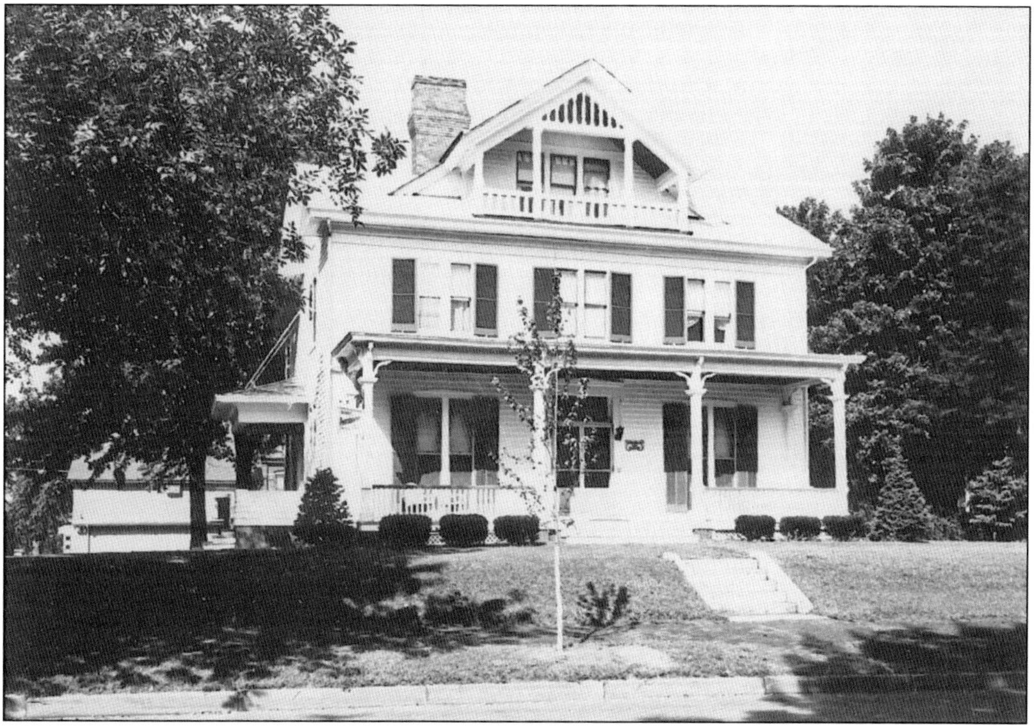

This former home of Amos Green, located at 505 North Eighth Street, still stands today. Green had a lumberyard on the northwest corner of Sixth and Maine Streets before the Opera House was built there.

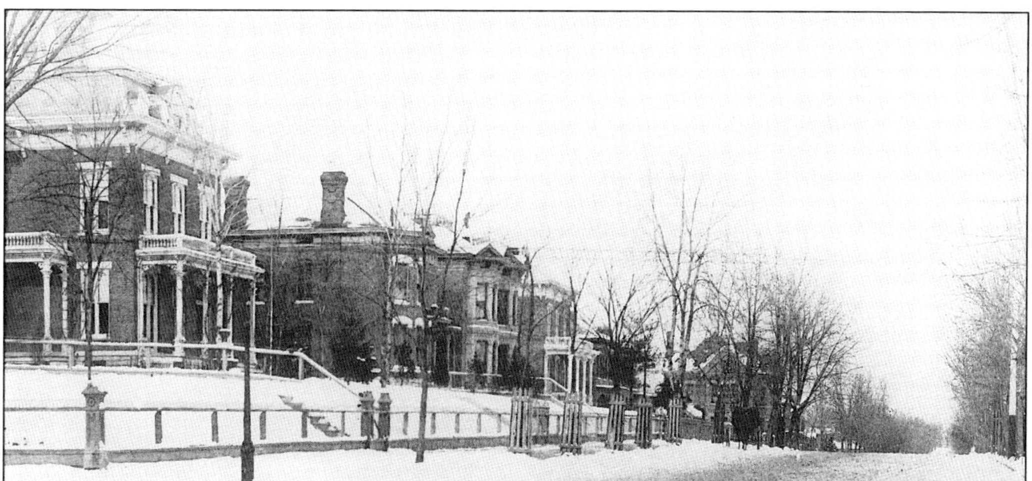

This picture of Sixth Street, looking north from Elm, shows the homes built by many prominent citizens at that time. As the city grew eastward, so did much of the population, and many of these homes were turned into apartment houses and allowed to deteriorate. Just in the last few years, several residents have seen the potential in these beautiful old homes and have undertaken the renovation of many of them.

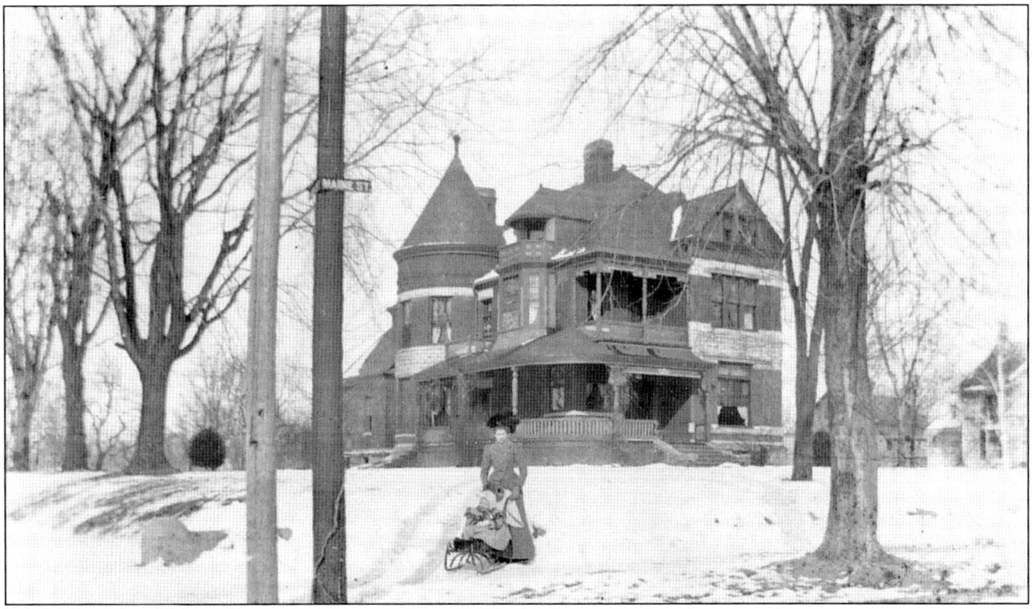

This is the Professor D.L. Musselman home at 2203 Maine Street. He was president of the Gem City Business College. There were three sons, D. Lafayette, Virgil George, and Thomas Edgar, and one daughter, Hattie.

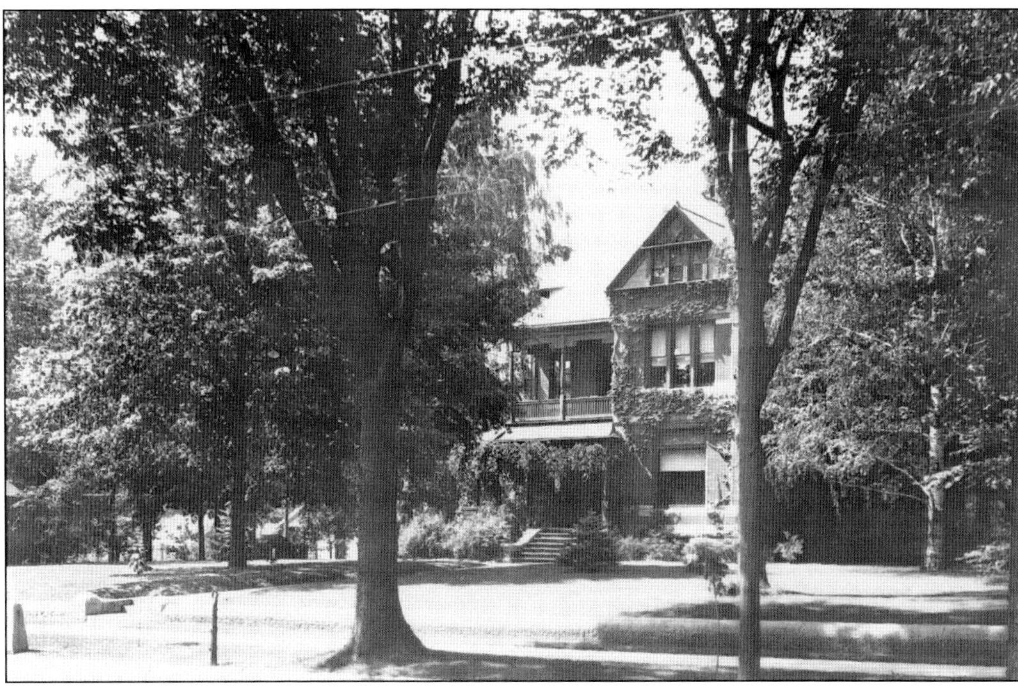

The D.L. Musselman home at 2203 Maine Street is seen here on a summer day.

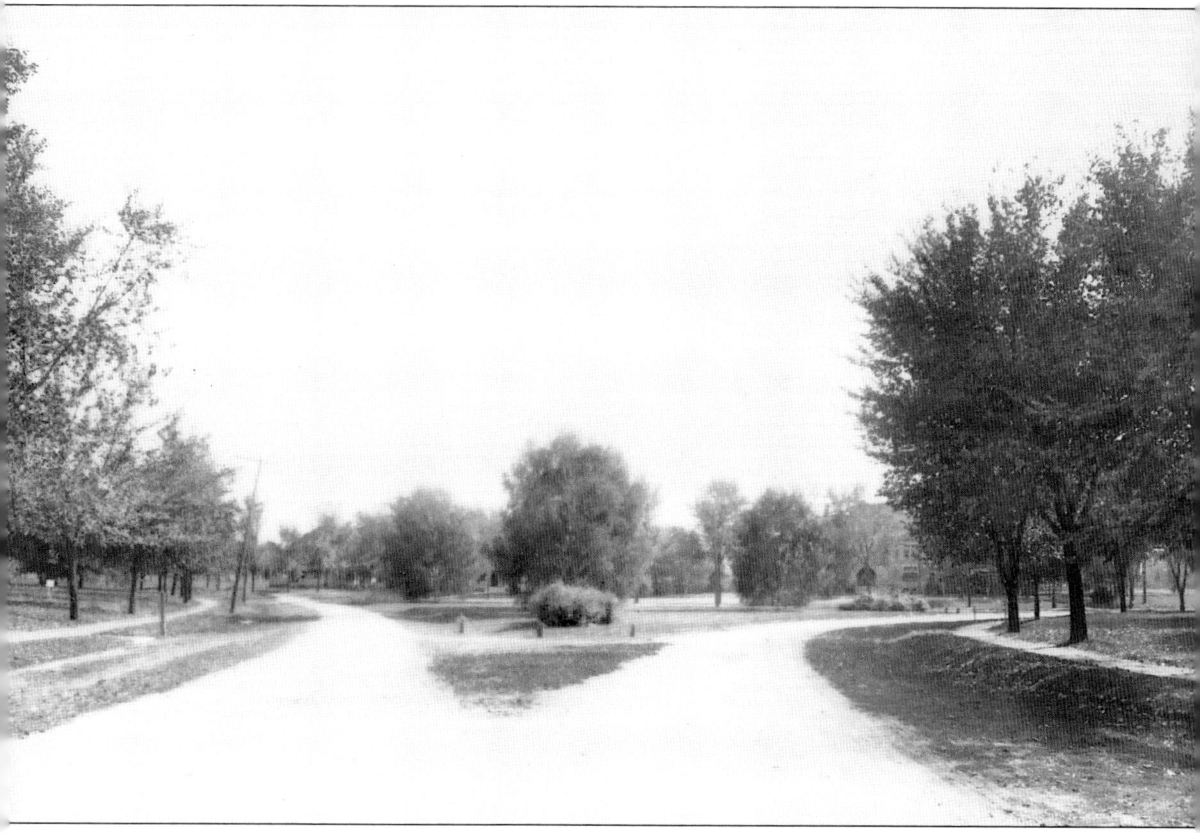

The Lawndale area is shown here after it was graded, drained, streets laid out, and trees planted, but before many houses were built. Before this area was developed, it was marshy. Many hunters shot ducks in the triangular area of Jersey, East, and West Avenues in Lawndale.

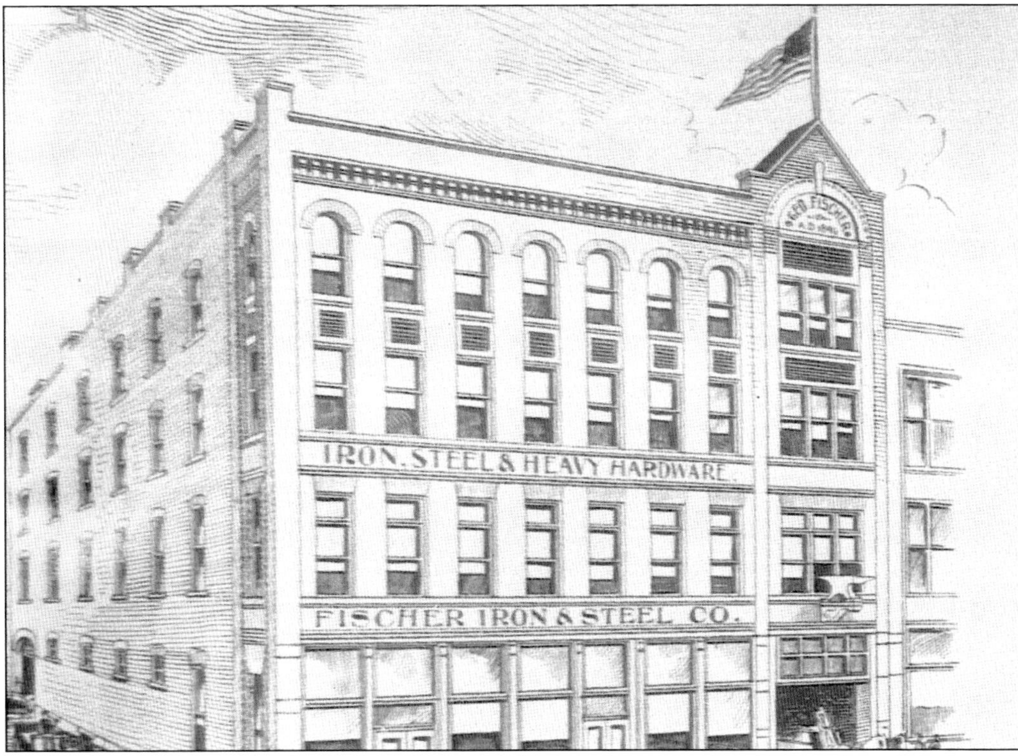

George Fischer started in business for himself selling stoves, grates, and house furnishings at 625 Maine Street, later moving to 521 Maine Street. In 1890, he bought out the Lemly Brothers hardware business at 217-221 Maine Street. By 1896, he had decided to construct a large, four-story brick building at 121-25 South Fifth Street, shown here, where the firm prospered. It was later purchased by Tenk Hardware Co.

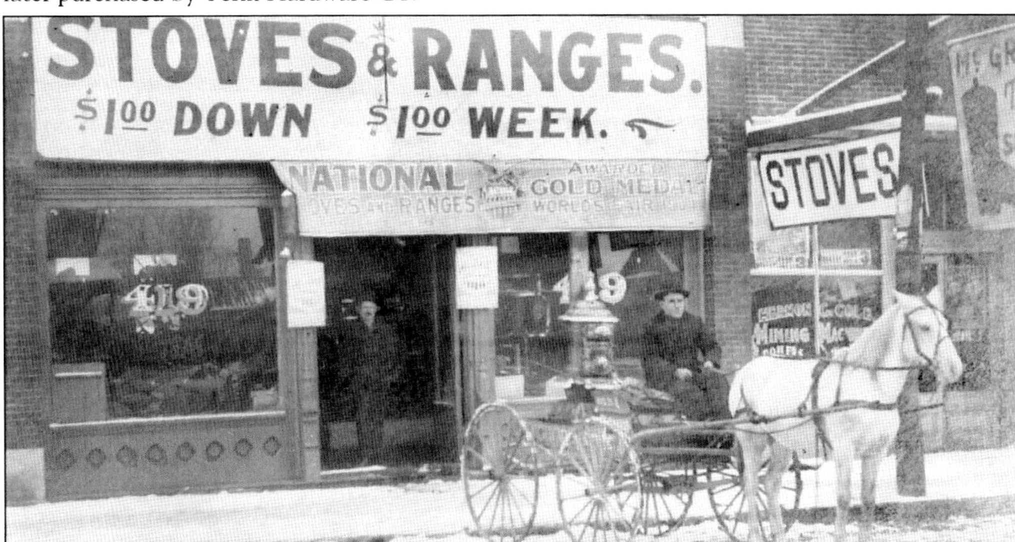

At one time, Fischer formed a partnership with John Grant in the hardware business on Hampshire Street. The sign advertises National Stoves and Ranges, $1 down, $1 week; they were awarded a Gold Medal at the World's Fair.

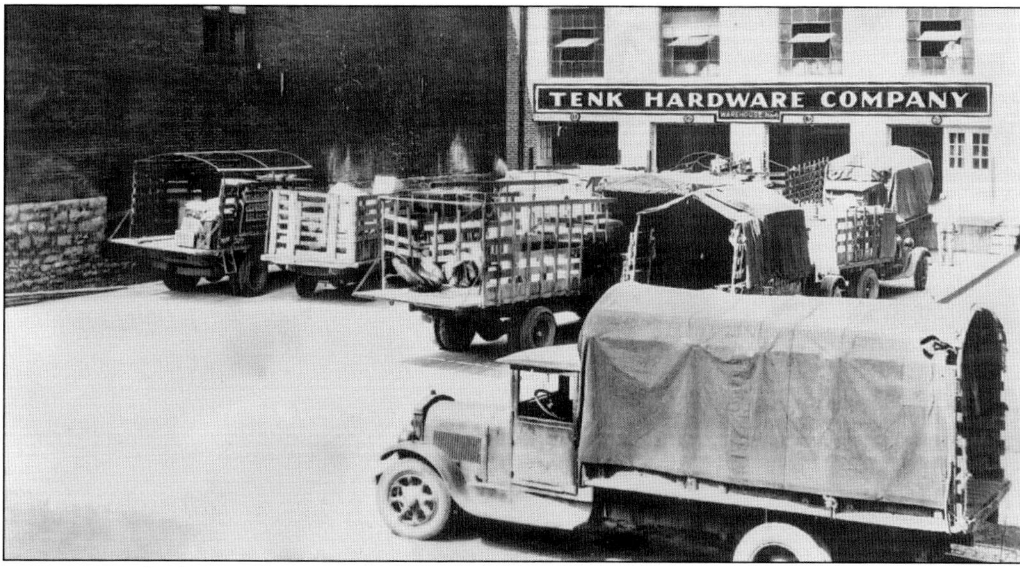

Henry Jr. and John Herman Tenk founded the Tenk Hardware Co. in the 1860s at 512 Maine Street. In 1918, the company purchased the Fischer building at 121-23 South Fifth Street for the wholesale division. There were two warehouses, one at 511 Jersey Street, and the other at 610-616 Jersey Street. The building at 121-23 South Fifth Street was razed for the parking deck located there today.

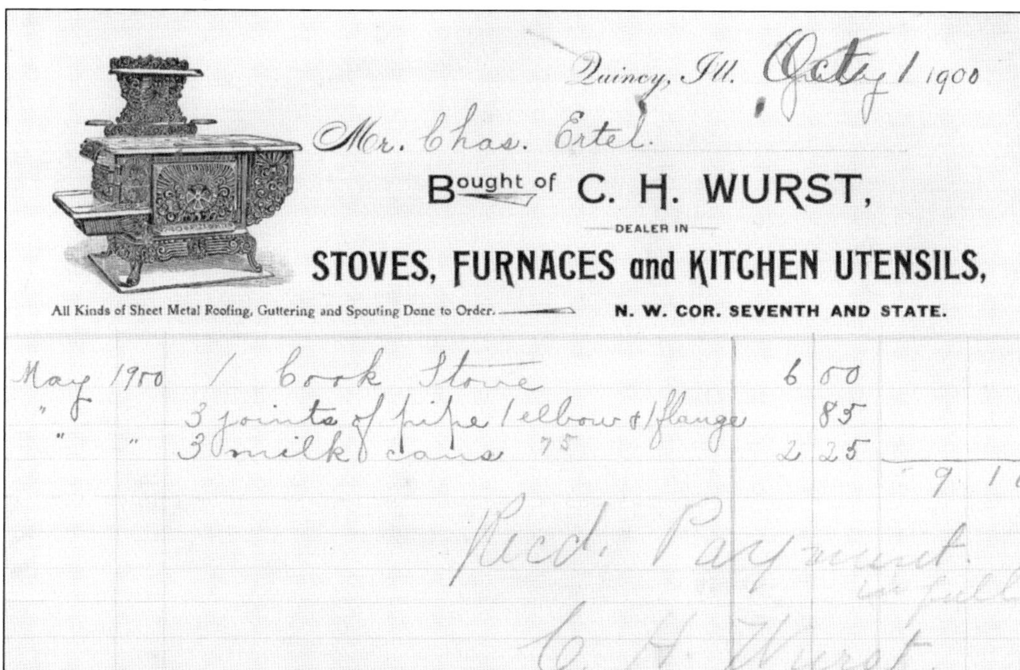

Quincy, Ill. Octr 1 1900

Mr. Chas. Ertel.

Bought of C. H. WURST,

DEALER IN

STOVES, FURNACES and KITCHEN UTENSILS,

All Kinds of Sheet Metal Roofing, Guttering and Spouting Done to Order.

N. W. COR. SEVENTH AND STATE.

May 1900	1 Cook Stove	6 00
"	3 joints of pipe 1 elbow & 1 flange	85
" "	3 milk cans 75	2 25
		9 10

Recd. Payment in full

C. H. Wurst.

The C.H. Wurst Co. operated on the northwest corner of Seventh and State Streets for many years. Their tin shop, which handled all kinds of sheet metal, roofing, guttering, and spouting, was on Seventh Street directly north of the store. This October 1, 1900, receipt indicates the sale of a cook stove for $6, three joints of pipe, and three milk cans to Mr. Chas. Ertel for a total of $9.10.

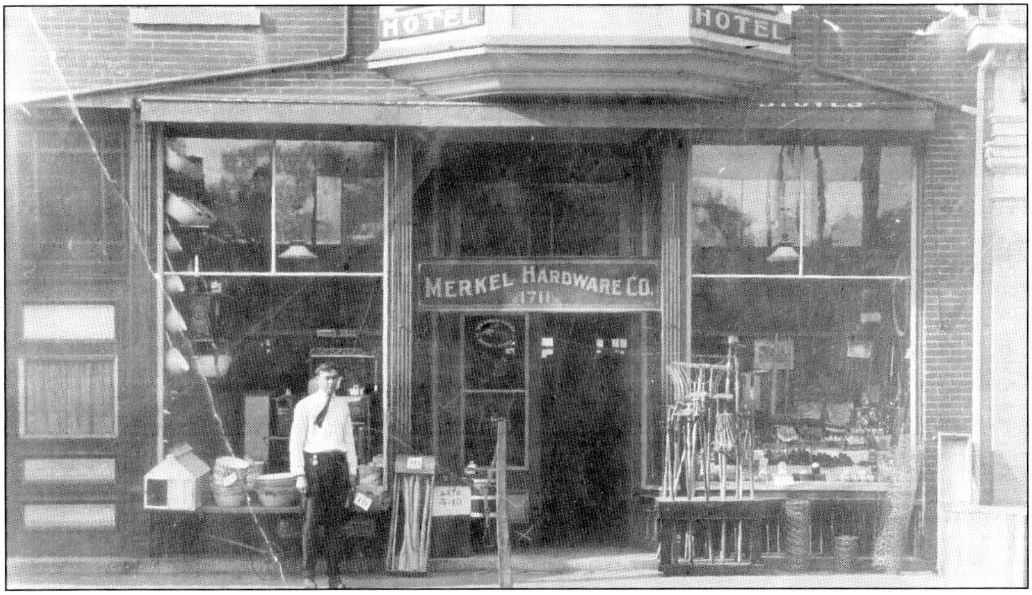

The Merkel Hardware Co. store, located at 1711 Broadway, is shown here in this 1910 photograph with the East Broadway Hotel on the second floor. Note the wide range of items for sale, from brooms and mops to baseball bats and chicken coops.

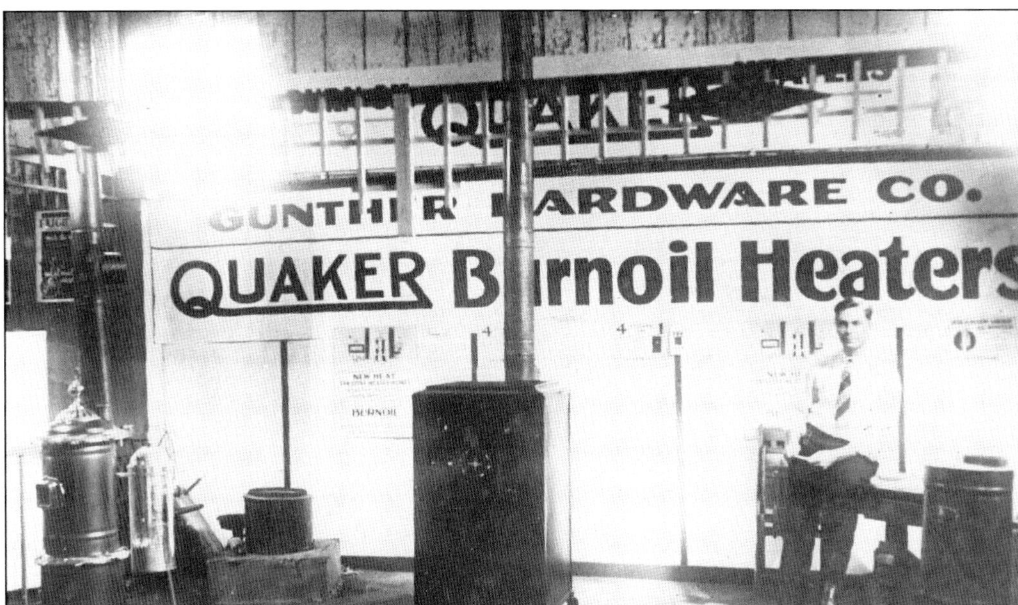

Gunther Hardware Co. was started by Robert Gunther in the 1880s. By 1899, the store had moved to 505 Hampshire Street, where it remained for many years. The Japan Photographic Art Studio took this picture advertising Quaker Burnoil Heaters in 1918. M. Yamaguchie was the proprietor of the art studio, which was located upstairs of the Gunther Hardware Co. at 505 1/2 Hampshire.

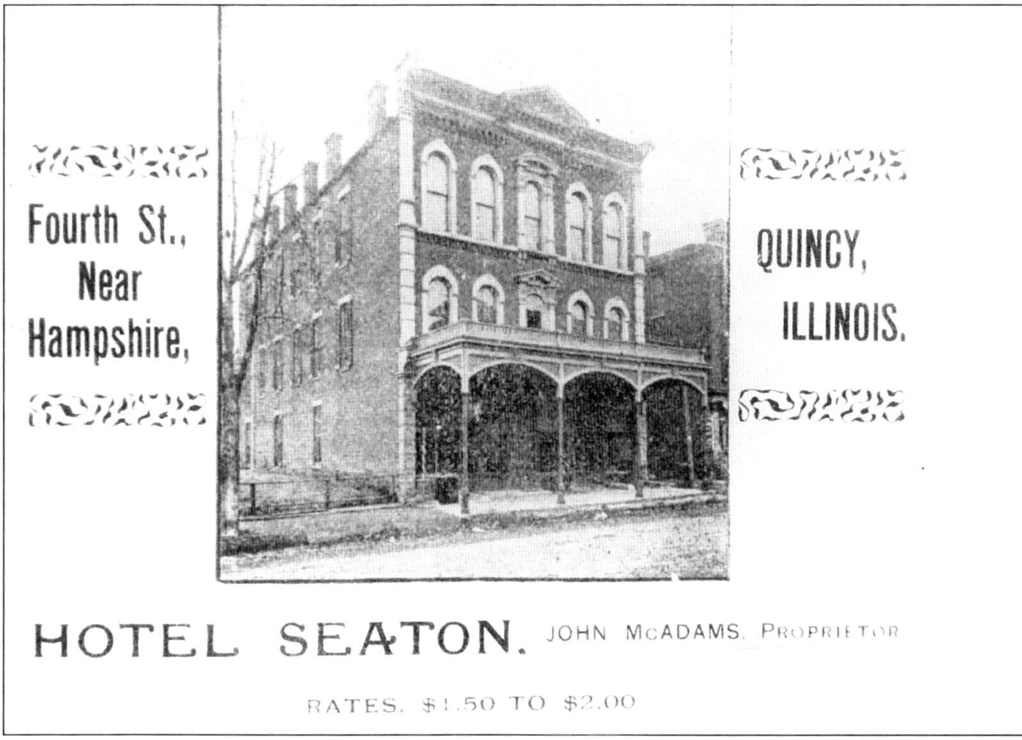

Once known as the New Windsor Hotel, the Hotel Seaton, shown in this 1892 photograph, was located on the east side of Fourth Street between Hampshire and Vermont Streets. John McAdams was proprietor of the hotel and offered rates from $1.50 to $2. McAdams served as a member of the General Assembly of 1880-1881, thereafter located in Quincy. In 1897, he was elected to the state senate.

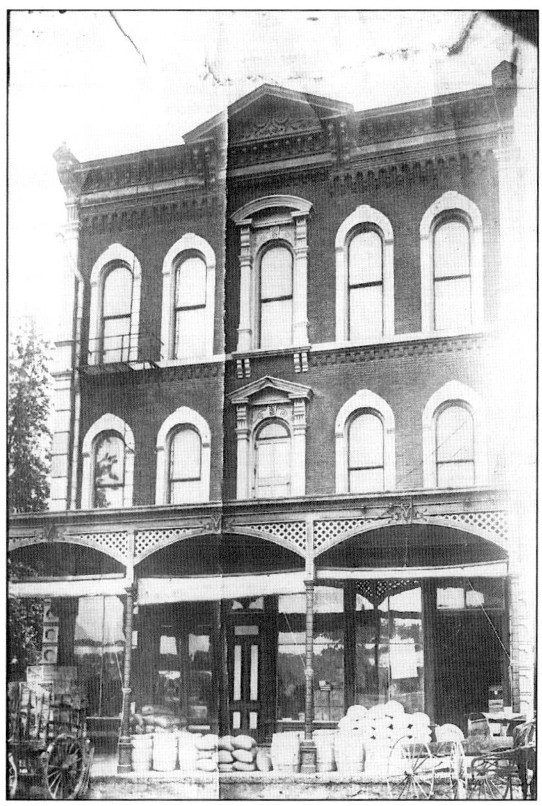

The N. Kohl Grocer Co. bought the building at 218-220 North Fourth Street in 1896 and remodeled it for their wholesale grocery business. After a bad fire in 1920, the front of the building was changed somewhat when the old-time wooden awning was removed.

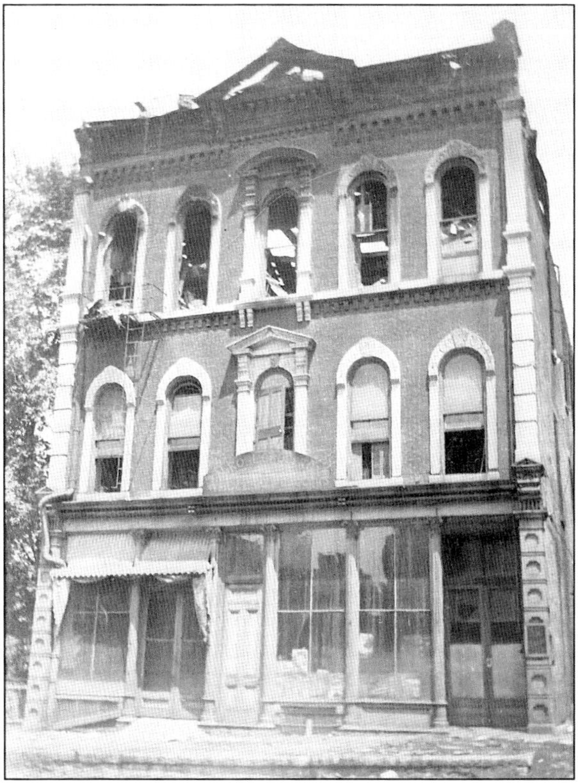

In addition to the fire mentioned in 1920, there was another fire in 1919 that saw hundreds of thousands of matches in wooden boxes go up in flames. Another fire in 1938 washed off the labels from many cans and bottles.

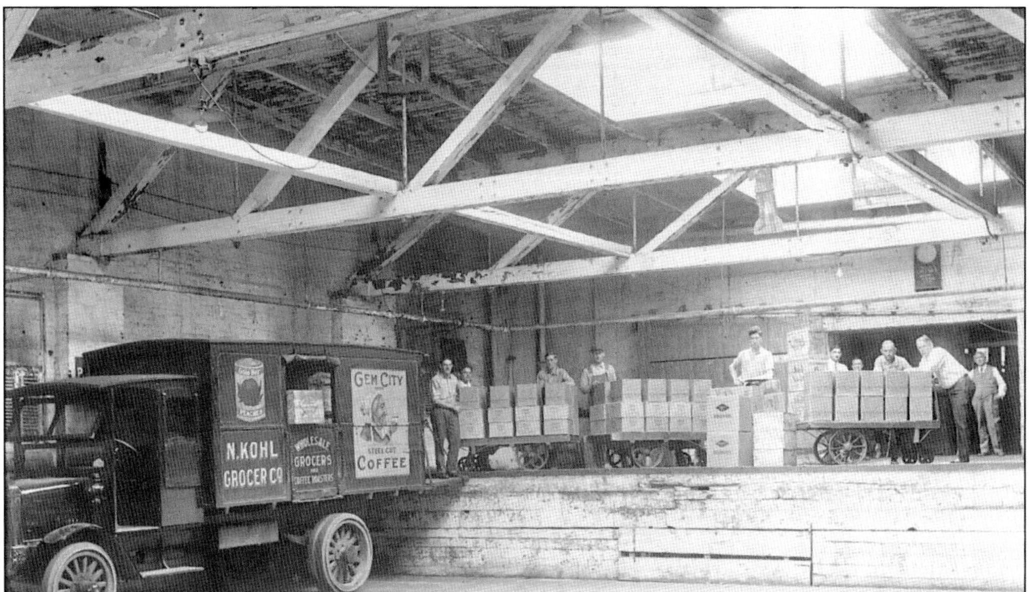

The N. Kohl Grocer Co. changed its name to Kohl Wholesale Co. in 1985. It also moved to 130 Jersey Street that year. They had been at the Fourth Street location for about 90 years. The front part of the warehouse on Fourth Street burned to the ground in a February 1990 fire. This picture shows workmen on the loading platform with a delivery truck, which advertises "Gem City Steel Cut Coffee" and "Gold Bar Peaches."

This was a progress report picture taken of the "New Tremont," or Hotel Quincy as it was later renamed, on December 1, 1910, for the C.L. Gray Construction Co. This hotel replaced the old Tremont Hotel, which burned June 22, 1904, claiming the lives of Elizabeth Welch, principal of Jefferson School, and Mary Welch, principal of Jackson School. Doors to the "New Tremont," or "Hotel Quincy," were opened to the public May 15, 1911.

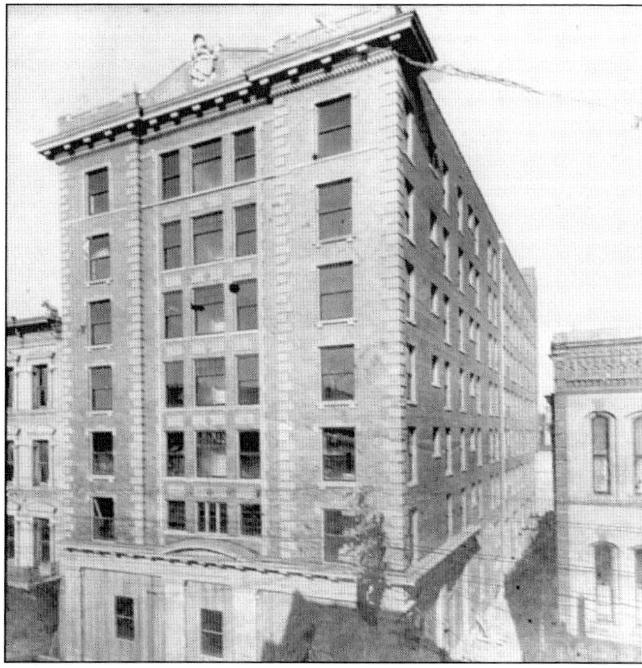

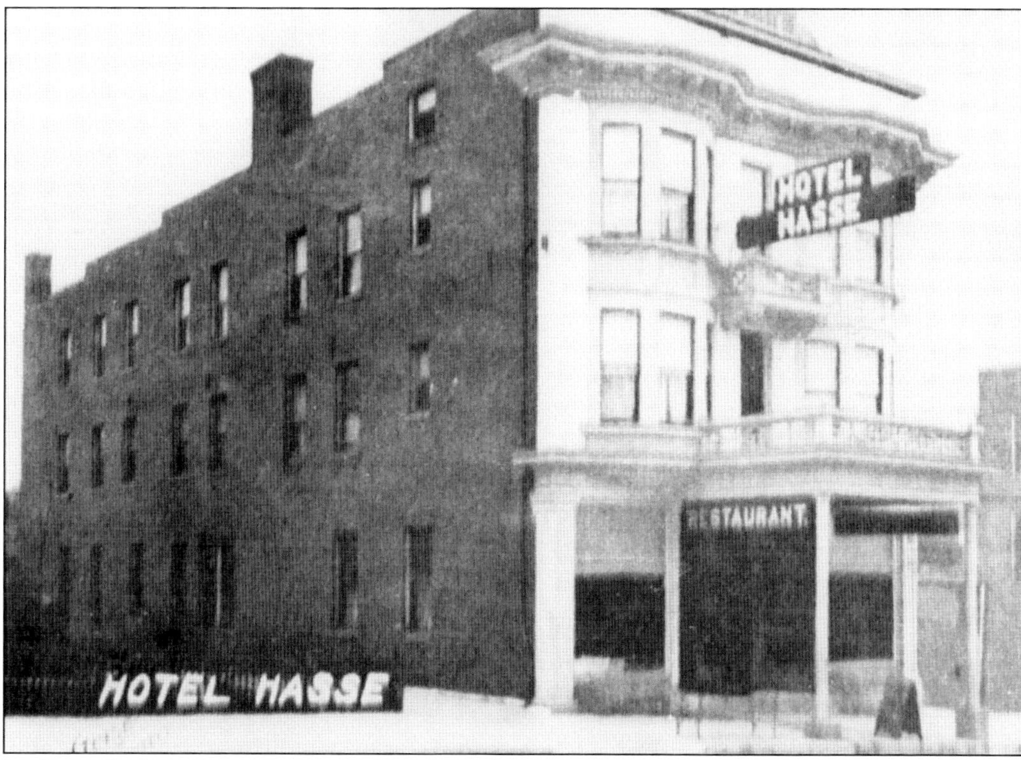

In the early days, Front Street was known as the Levee and was a very busy place. Several hotels were built on Front Street, as well as adjacent streets, to handle the trade from the steamboats and railway depots. One of those was the Hotel Hasse at 218-220 Oak Street, which operated for about 30 years.

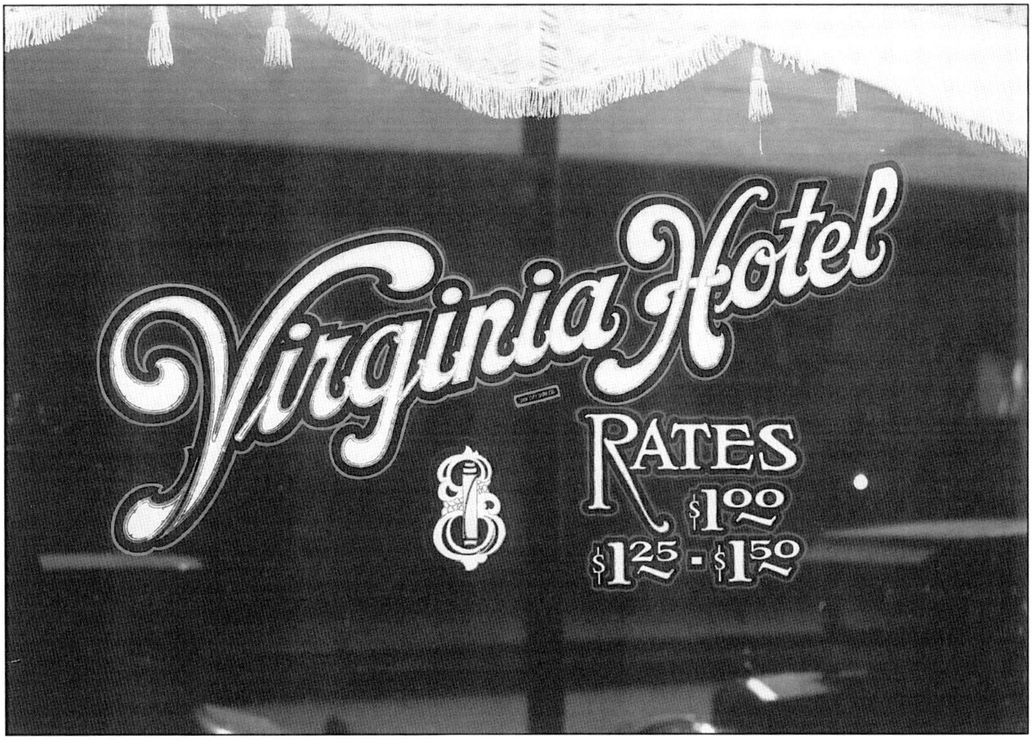

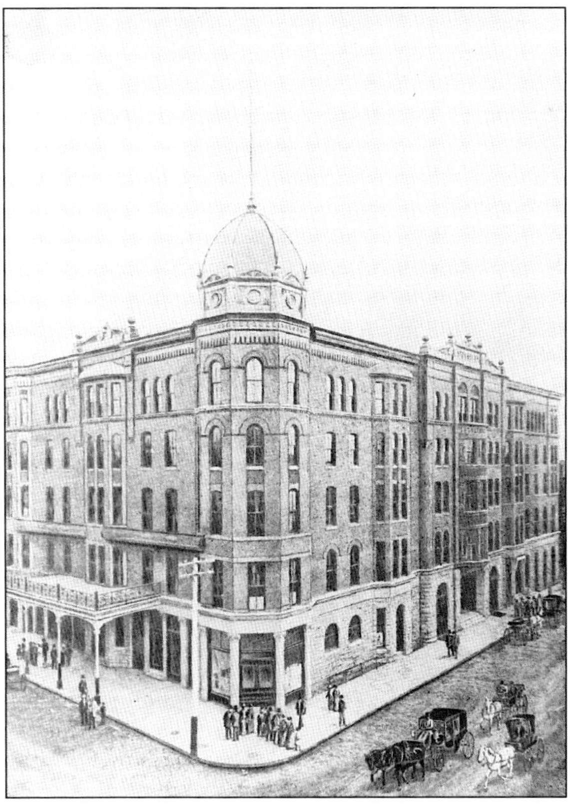

Another hotel in the Levee area was the Virginia Hotel at 528-36 North Second Street. It is believed the Virginia Hotel replaced the Moecker Hotel in this location and that the name changed to Virginia in 1918.

One of the most lavish hotels of its day, the Hotel Newcomb opened March 5, 1889, on the southeast corner of Fourth and Maine Streets. It was named for Richard Newcomb, president of the Quincy Hotel Company. The Quincy House preceded the Hotel Newcomb from 1838 to 1883.

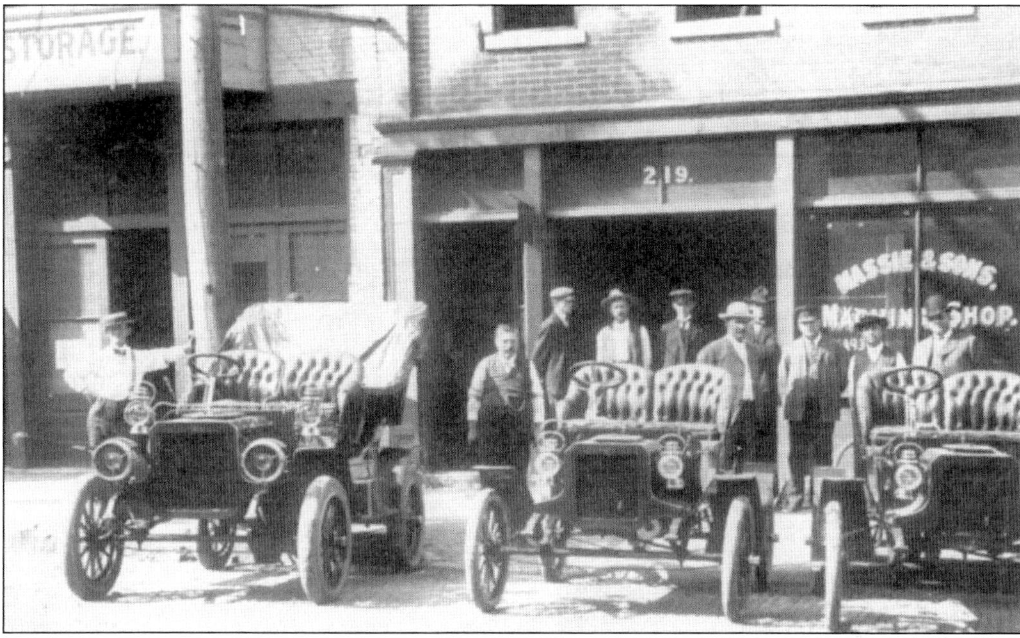

One of the first "horseless carriages" to be sold in Quincy was the Reo, shown here in front of Massie Machine Shop at 219 North Fourth Street in 1907. However, in the beginning, automobiles were an expensive luxury and not always popular. Many roads were posted with such signs as "The automobile is the curse of the country road."

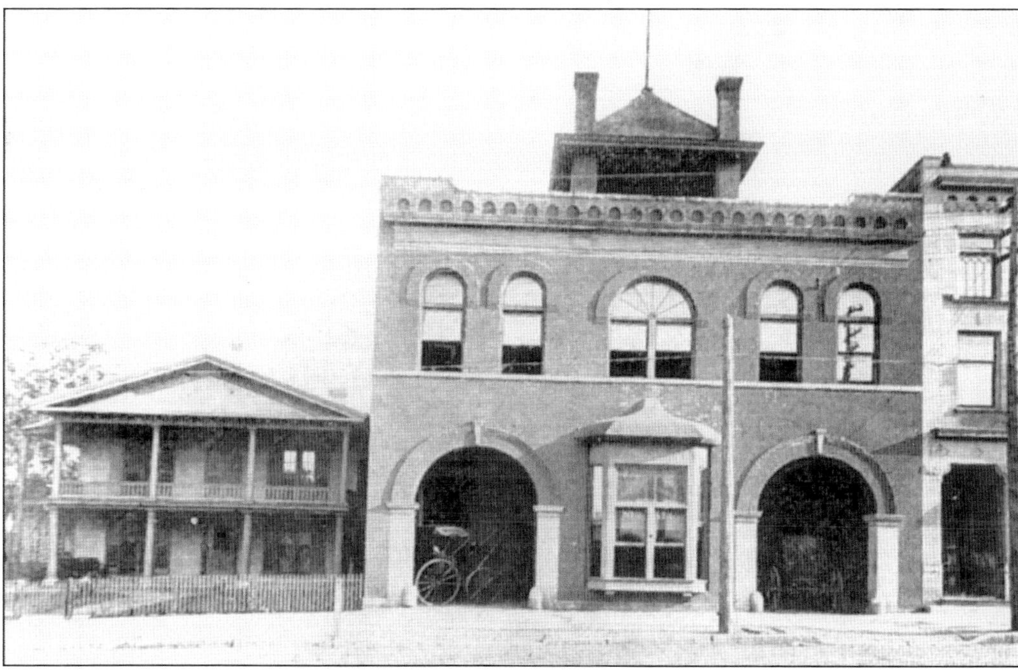

Even though the automobile was starting to come onto the scene, the horse was still more dependable and cheaper to own. Several livery stables were in operation, including the Palace Livery Stables at 812-814 Maine, owned by Henry Wiskirchen. Wiskirchen lived in the house to the left at 818 Maine.

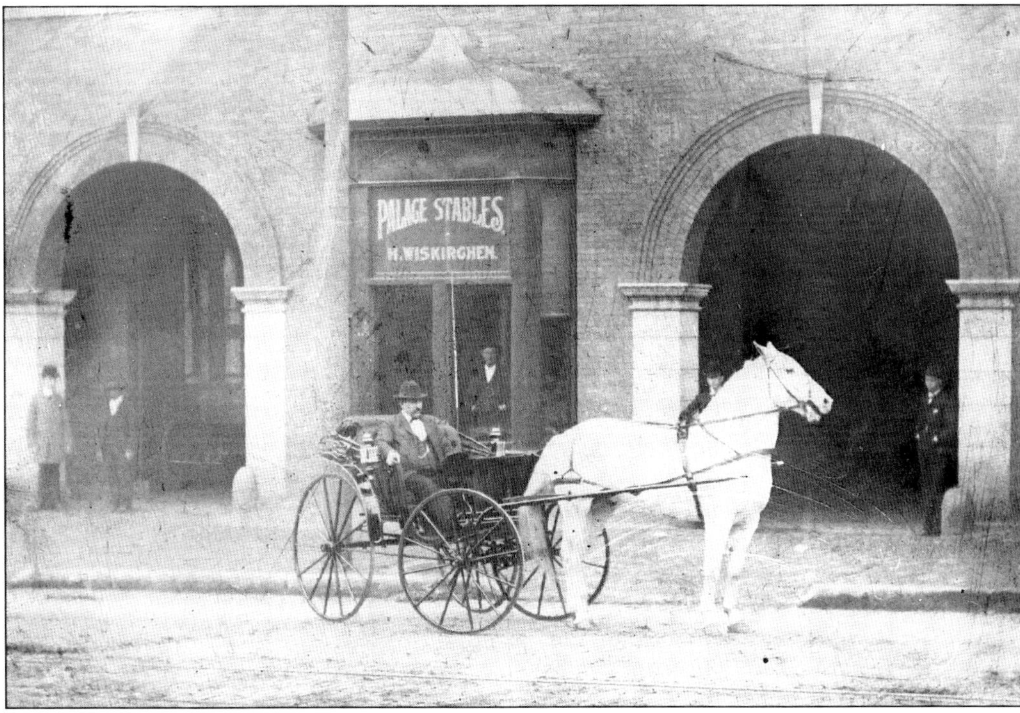

The Henry Wiskirchen Palace Livery Stable was erected in 1897. Mr. Wiskirchen is seen driving Dexter in front of the Palace Stables, which were located at 812-814 Maine Street. Dexter was a white Arabian with a pink nose, the favorite of several presidents and dignitaries who were transported by the Palace Stables when they visited Quincy.

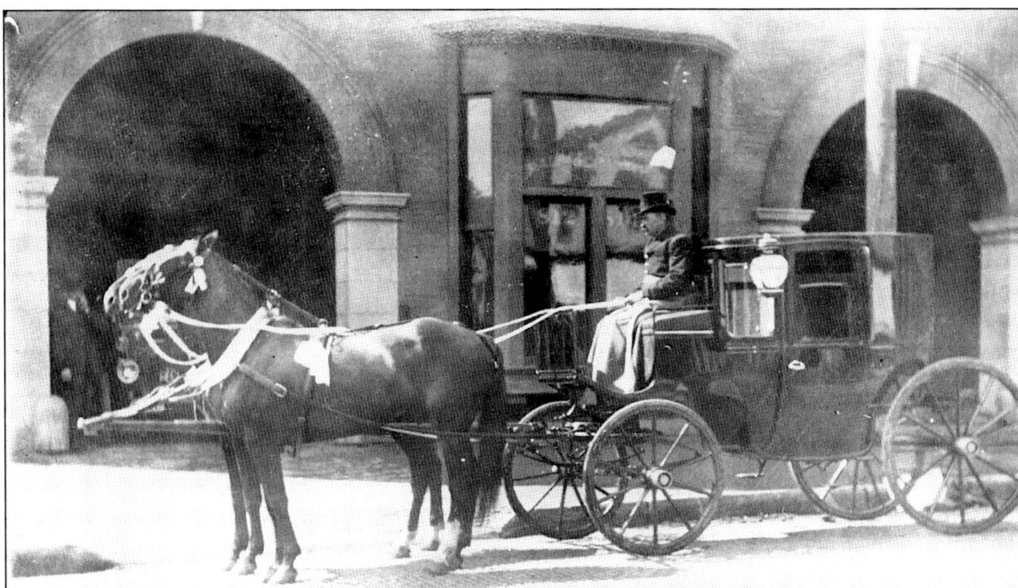

John Luke is driving this special bridesmaids' carriage with white collars for the horses. Many of the carriages owned by Mr. Wiskirchen cost more than a $1,000. Later, Fink's Garage was in this 812 Maine Street building.

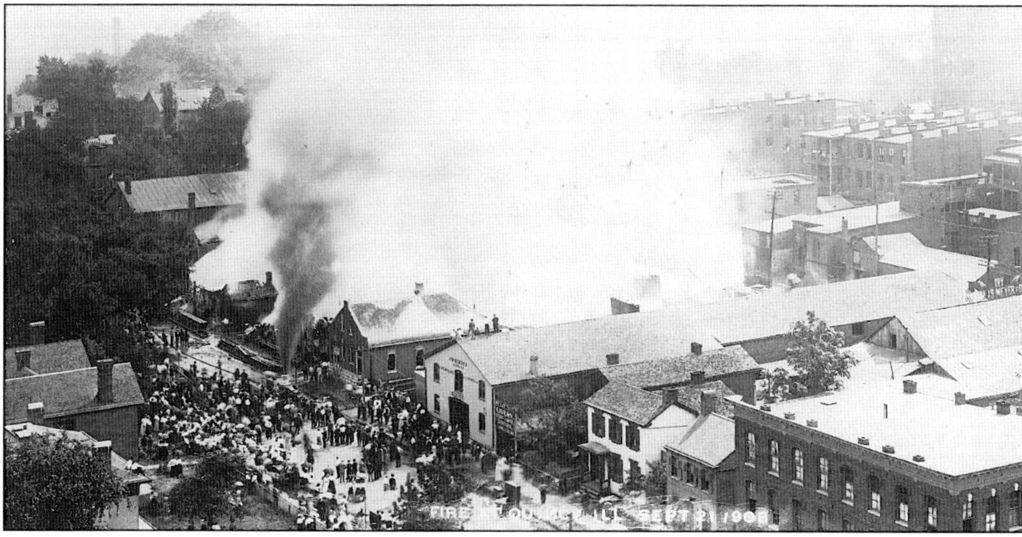

At the turn of the century, Moller and Vandenboom Lumber Co. had lumberyards on Vermont between Sixth and Seventh Streets, at Third and Vermont, at Third and Broadway, and a wholesale yard on the Quincy Bay. One of the worst fires the city has witnessed occurred at their yard on Vermont between Sixth and Seventh Streets on September 21, 1908. The next major fire suffered by the company was on January 6, 1912, with still another on a bitter cold night on January 31, 1935.

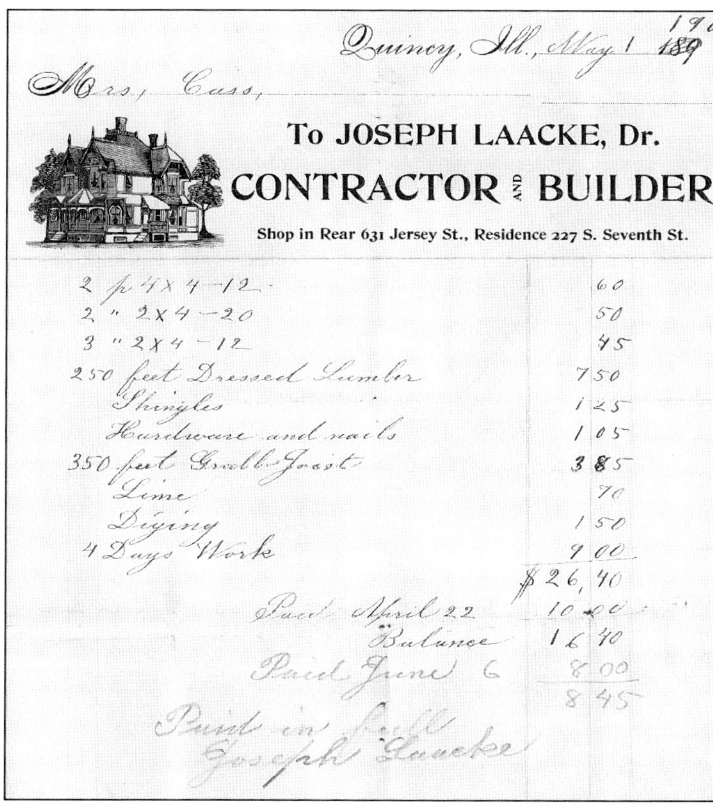

Quincy, Ill., May 1 1901

Mrs. Cass,

To JOSEPH LAACKE, Dr.

CONTRACTOR AND BUILDER,

Shop in Rear 631 Jersey St., Residence 227 S. Seventh St.

2 pc 4 x 4 - 12	60
2 " 2 x 4 - 20	50
3 " 2 x 4 - 12	45
250 feet Dressed Lumber	7 50
Shingles	1 25
Hardware and nails	1 05
350 feet Grubb-Joist	3 85
Lime	70
Diging	1 50
4 Days Work	9 00
	$26, 40
Paid April 22	10 00
Balance	16 40
Paid June 6	8 00
	8 45

Paid in full
Joseph Laacke

For many years before the turn of the century, Joseph Laacke was a well-known contractor and builder. This bill dated May 1, 1901, to a Mrs. Cass, charged a total of $26.40. It included 250 feet of dressed lumber for $7.50, shingles for $1.25, hardware and nails for $1.05, diging (sic) for $1.50, and four days work at $9.

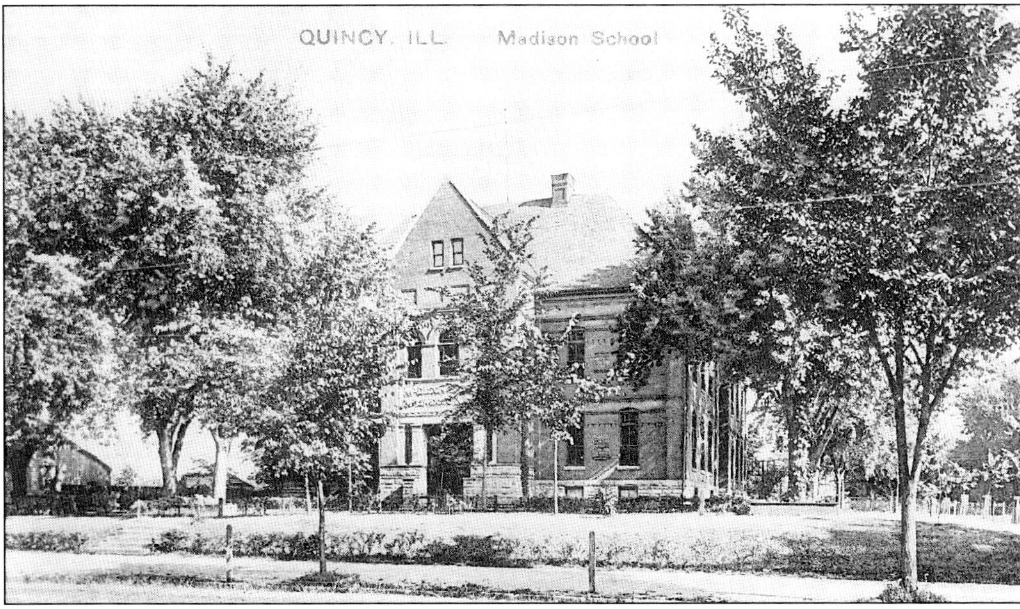

Madison School at Twenty-fifth and Maine Streets was named for Pres. James Madison. The original structure had only two rooms, but a new building was erected c. 1890 at a cost of $9,000. In 1898, four more rooms were added on the north, and in 1925, a modern addition, costing $171,000 was built to provide eight more classrooms, a gymnasium, a heating plant, and an auditorium.

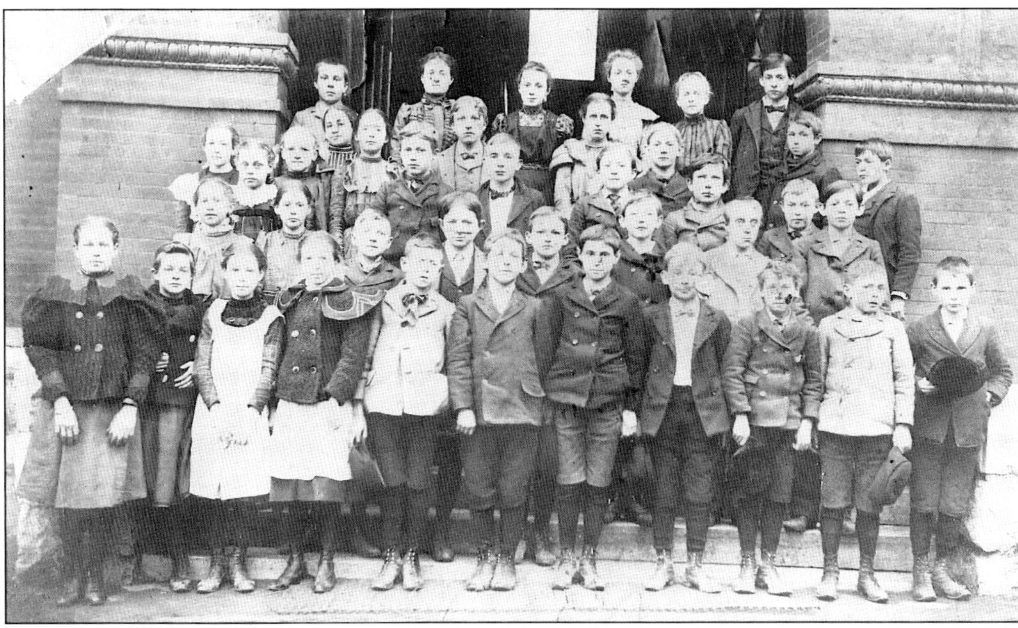

Irving School, located on Payson Avenue between Eighth and Ninth Streets, was named for novelist and historian Washington Irving. This group of sixth graders, photographed in 1899, stands in front of the old building, which was erected in 1864. In 1919, the old building was torn down and a new structure was erected at a cost of $152,000.

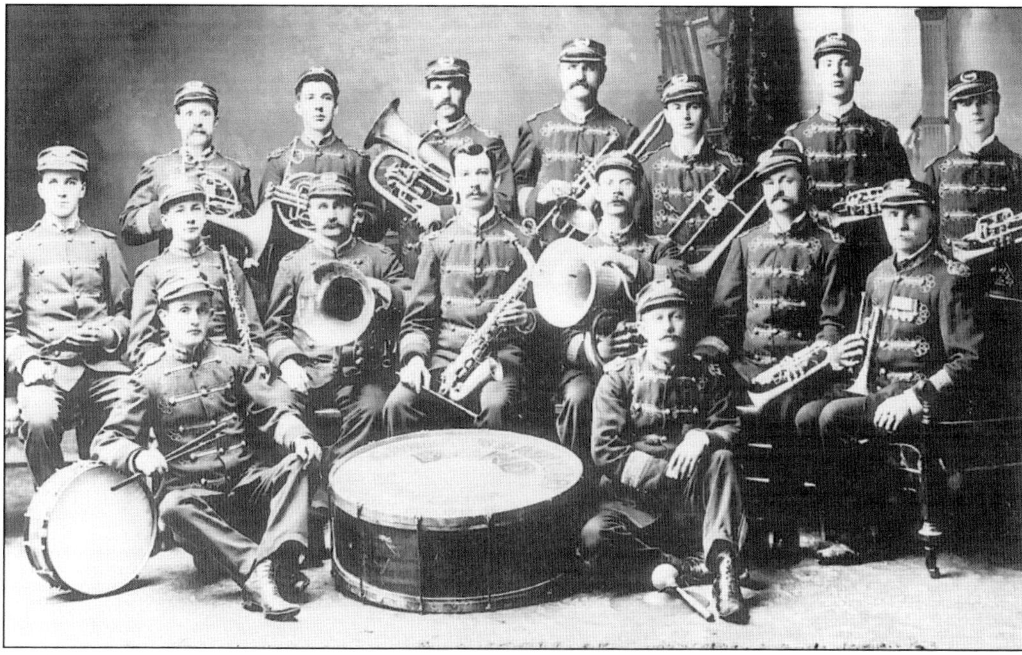

Carl Gardner, born in Germany in 1868, studied in Europe and came to America as a young violinist. In 1890, he accepted an offer to direct the orchestra in Doerr's Opera House at Sixth and Maine Streets. He also organized and directed this military concert band. Players shown, from left to right, are as follows: (front row) Oscar Schilling, snare drums; and Albert Schilling, bass drum; (second row) Joseph Weiler, flute; Charles Weiler, clarinet; Wilbur Thompson, baritone; Carl Gardner, director; Pat Lenane, tuba; A. Stimpson, cornet; and Barney Krebber, cornet; (back row) B. McCoy, melophone; Albert Gardner, melophone; Robert Broemmer, baritone; John Holtschlag, trombone; Alfred Call, trombone; Ferdinand Gardner, cornet; and Ernest Call, cornet.

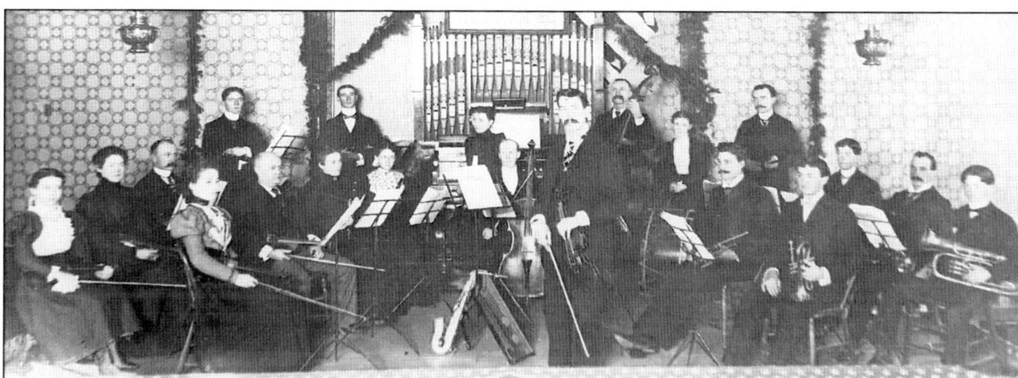

Carl Gardner also directed the Mendon Congregational Church Orchestra in the 1890s. Seen here, from left to right, are as follows: (front circle) Willa Wible, violin; S.F. Chittenden, violin; Olive Ely, flute; E.R. Chittenden, flute; W.G. Gay, cello; Carl Gardner, leader; Rolla Henderson, cornet; and Ralph McIntyre, cornet; (rear circle) Cecelia Pepple, violin; Sadie Harrison, violin; George Chittenden, viola; Julian Boyer, clarinet; Oliver Quinn, clarinet; S.F. Chittenden, piano and organ; Thomas Gilliland, string bass; Sadie Pepple, bass drum; Charles Robertson, snare drum; John McIntyre, cornet; Gilbert Starr, French horn; and Charles McIntyre, French horn.

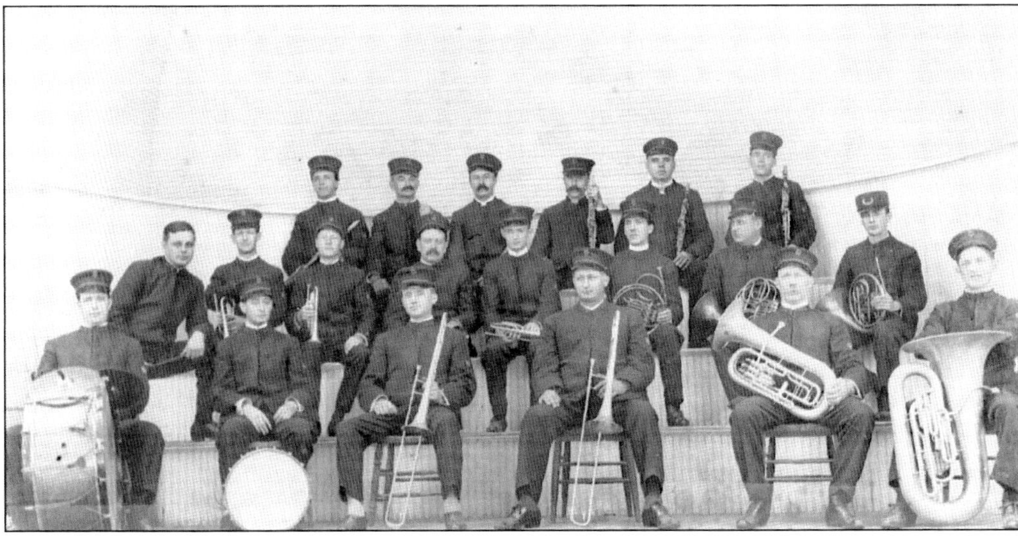

About the turn of the century, Quincy had several bands, including the Quincy City Band, shown here at Baldwin Park, *c.* 1908. Band members included in this photo are as follows: (front row) Cliff Weller, Jos. Williams, Chas. Edw. Hoadley, Clarence Buttz, Wilbur Thompson, and Harry Bourne; (second row) leader Albert Carl Fischer, Victor Anthony, George Hoffman, William Edward Gillespie, Clarence Warner, Albert Gardner, Oliver Jennings, and Julius Gardner; (back row) Joseph Weiler, Frank Holtschlag, Barney Damhorst, John Weller, M.E. Swords, and Maurice Wingert.

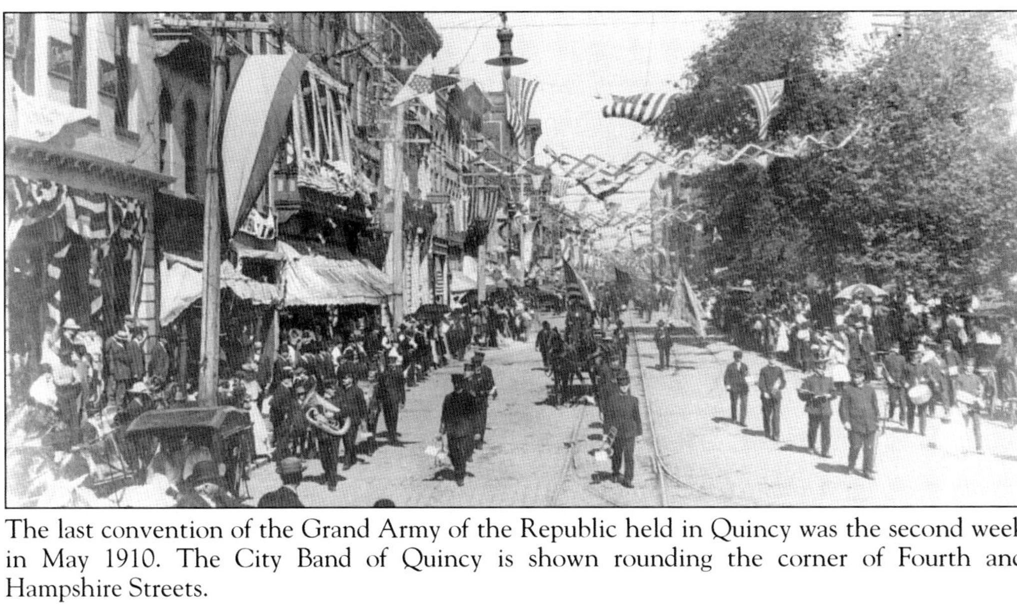

The last convention of the Grand Army of the Republic held in Quincy was the second week in May 1910. The City Band of Quincy is shown rounding the corner of Fourth and Hampshire Streets.

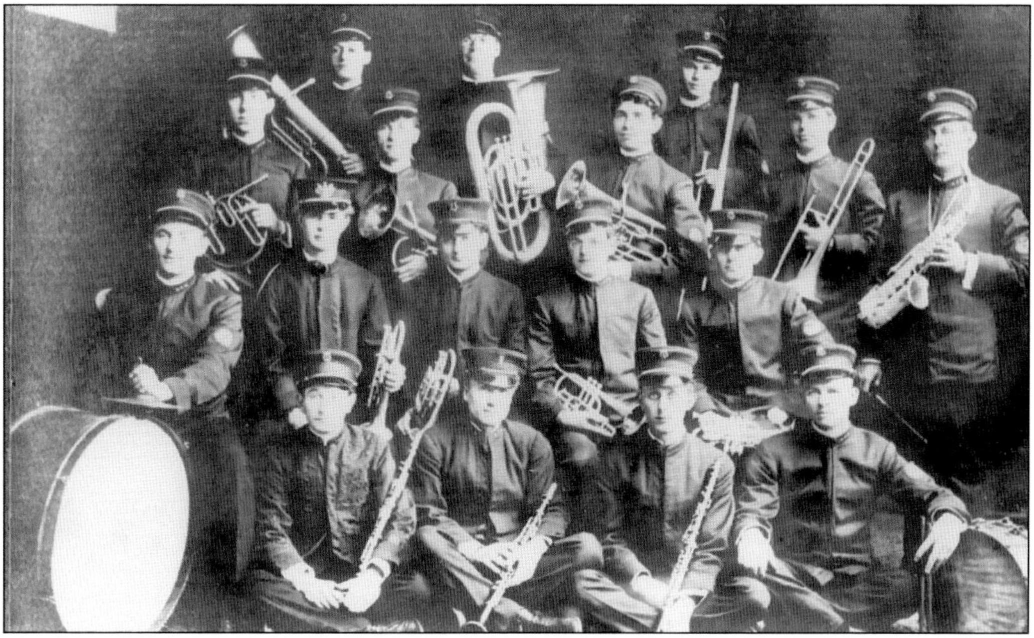

At the turn of the century and during the years immediately following, Labor Day was celebrated with large parades, picnics, and oratory. Many Union groups took part in the Quincy celebrations, including the Iron Molders and the Iron Molders' Band. The Iron Molders' Band did not always consist entirely of members of the molders' trade, but many times was joined by the Musicians' Union members, as is the case in this photograph. Harry Mayhall is the leader of this group.

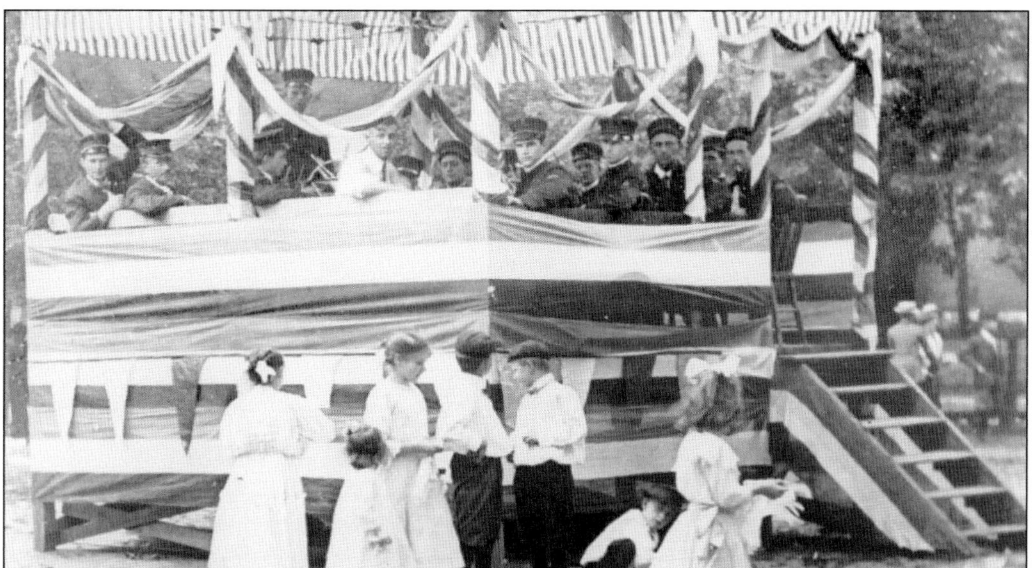

The Iron Molders' Band not only played for Labor Day celebrations, but also for picnics sponsored by various other organizations. Arthur Coffman (standing center) led the Iron Molders' Band. They are believed to be playing for a St. Francis picnic.

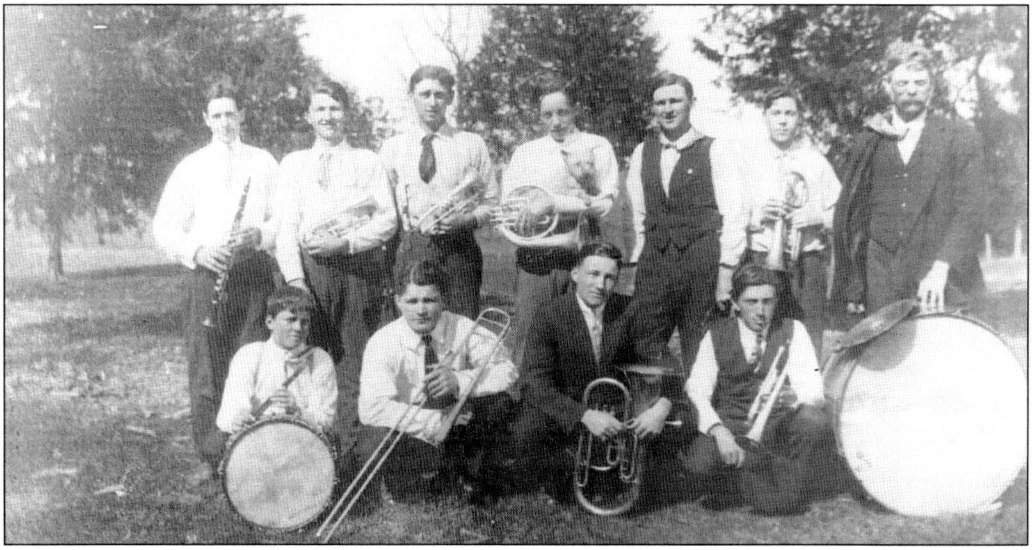

In the 1898 city directory, there are ten brick makers listed: Frederick Biermann, Bernard Brackensick, Damhorst Bros., Gem City Paving Brick Co., Hummert, Schmits & Co., Hummer & Sanders, Henry Menne, Quincy Brick Exchange, Quincy Press Brick Co., and Stroot Bros. (John and August). The Brickyard Band, shown here *c.* 1910–12, was organized by William Spilker; most original members worked at Chas. Prante's brickyard at 16th and Jefferson Streets. Shown here, from left to right, are as follows: (front row) Russell Burgess, Harvey Burgess, Howard Burgess, and Carl Bucher; (standing) Al Wolf, Edward Spilker, William Spilker, Otto Oelke, Fred Spilker, Edwin Huechteman, and James Genteman.

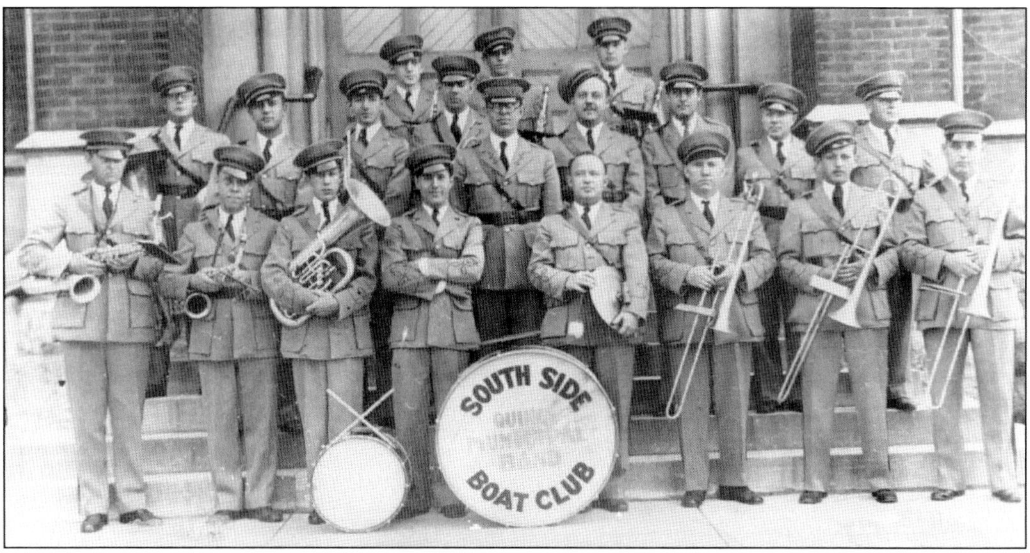

The South Side Boat Club Band was directed by Andrew Musholt for many years. The members shown here, from left to right, are as follows: (front row) Paul Tushaus, John Schultheis, John Haerle, John Musolino Jr., Ray Lampe, Riley Purdy, Marion Schuecking, and Robert Maier; (second row) Adam Weisenberger, Norbert Ott, Joe Bonansinga, Ben Schuecking, Andrew Musholt (with glasses), Melvin Blackwood, Carl Hibbard, Charles Abbott, and George Ringler; (top row) Richard Hoener, Robert Schuering, and Ralph Tushaus. Ray A. Welsh, not pictured here, was drum major and later would become police chief.

Five

World War I 1917–1918

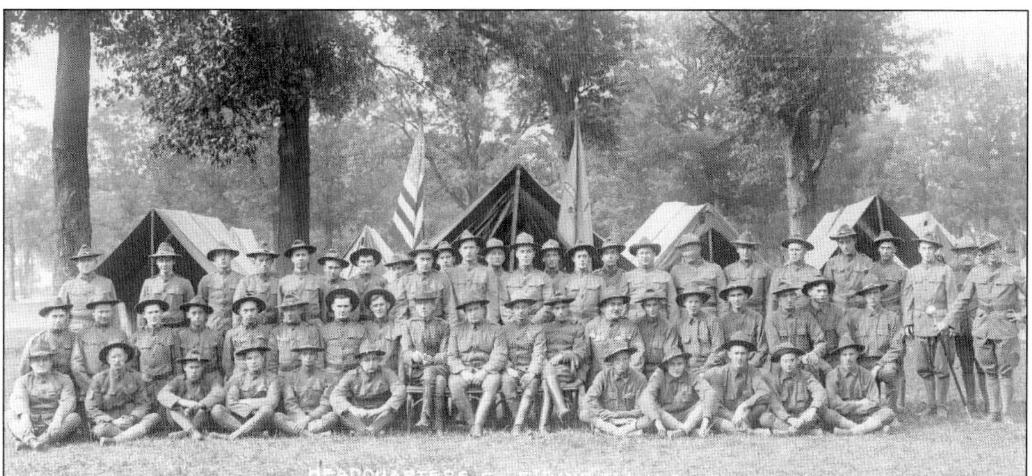

In 1873, Quincy was allotted Company D, Fifth Illinois Infantry, which later changed to Company F. The Machine Gun Company and the nucleus of the Headquarters Company were quartered in the Fifth Infantry Armory on Jersey Street. Quincy's General Henry R. Hill commanded the Brigade Headquarters. He was killed in action in France in 1918. This picture of the Headquarters Co., Fifth Infantry, Illinois National Guard, was taken in 1915 during camp in Springfield.

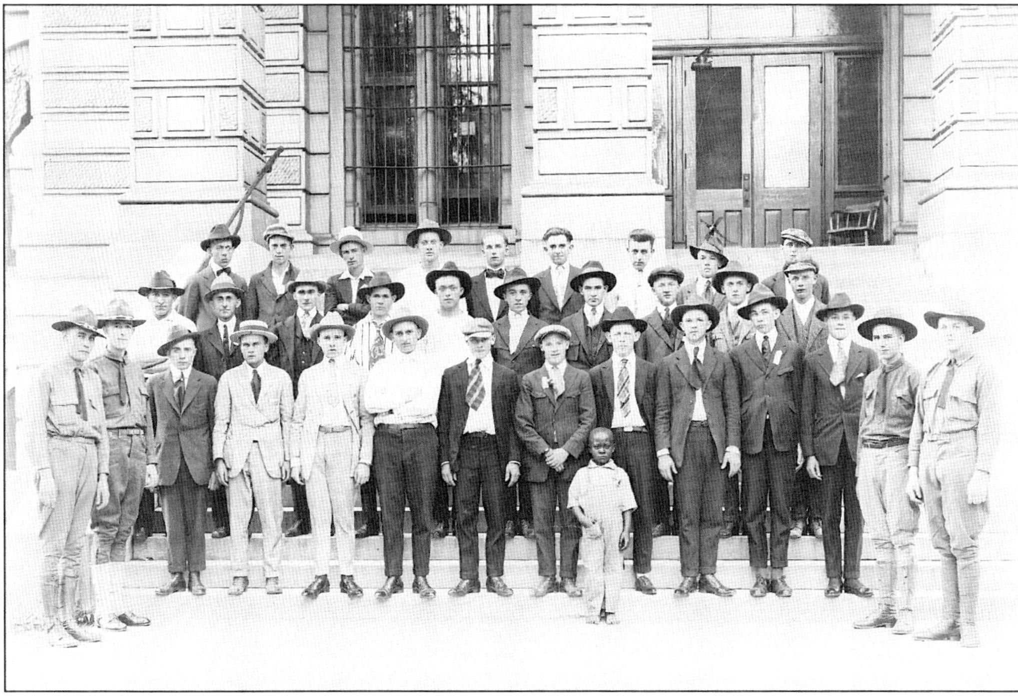

This picture, taken on the steps of the Adams County Courthouse, shows an induction group before WW I was declared by President Woodrow Wilson. The only man identified is James Smith, second from right, top row.

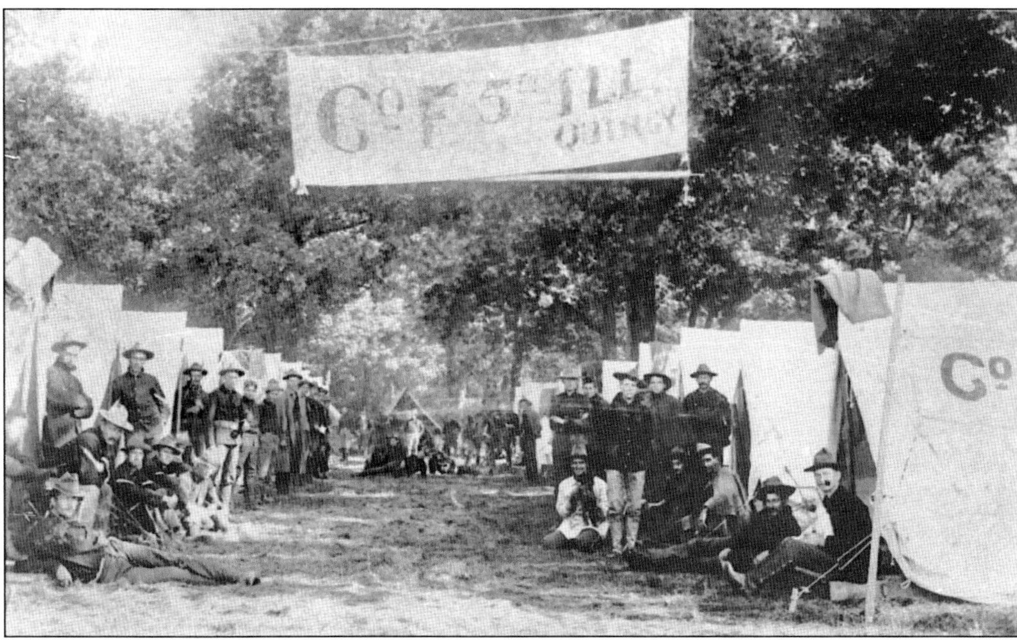

In 1917, the Fifth Infantry Regiment was called into service. Part of Company F went to Beardstown to guard the bridge there, while the rest crossed the river from Quincy to Sherman Park to guard the railroad bridge at that point. The site of this camp remains unknown, but it is believed that it was the camp located across the river.

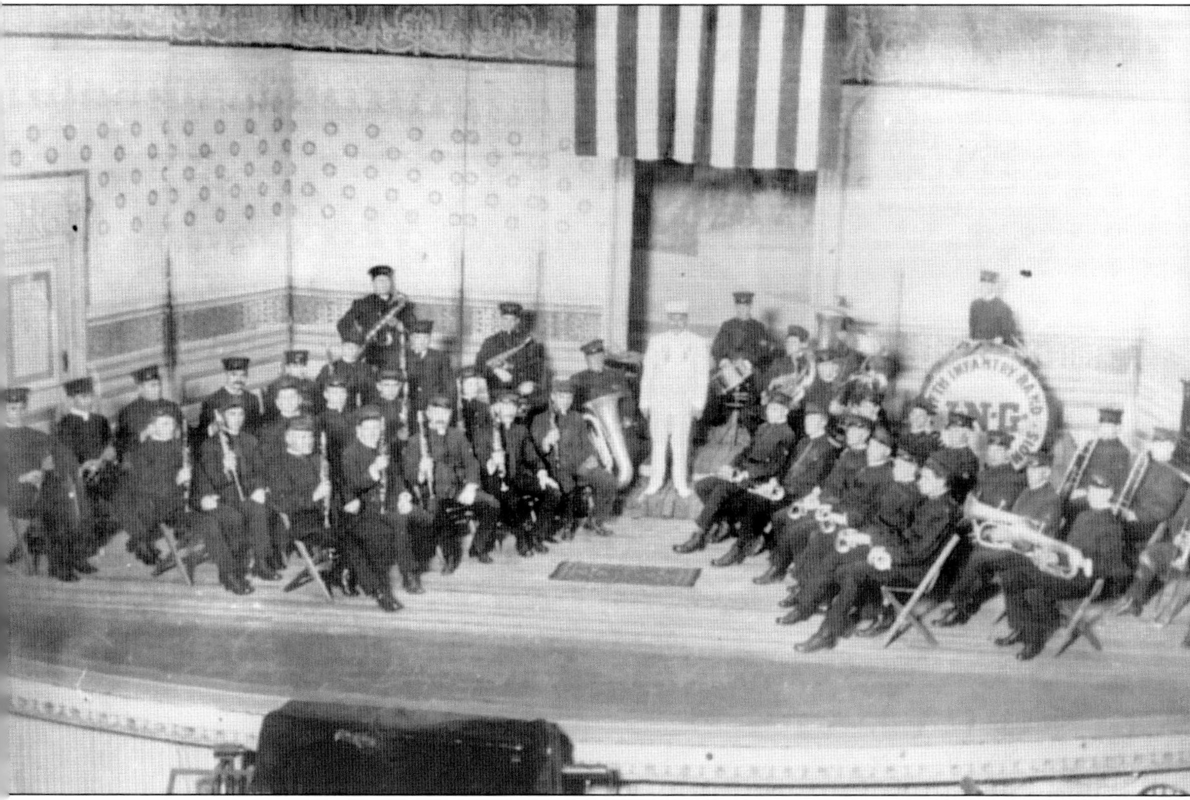

The Fifth Regimental Band, the Illinois National Guard, played a concert in the Empire Theater on November 21, 1913. Emil Reinkendorff was director. Personnel identified are as follows: (flutes) Joseph Weiler, Walter Glass, and C.W. Sullivan; (oboe) Benj. Southcott; (Eb clarinet) John C. Weller; (Bb clarinets) Dennis Markillie, Arthur Irwin, Barney Damhorst, Frank Holtschlag, J. Doane Edie, Fred W. Miller, Charles Weiler, Mike Cavanagh, Maurice Wingert, Louis Keis, and John Corbett; (alto sax) Fred Freiburg; (baritone sax.) J. Earl Caldwell; (cornets) Frank Wolter, Bert Ferguson, George Hoffman, Ollie Ferguson, and Emmett Kientzle; (horns) Oliver Jennings and Edw. Green; (baritones) Wilbur Thompson and J.W. Richards; (trombones) Clarence Buttz, Charles Hoadley, and Eben Turner; (tubas) Harry Bourne, Joseph Helfrich, and Adam Weisenburger; (drums) Joseph Williams and Cliff Weller.

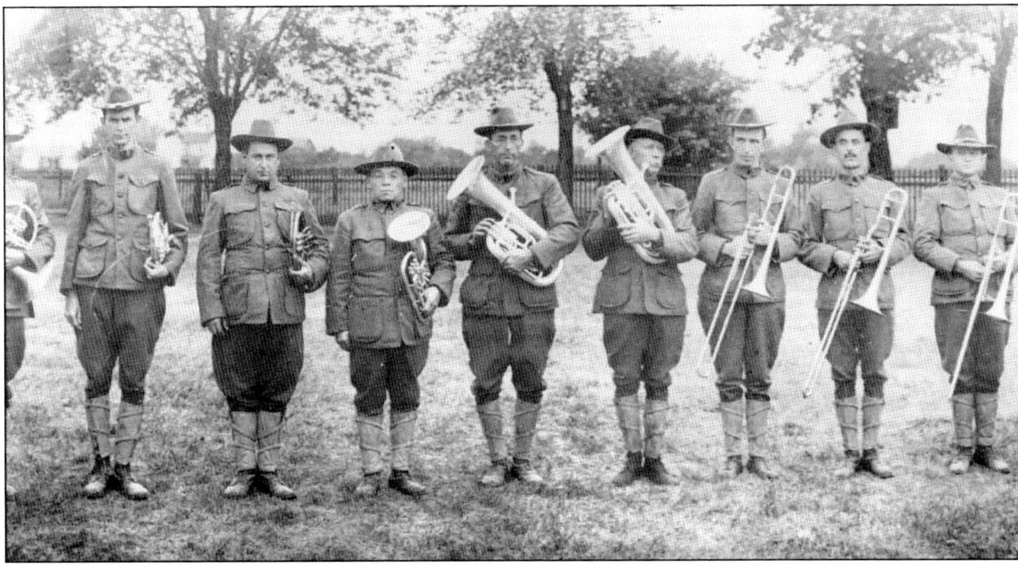

The members of the Fifth Infantry Band, Illinois National Guard, from left to right, are as follows: (alto horns) Fred W. Orr, Oliver G. Jennings, Max Rischar; (baritones) William Richards and Wilbur Thompson; (trombones) Marcus Weeks, James Stott, and C.E. Hoadley.

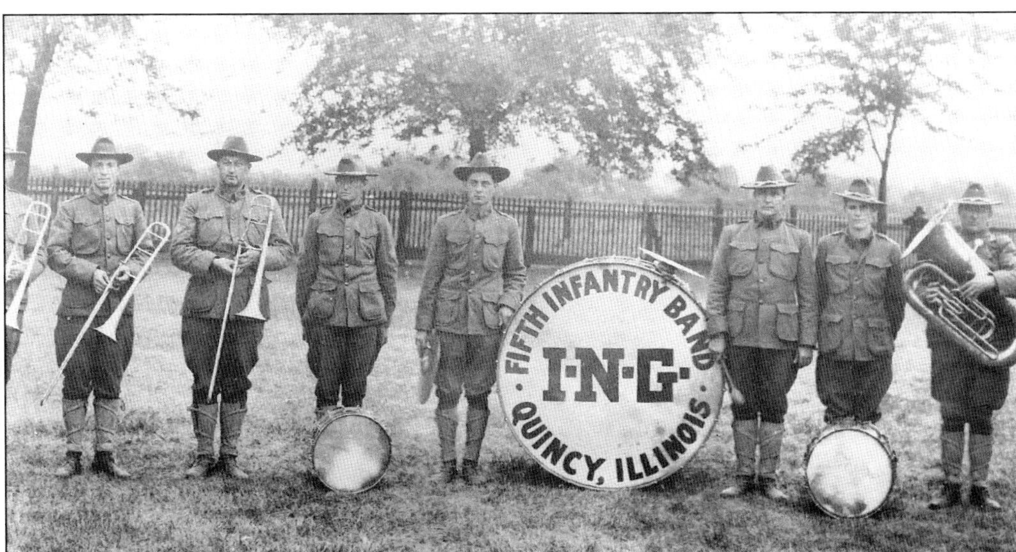

Pictured here, from left to right, are as follows: (trombones) Leslie Mayhall and Clarence G. Buttz; (snare drum) Joseph K. Williams; (cymbals) Albert D. Buttz; (bass drum) Cliff Weller; (snare drum) James Maderis; and (tuba) Joseph Helfrich.

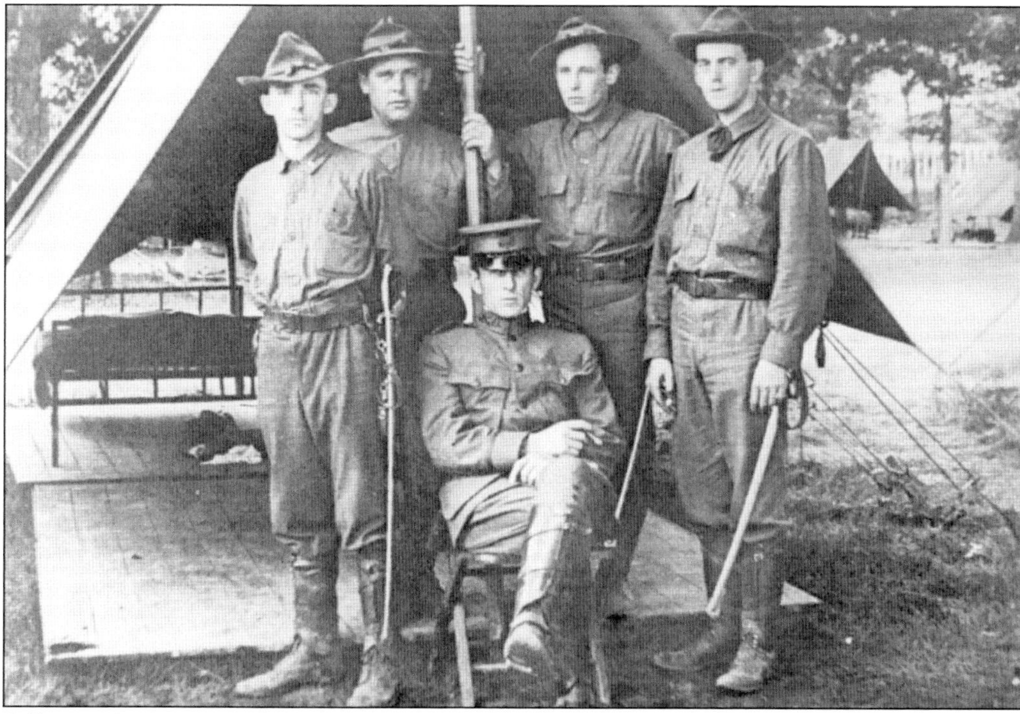

Officers of Company F, shown here from left to right, are as follows: (sitting) Major William Yarbrough; (standing) Capt. Laurence Smith, Second Lt. Albert Zoller, First Lt. Frank Alexander, and Capt. Bert Stiles, Gatling Gun Platoon, Fifth Regiment. All except Stiles followed Henry Hill as captain of Company F, Illinois National Guard.

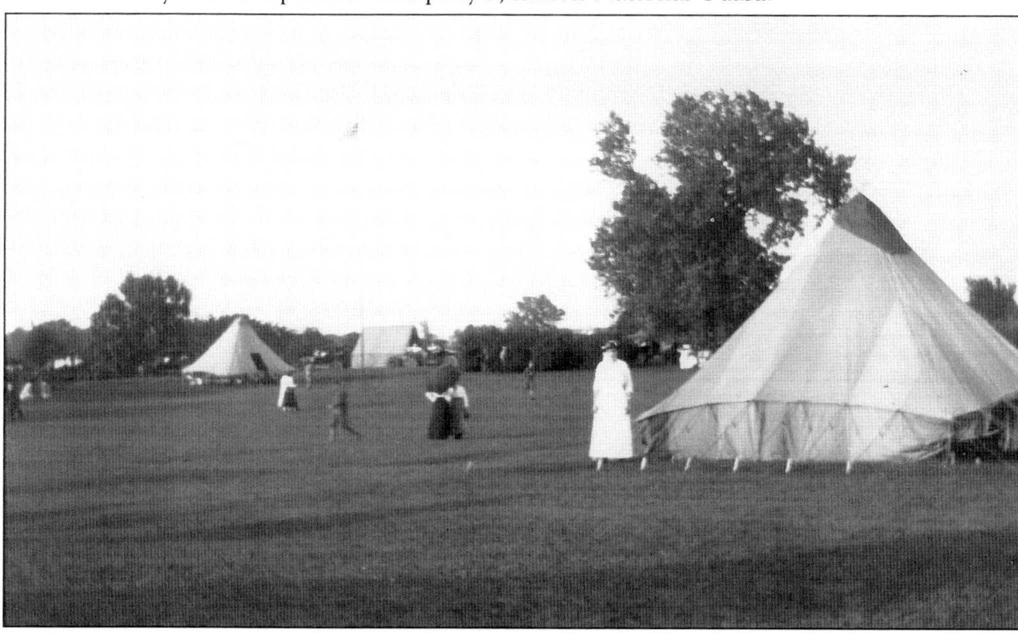

High water forced the soldiers guarding the railroad bridge to move from their camp site at Sherman Park. Camp Parker in Parker Heights Park, on the northwest part of Quincy, was established when Sherman Park became unsuitable. This photograph was taken in 1917.

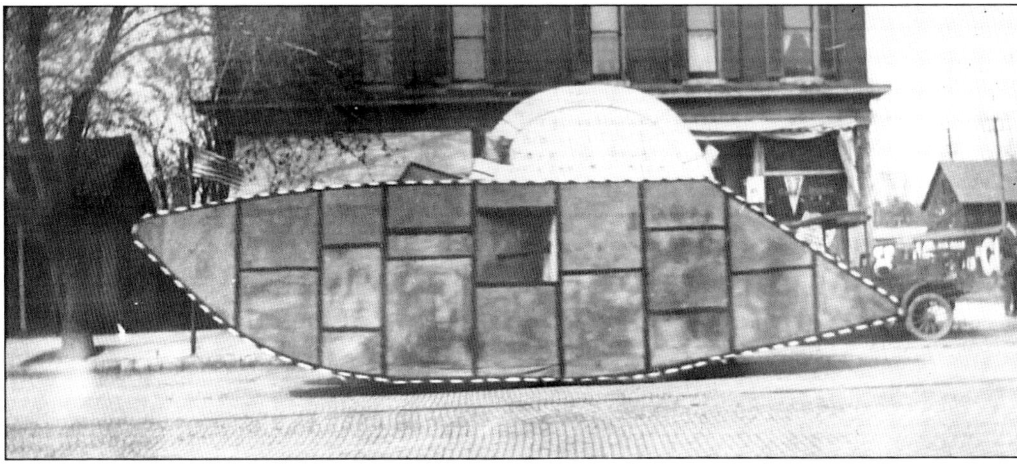

During WW I, there were several Liberty Loan War Bond Drives to obtain money to carry on the war. The Third Liberty Loan Drive was held in April 1918 and featured a huge parade on April 13, 1918. This replica of a war tank, made by Frank Einhaus & Son, has a 1913 Overland car inside. Pictured at Eighteenth and Broadway, Chas. Ross Saloon and Herman Rakers Bakery next door can be seen on the northwest corner.

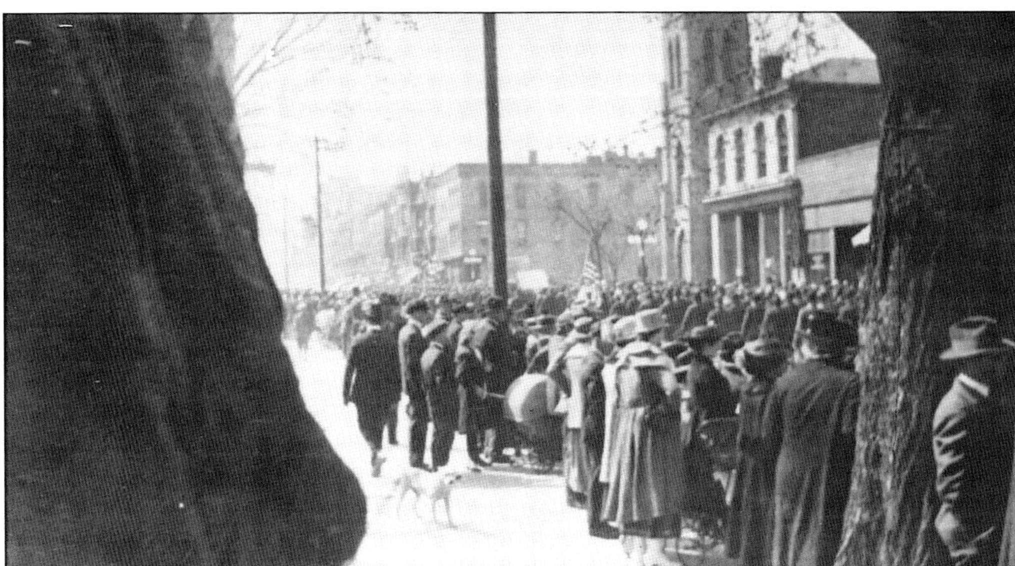

The crowd is gathered for the Liberty Loan parade on April 13, 1918, on Hampshire Street between Seventh and Eighth Streets. St. Johns Episcopal Church may be seen in the background.

Six

1920s–1930s

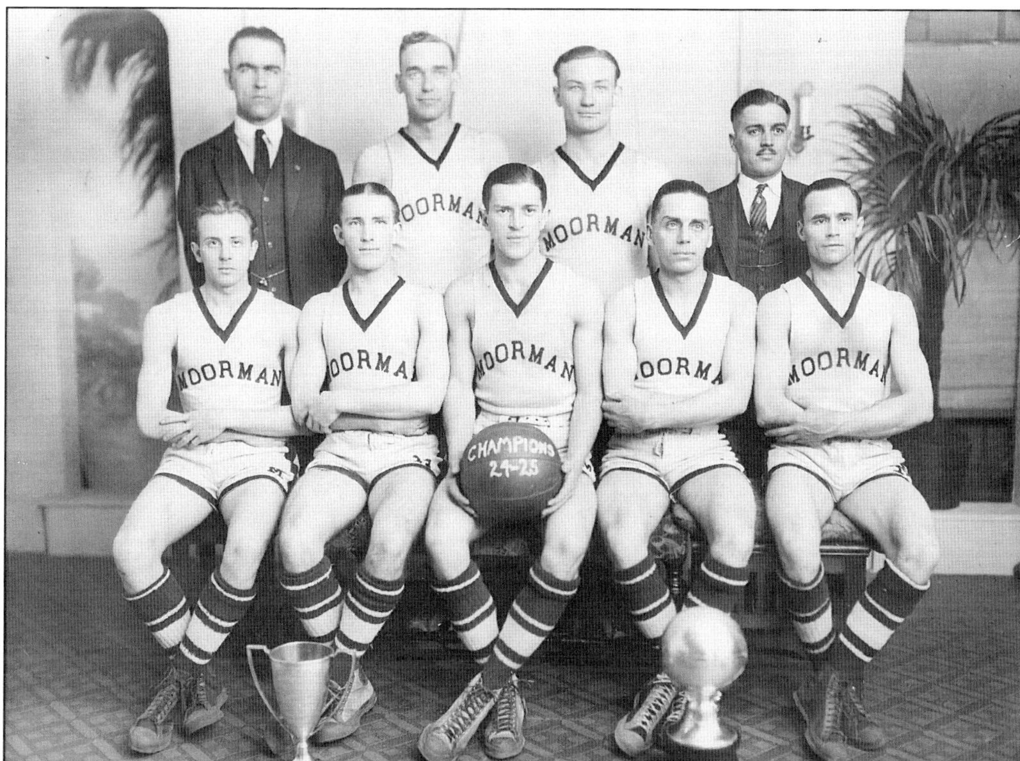

Basketball was introduced to Quincy in 1896, when the first game was played in the old German YMCA (later the Labor Temple building) at Ninth and State Streets. In time, the city, church, industrial, and commercial leagues were formed. The Moorman Manufacturing team was the champion in the Industrial League in 1924–25. Members included in this photo are Abe Merkel, Claude Holmes, Dick Elder, Ercell Day, John Suhren, Merle Austin, Art Adams, Ed Stewart, and Fly Hoffman. Most of the games in the 1920s and 1930s were played in the Armory on Jersey Street between Fourth and Fifth Street.

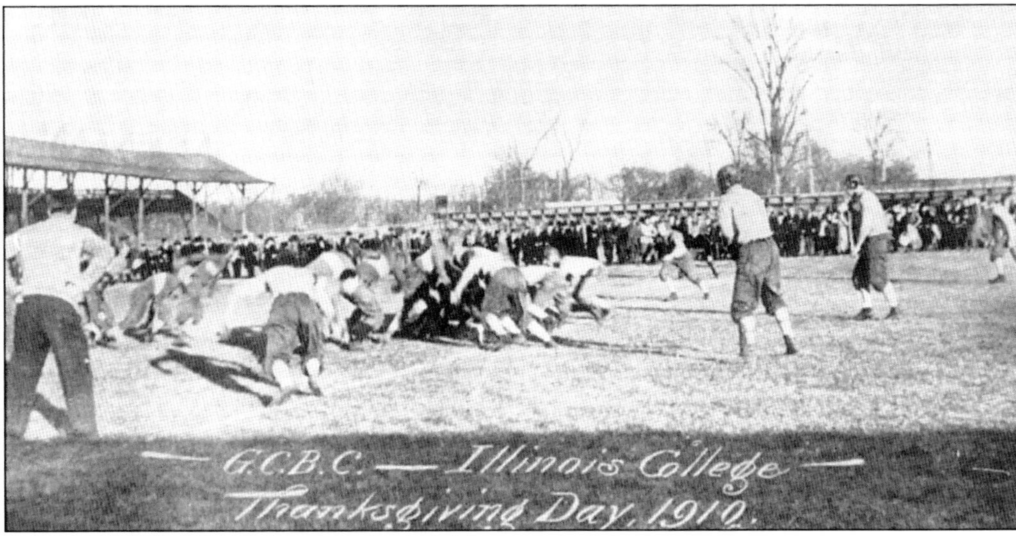

Gem City Business College placed its first football team in the field in 1895. They played both college and high school teams. In that year, Quincy High lost in a 16-0 match with Gem City Business College. The college's fall schedule usually ended with a game on Thanksgiving Day, as it did in 1910 when they beat Illinois College 53-0!

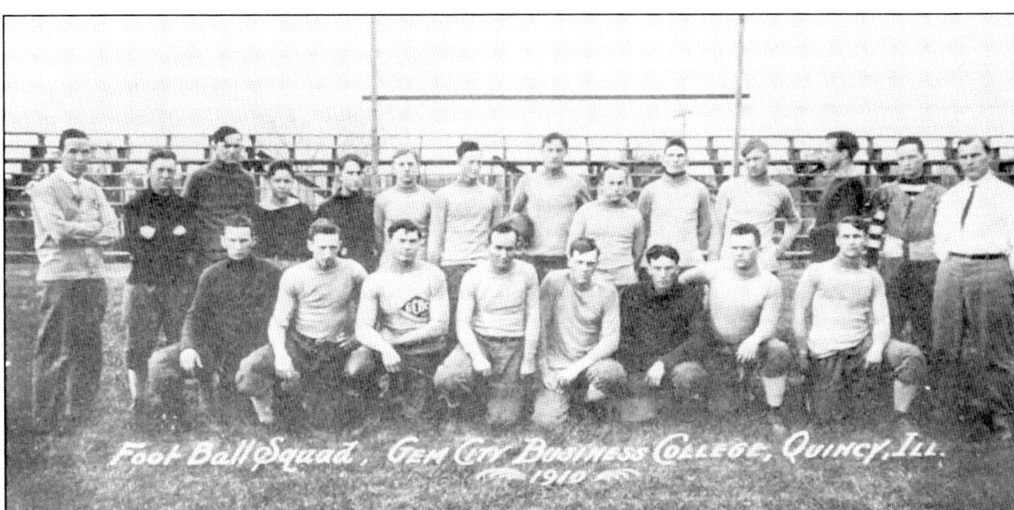

In fact, the Gem City Business College team was unbeaten in 1910. They played Monroe City, Missouri, 33-5; Carthage College, 3-0; Lewistown, Missouri, High School, 78-0; Christian University at Canton, Missouri, 9-0; Carthage College at Quincy, 20-0; and Illinois College at Quincy 53-0.

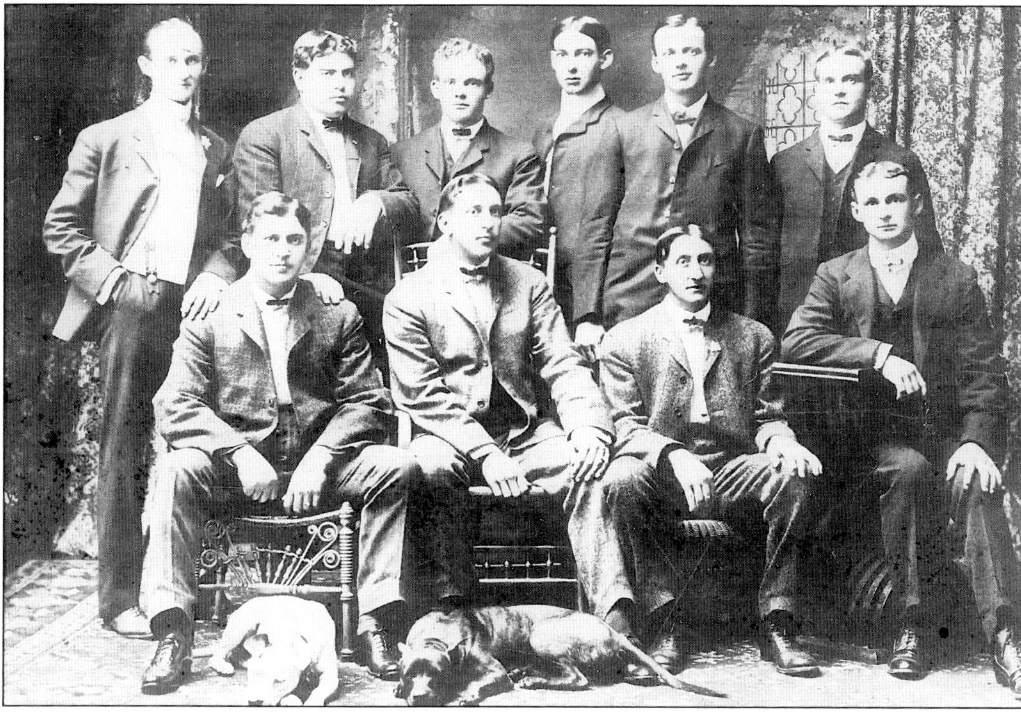

All of the baseball players are not identified in this 1903 photograph. The following, from left to right, are identified: (front row) Charles Lutenberg, Harry Hofer, Fred Bickelhaupt, and James Monahan; (back row) Walter Wich and James Hackett. Lutenberg had a professional career with the Pittsburgh Pirates, Oakland, California, and Denver. The big leagues also scouted Bickelhaupt, but he was making more money as a tool sharpener in Quincy than they could offer.

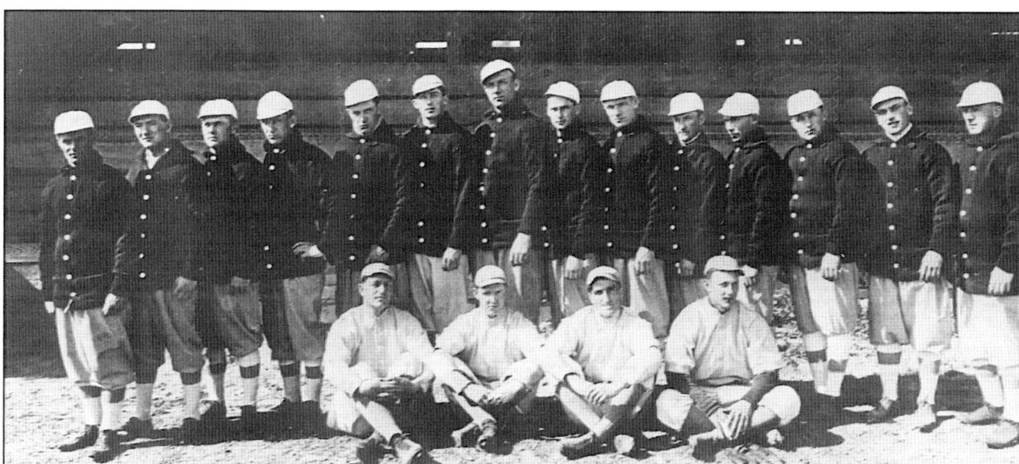

The Quincy Gems played the Burlington Club at Sportman's Park on September 11, 1910. Ed Walker, the tall man in center of this picture, was the hurler who pitched a very good game, but the newspaper reported that the many errors on the part of the Burlington team cost them the game. Other towns in this league were Ottumwa, Hannibal, Galesburg, Keokuk, Monmouth, and Kewanee.

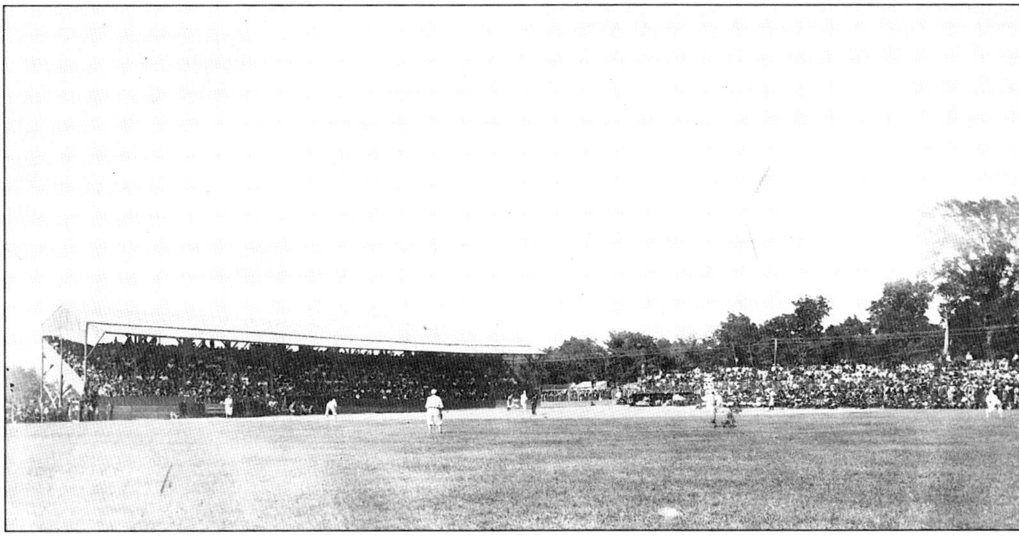

Sportsman Park, located between Seventeenth and Eighteenth Streets, and Cherry and Cedar Streets, is shown here, *c.* 1910. The park was first established as baseball grounds in 1888, with a grandstand and fence being added in 1889. Quincy had other baseball parks in the early years of the game, namely on Seventh and Eighth, Spruce and Sycamore (where neighbors protested Sunday games to no avail); Fifteenth and Spring Streets; Sixteenth and State Streets; Tenth and Jackson Streets; Fourth and Locust Streets; South Sixth Street; and Singleton Park, later Baldwin Park, at Thirtieth and Maine Streets.

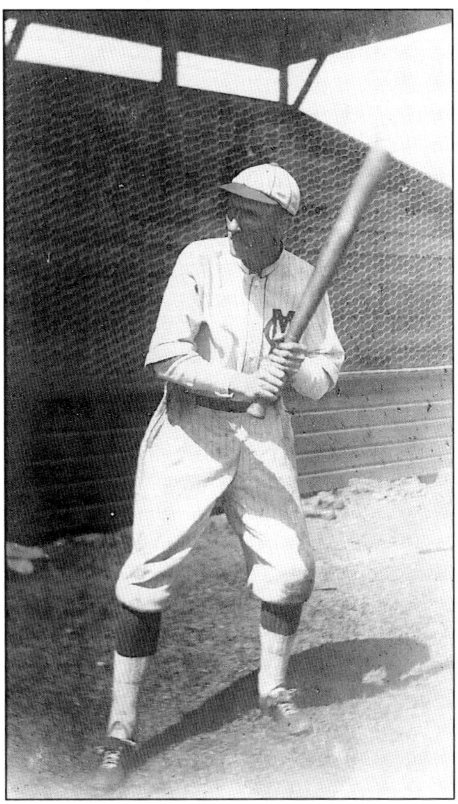

In 1922, Quincy's Moose-Gems were champions of the Illmo League. In a game played against Palmyra at Baldwin Park, the winning run was scored by George "Skinny" Sohn in the eleventh inning. Sohn worked as a railroad switchman during the winter months, and played semi-pro baseball during the summer months. Other players who contributed to the Quincy win were pitcher Dutch Kemner, Ferd Niemann, and John Nessler.

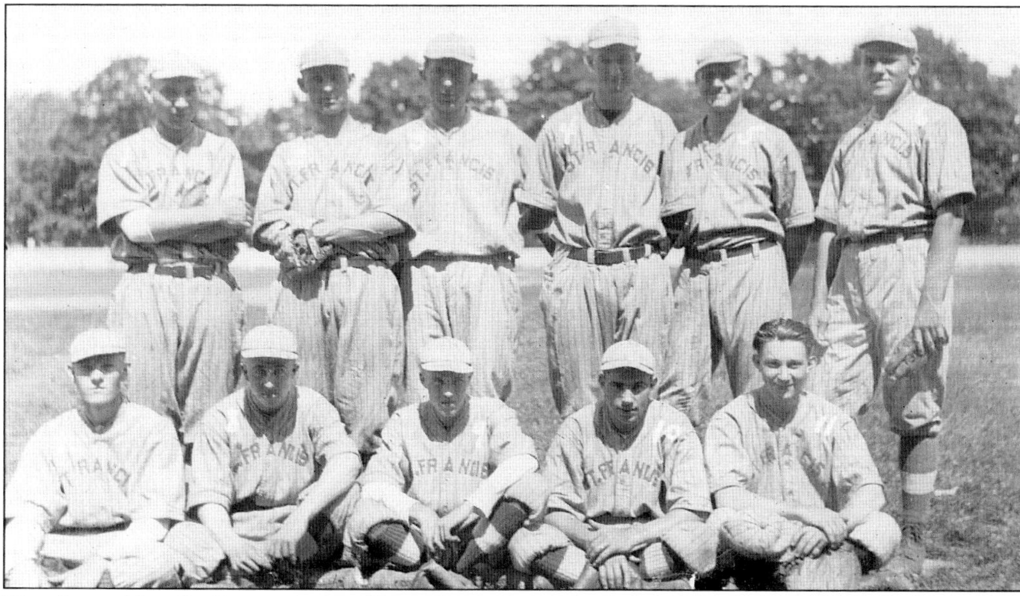

The date of this St. Francis baseball team picture is unknown. At one time, many of the Catholic churches had baseball teams in the Parish League. Most of the games were played at Nauert's Park or Bickhaus Park.

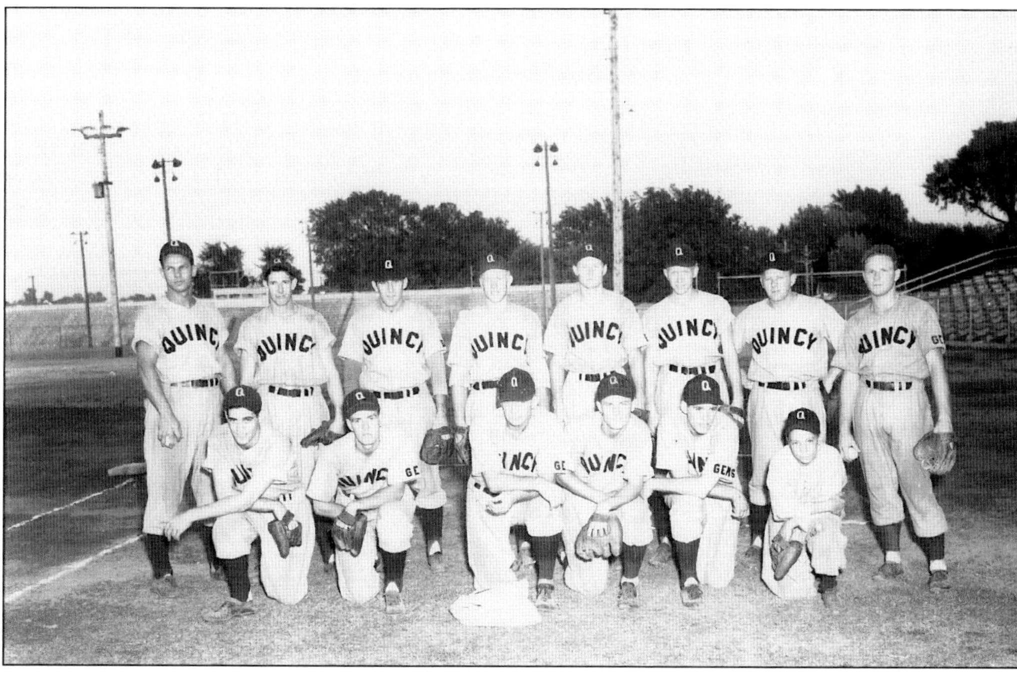

This undated photograph shows Quincy continuing to enjoy the Quincy Gems baseball games. More than 100,000 fans attended the Gems games last year, with an average of 3,000 per game. Today, the Gems are made up of collegiate players and are entering their fourth season in the Central Illinois Collegiate League. Games are played in "Q" Stadium, at Eighteenth and Spruce Streets, which was built in 1930. The stadium underwent major improvements in 1996, thanks to a generous donation from Bernie and Isabelle Willer.

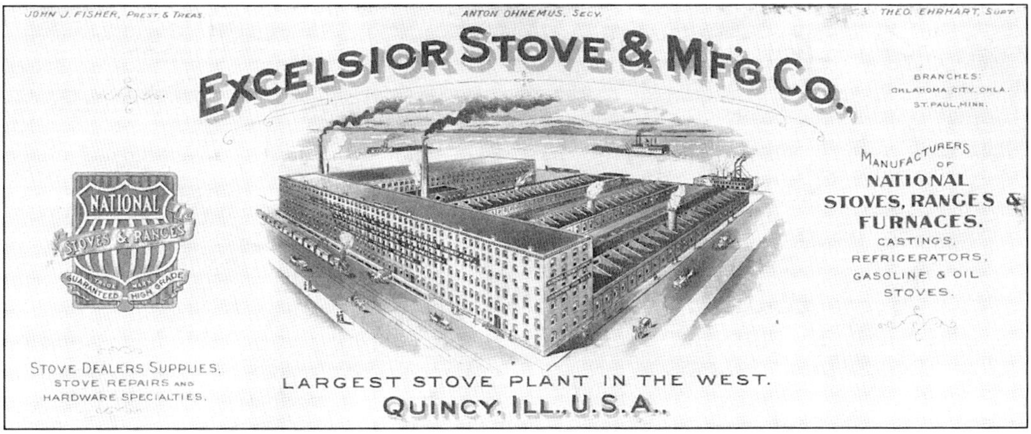

Quincy was one of the first cities in the "new West" that engaged in stove manufacturing. The Excelsior Stove Co. was first established as the Excelsior Stove Repair; the name changed to the Excelsior Stove and Manufacturing Company in 1896. John Fisher was president and treasurer; Nicholas Kohl was vice president; Anton Ohnemus was secretary; and Theodore Ehrhart was superintendent. The company employed 400 men with the office and foundry at 509-615 South Front Street. Quincyans usually referred to the company as the "Ex."

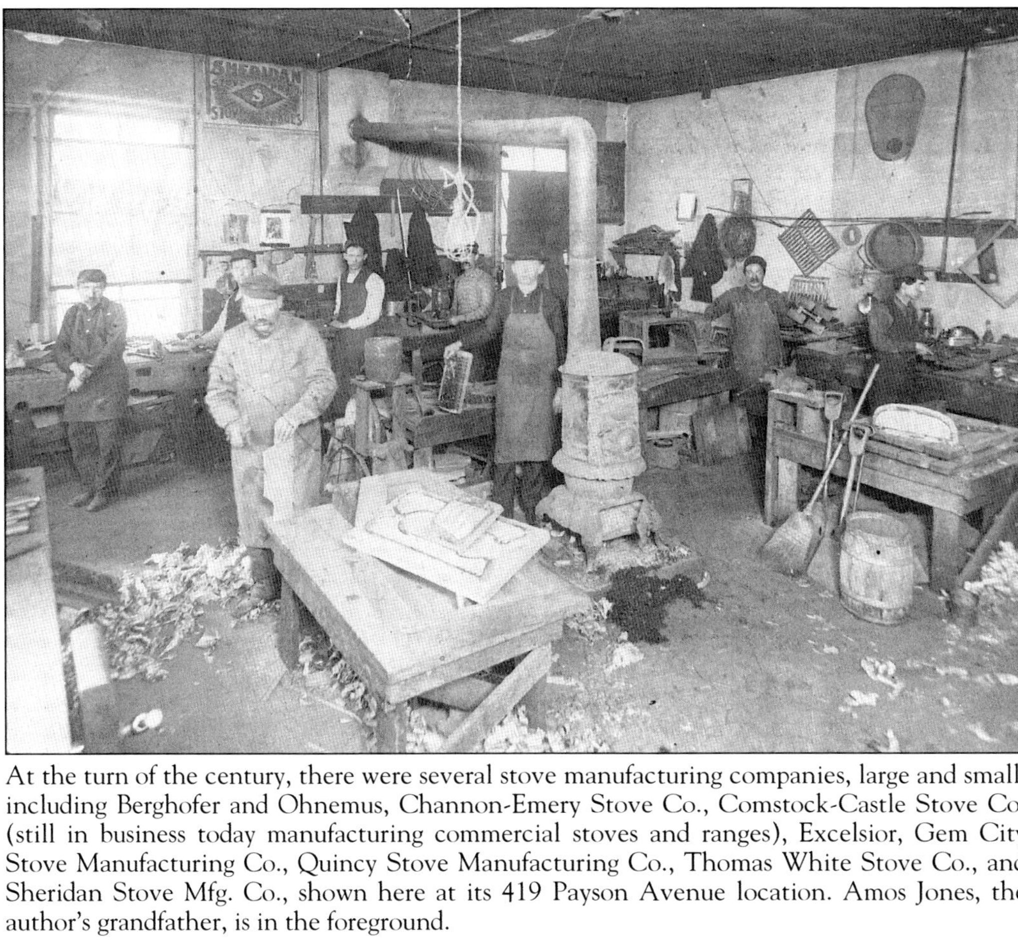

At the turn of the century, there were several stove manufacturing companies, large and small, including Berghofer and Ohnemus, Channon-Emery Stove Co., Comstock-Castle Stove Co. (still in business today manufacturing commercial stoves and ranges), Excelsior, Gem City Stove Manufacturing Co., Quincy Stove Manufacturing Co., Thomas White Stove Co., and Sheridan Stove Mfg. Co., shown here at its 419 Payson Avenue location. Amos Jones, the author's grandfather, is in the foreground.

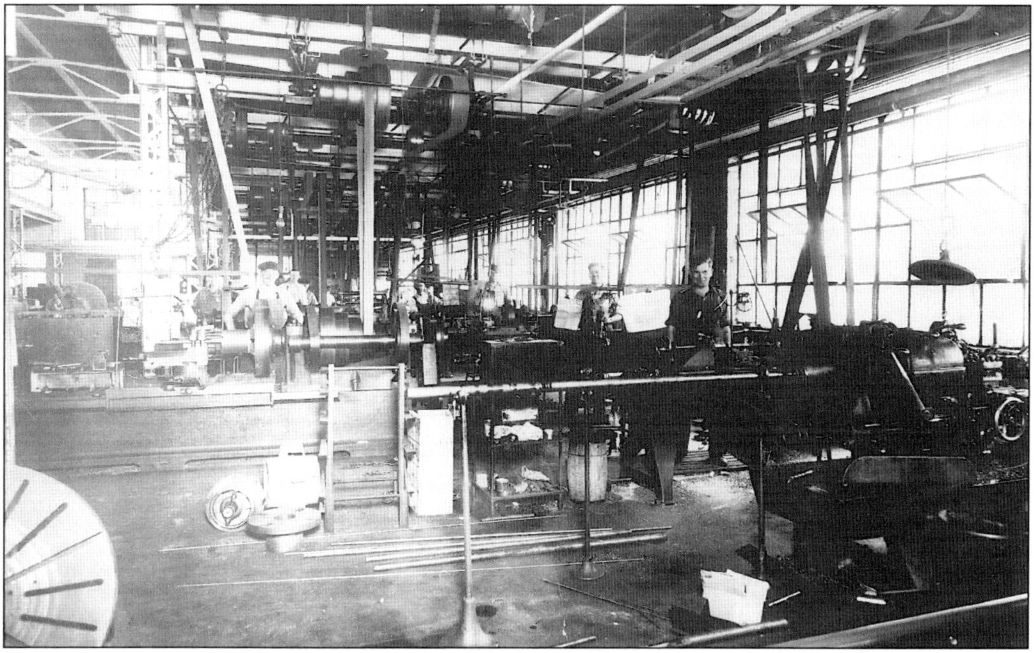

This is believed to be the Dayton-Dowd plant, located at 115-117 York Street. Dayton-Dowd Co. manufactured pumps and small engines; it was a large employer in Quincy until it moved to Indianapolis in the early 1940s.

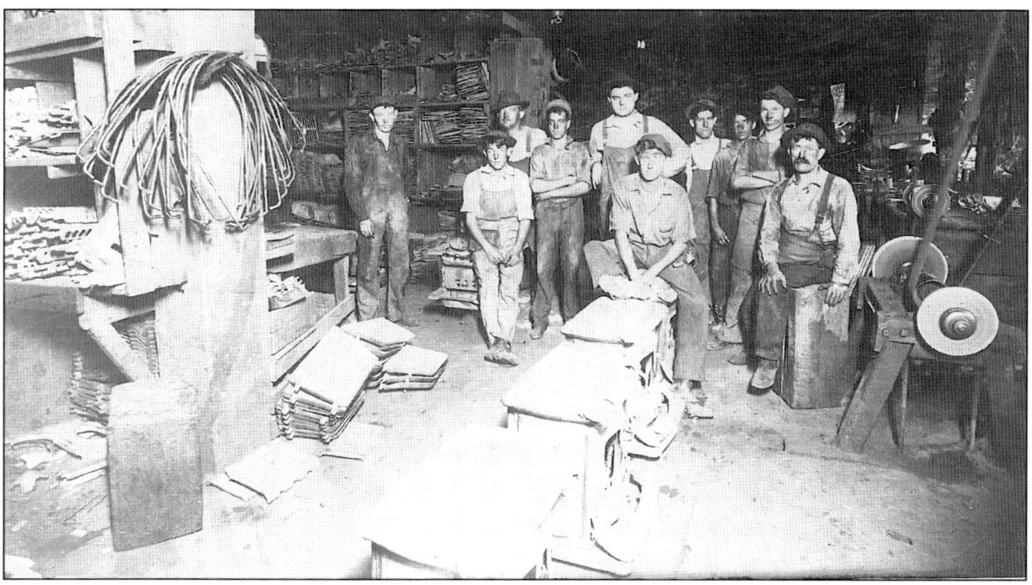

This picture shows the interior of a local stove foundry and employees. One of these employees, William Krueger, was a long-time employee of the Channon-Emery Stove Company, as well as the Comstock-Castle Stove Company.

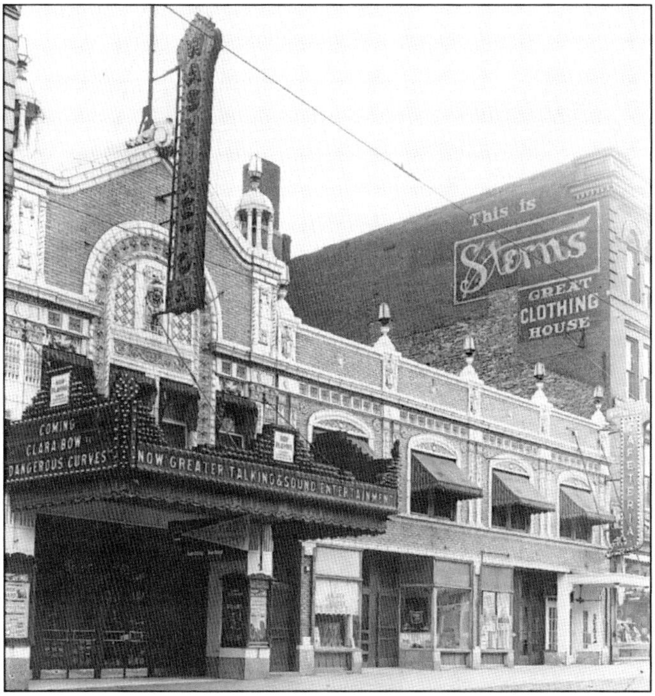

The Washington Square Theatre at 425 Hampshire Street opened in 1924. Later, Walter Tanner moved to Quincy to play organ in the new theatre. This 1929 picture announces these coming attractions: Clara Bow in *Dangerous Curves* and *The Follies of 1929*. Directly to the right, or east, is the Washington Beauty Shoppe, then the Underwood Typewriter shop, the Washington Cafeteria (which was in the basement), and Sterns Great Clothing House.

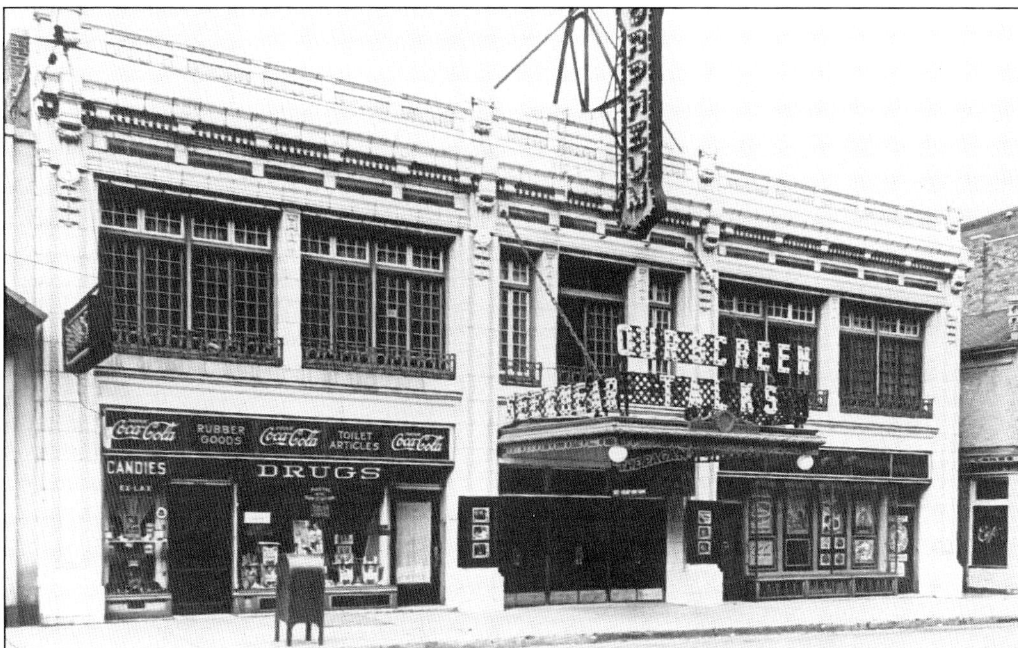

The Orpheum Theater, located at 620 Hampshire Street, opened on Christmas Eve in 1914 with vaudeville acts. They later began showing silent films. The first "talking" motion picture was shown on July 7, 1929. From that time on, it was a movie theater until it closed in 1954. Jack Benny played here one time on the vaudeville circuit, playing a few bars of "Love in Bloom." He then paused and said, "And then there's Kreisler." To the left of the theater is the Kiefer Pharmacy.

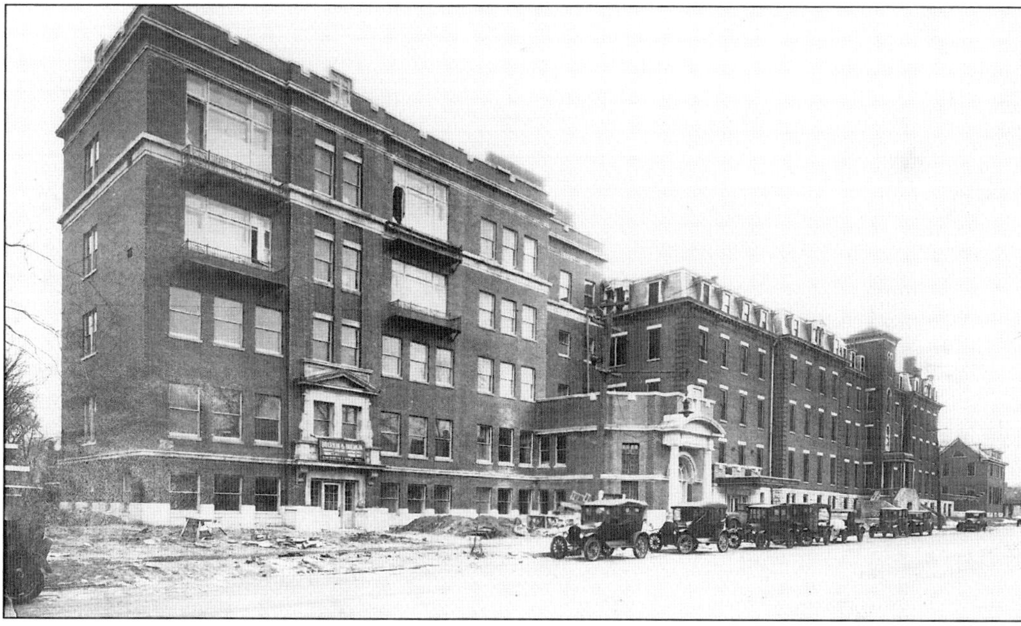

St. Mary Hospital had its beginning in the Bishop's house at Eighth and Vermont Streets, but the cornerstone for the new building on Broadway at Fourteenth was laid May 5, 1867. The 50-bed hospital opened in October that year. Additions were made as the need arose; the one occurring here took place in 1930. Buerkin and Buerkin were the general contractors.

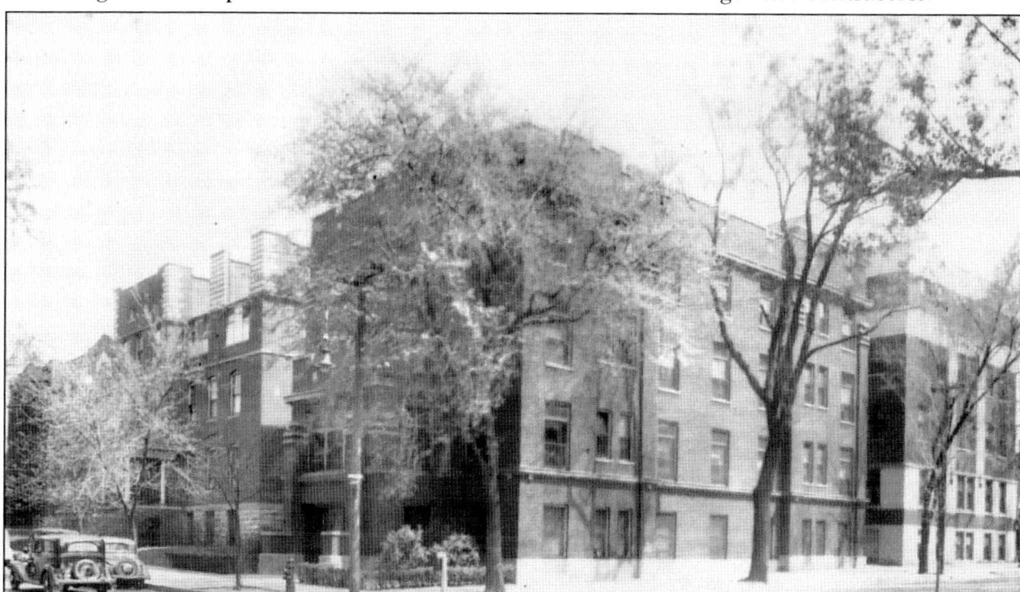

Blessing Hospital opened in 1875, after having been built on land and by funds donated by Mathias and Sarah Denman. It was first known as Blessing Hospital; after Mrs. Denman's death it was called the Sarah Denman Hospital, but in 1885, it again became Blessing Hospital. In 1895, an addition was made to the original building. Another addition, shown here on the southeast corner of Tenth and Spring Streets in 1920, provided an entrance on this corner for many years.

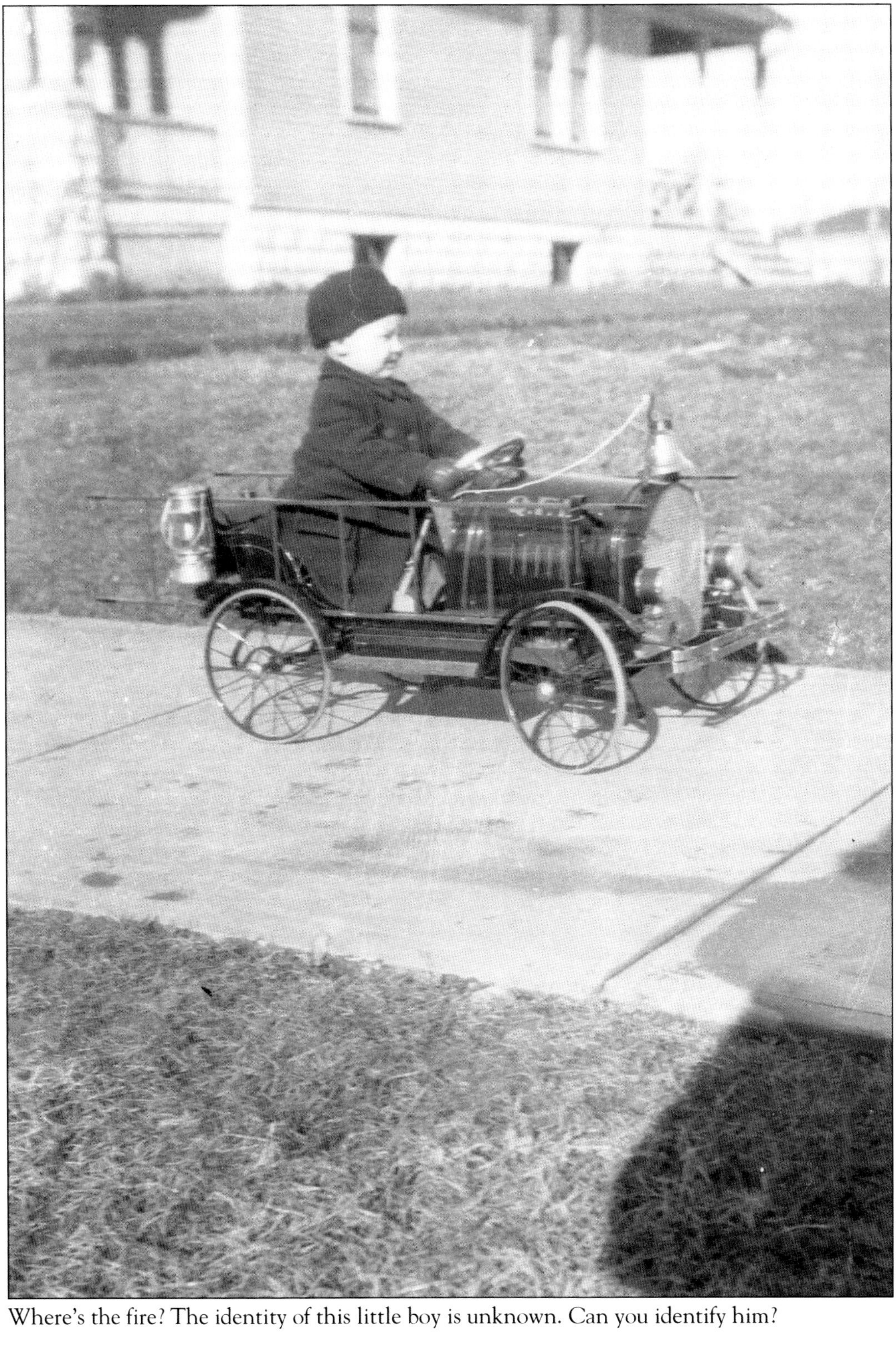

Where's the fire? The identity of this little boy is unknown. Can you identify him?

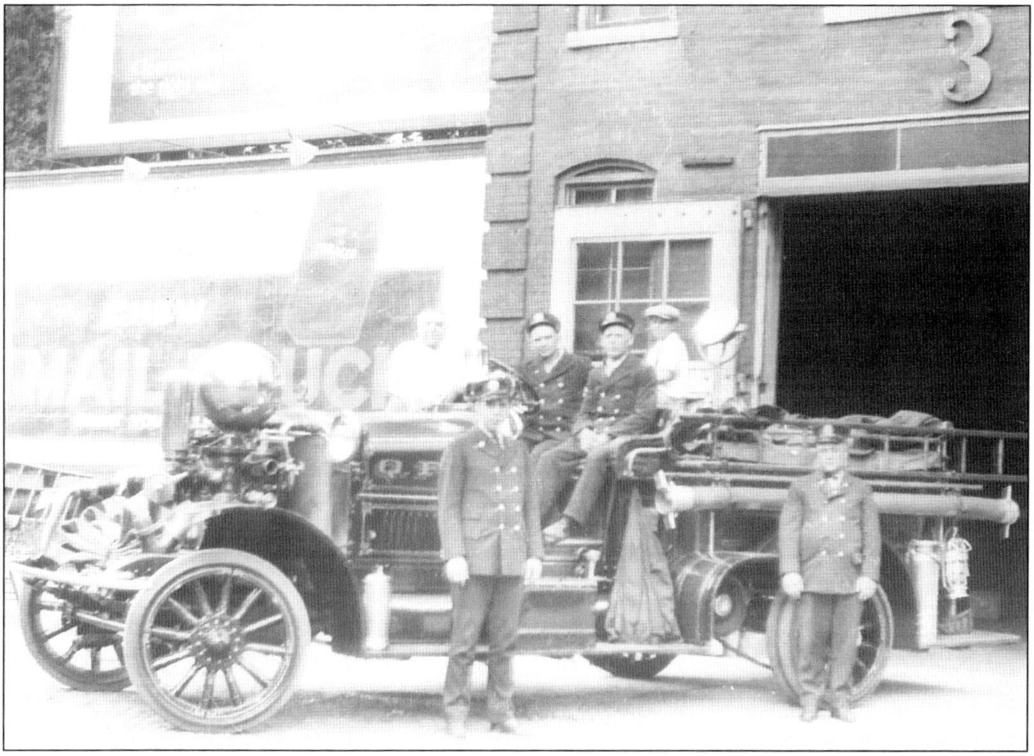

In the early years, fire equipment was named for prominent members of the community, such as the mayor or the aldermen. This pumper, purchased in November 1927, was named for Ald. Frank Knight. It is shown in front of the #3 firehouse on Eighth Street, between Maine and Jersey Streets. John Musolino is the man in the white shirt; Junior Musolino sits on top.

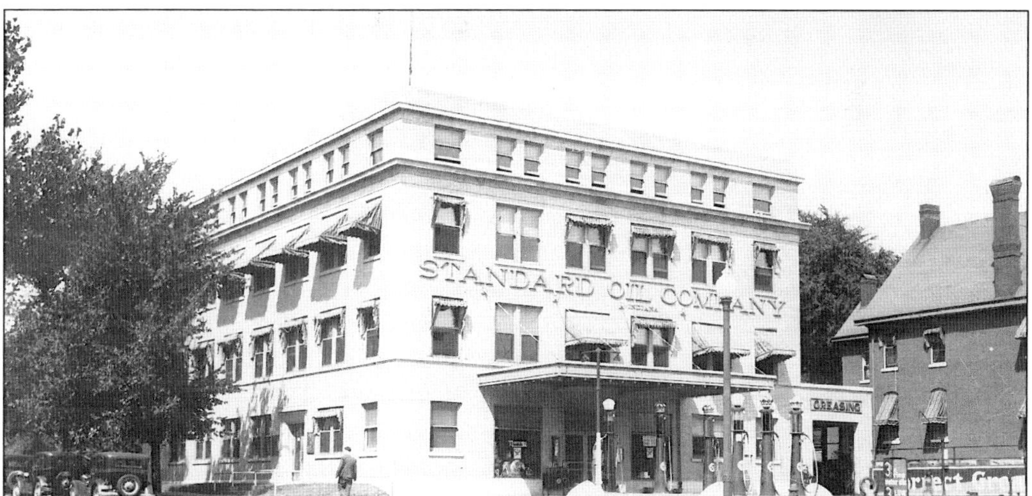

The Standard Oil Company erected this building at 1101 Maine Street in 1926 for its divisional office, with a service station in front. The Physicians and Surgeons Clinic bought and remodeled the building, *c.* 1946. Today, the building is a part of the Quincy Medical Group complex.

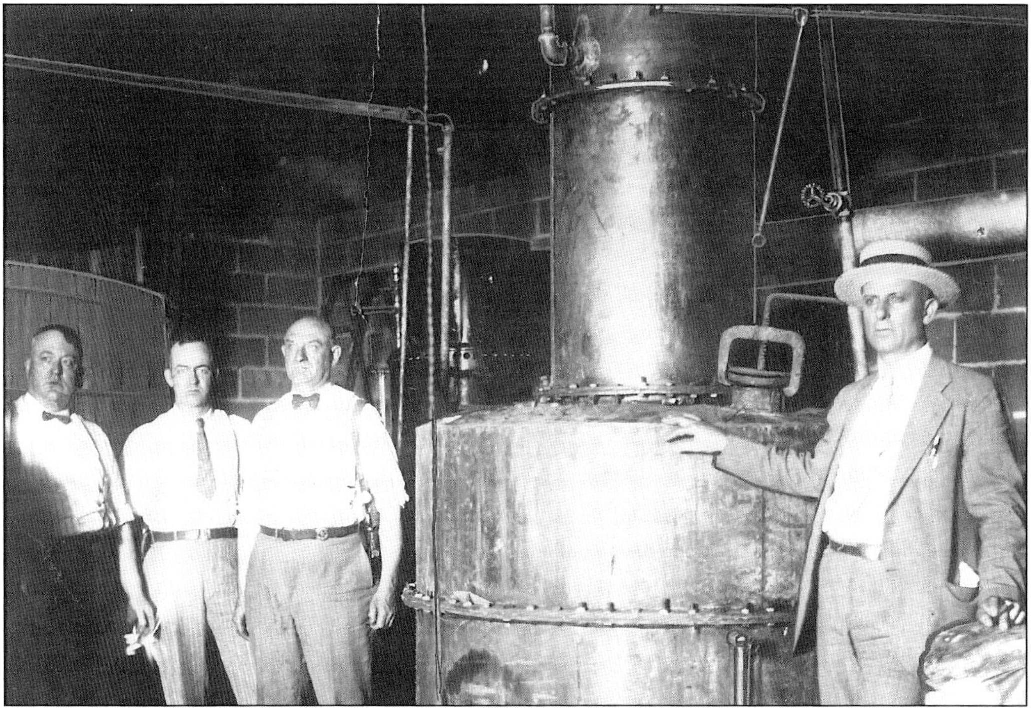

The Volstead Act of Congress in November 1918 made it illegal to make or sell beverages with distilled spirits. For the most part, the law was observed in Quincy, but there were some individuals who tried to make the product undercover. Federal agents and Quincy police raided a number of these "businesses." One of these was a former tin shop located at 1028 Broadway.

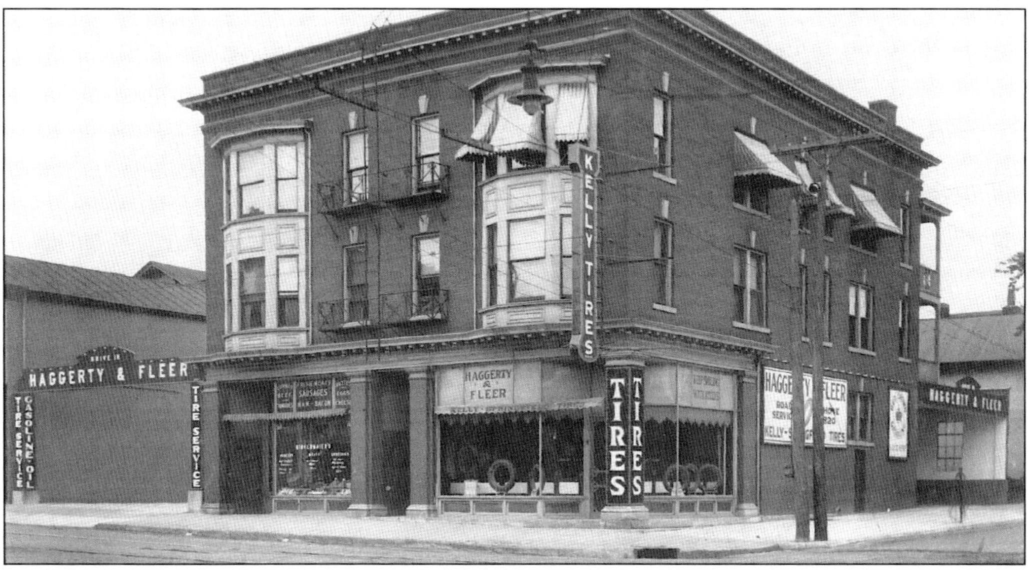

In the 1920s and 1930s, there were many small tire shops in Quincy. One of those, shown in this 1925 picture, was Haggerty & Fleer, located on the northwest corner of Ninth and Maine Streets. To the left is Birkenmaiers Meats and Groceries, before they moved across the street to 834 Maine Street. Signs advertise corned beef and tongues; sausages, ham, and bacon; and butter, eggs, and cheeses.

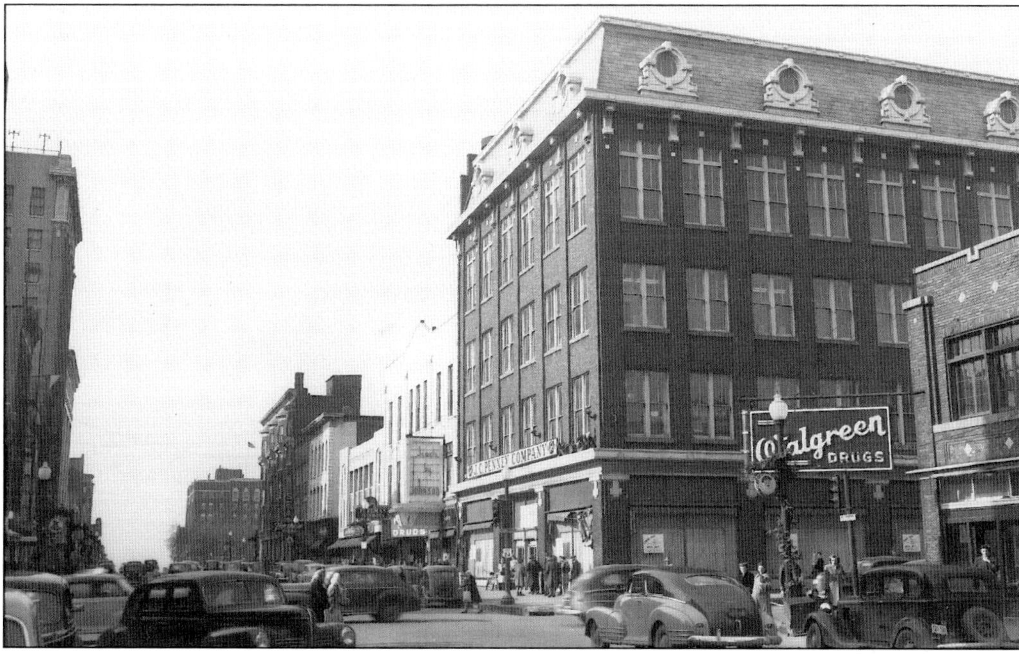

This late 1940s picture of the intersection of Sixth and Maine Streets shows the J.C. Penney department store on the northwest corner and Walgreen Drugs at 601 Maine Street. To the left of Penney's was Jewelry by Johnson (L.F. Johnson, manager), Kings Cut Rate Drugs, and Heintz Shoe Store.

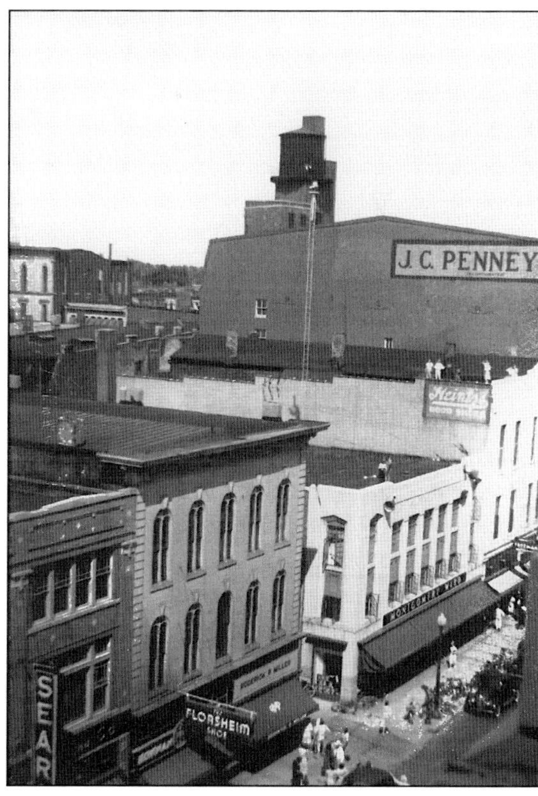

This late 1930s view of Maine Street between Fifth and Sixth Street looks northeast. Roderick P. Miller Women's Apparel may be see where it operates today at 515 Maine Street. To the left was the Bootery Shoe Store, and to the right, across the alley from Millers, was the Montgomery Ward department store, Heintz Shoes, and J.C. Penney.

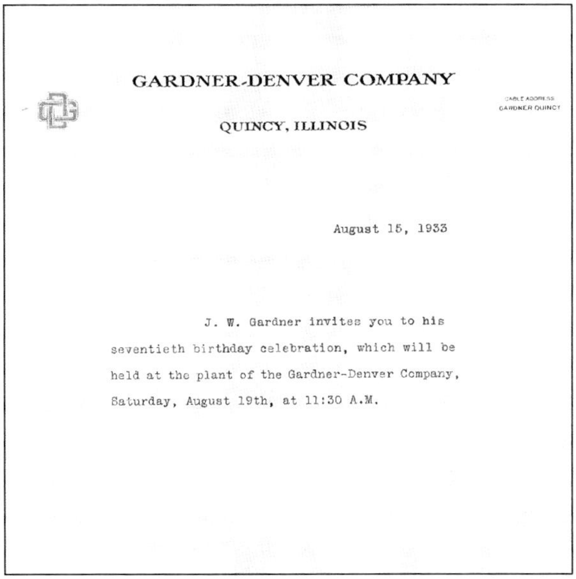

GARDNER-DENVER COMPANY

QUINCY, ILLINOIS

CABLE ADDRESS GARDNER QUINCY

August 15, 1933

J. W. Gardner invites you to his seventieth birthday celebration, which will be held at the plant of the Gardner-Denver Company, Saturday, August 19th, at 11:30 A.M.

All employees of Gardner-Denver Company received this invitation to J.W. Gardner's 70th birthday celebration on August 19, 1933. When Mr. Gardner took a lengthy vacation, he always sent or brought the employees gifts from his trip. William J. Landrum, the author's father, was the recipient of many of these gifts.

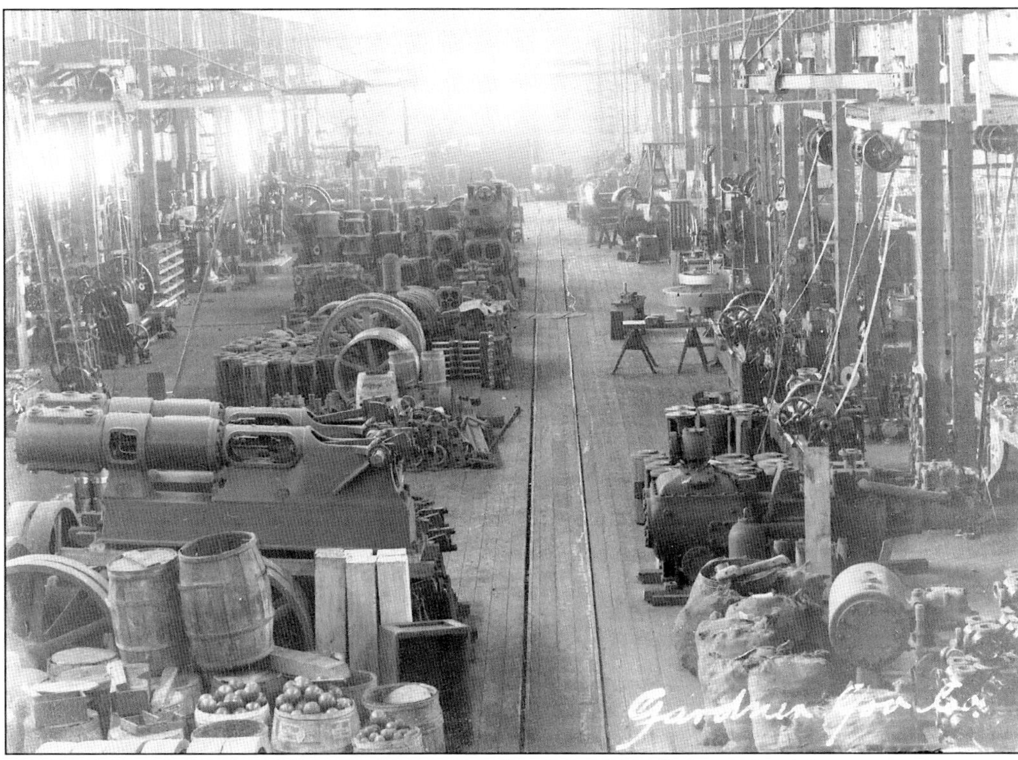

This is the interior of Gardner Governor Co., later Gardner-Denver Co. This company started before the Civil War, when Robert Gardner became a partner with John Robertson. They invented the balanced double-acting valve used on the governor of the steam engine. About 1870, Gardner bought out Robertson. At the time, the Gardner Steam Engine Governor shop was on the northwest corner of Fifth and Ohio Streets. The business prospered and a large plant was erected on Front Street by 1901. In 1927, the company merged with the Denver Rock Drill Co.; the name then became the Gardner-Denver Co.

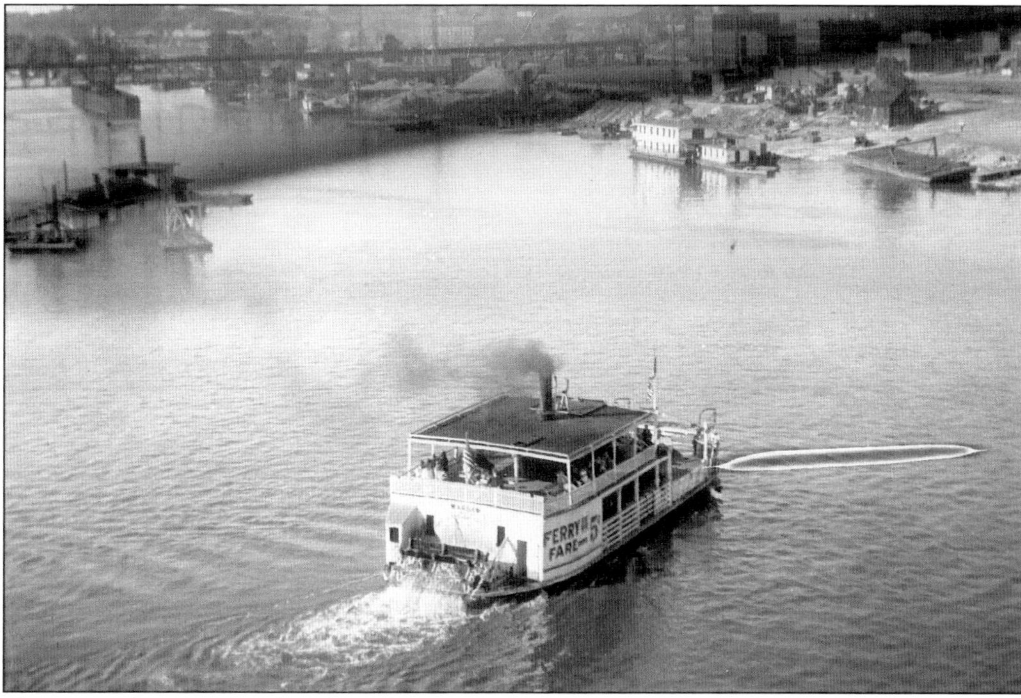

This 1930 photograph, taken from the Memorial Bridge, shows a ferry approaching the landing at the foot of Hampshire Street. Clat Adams operated several ferries over the years, including the *B.B.*, which was built in 1906 and sold in 1920. The *B.B.* had carried more than 12,000 passengers across the river to Sherman Park in West Quincy.

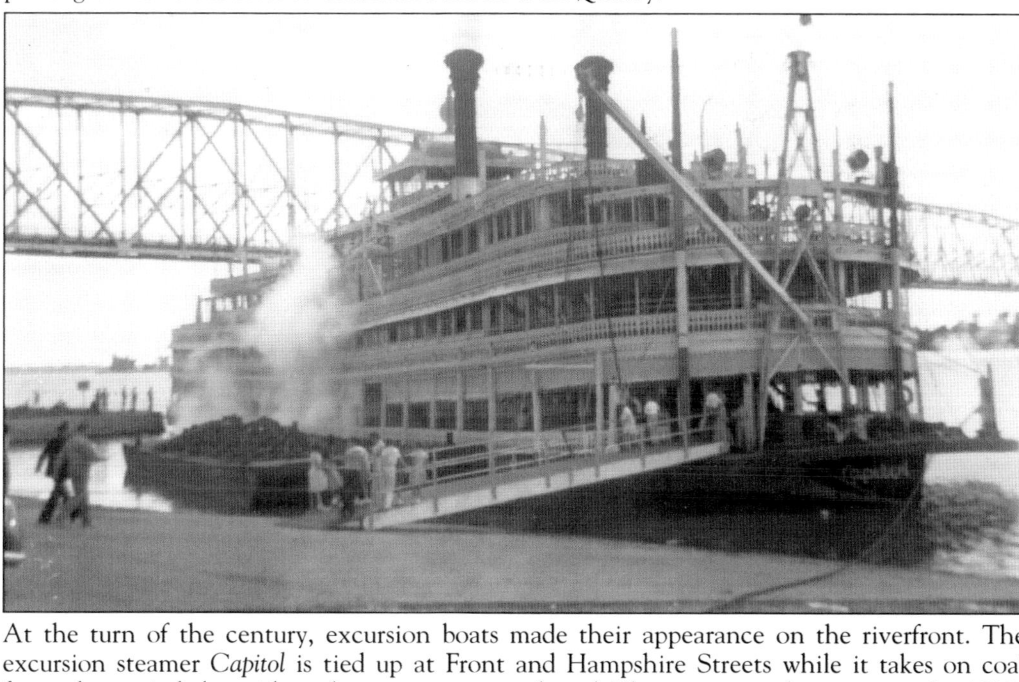

At the turn of the century, excursion boats made their appearance on the riverfront. The excursion steamer *Capitol* is tied up at Front and Hampshire Streets while it takes on coal from a barge tied alongside and passengers come aboard. This was a popular outing in the 1920s and 1930s.

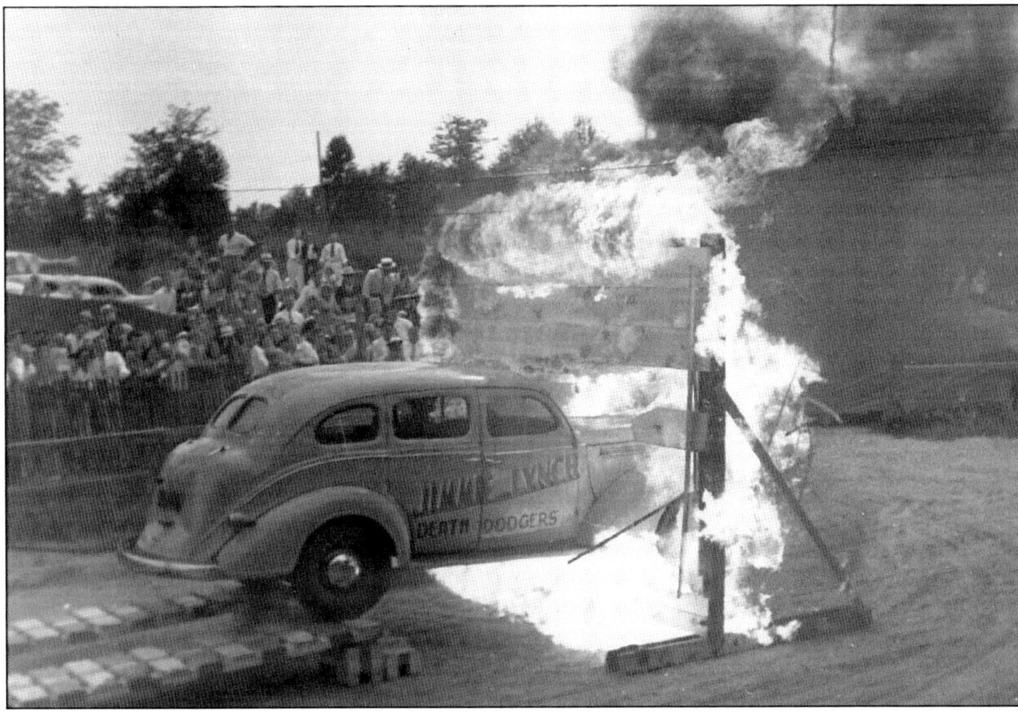

The Knights of Columbus barbecue continues to be a popular late-summer event. In earlier years, there were parades, horse racing, ball games, band concerts, and delicious barbecued beef sandwiches. Some of these activities are no longer held, but the barbecue sandwiches continue to be a "draw." In 1938, the Jimmie Lynch Death Dodgers was a crowd-pleasing attraction.

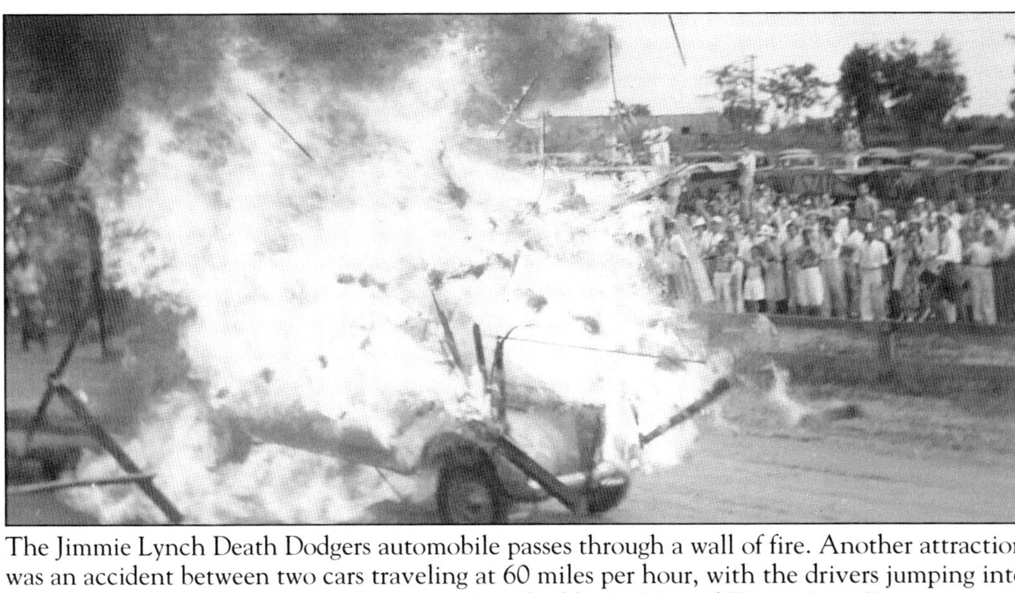

The Jimmie Lynch Death Dodgers automobile passes through a wall of fire. Another attraction was an accident between two cars traveling at 60 miles per hour, with the drivers jumping into the rear seats at the last minute. Cars were furnished by Jo-Jo's and Fierge Auto Parts.

Seven

World War II 1941–1945

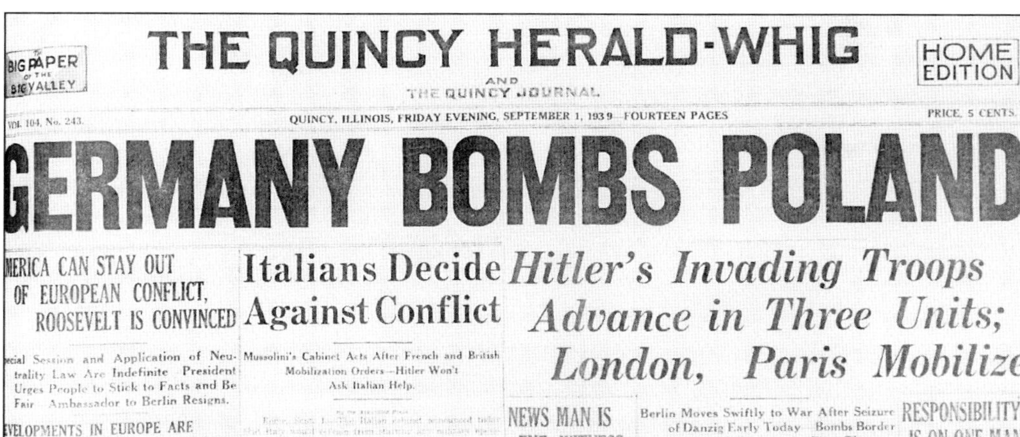

THE QUINCY HERALD-WHIG

AND THE QUINCY JOURNAL

BIG PAPER OF THE BIG VALLEY

HOME EDITION

VOL. 104, No. 243. QUINCY, ILLINOIS, FRIDAY EVENING, SEPTEMBER 1, 1939—FOURTEEN PAGES PRICE, 5 CENTS.

GERMANY BOMBS POLAND

MERICA CAN STAY OUT OF EUROPEAN CONFLICT, ROOSEVELT IS CONVINCED

ecial Session and Application of Neutrality Law Are Indefinite President Urges People to Stick to Facts and Be Fair—Ambassador to Berlin Resigns.

EVELOPMENTS IN EUROPE ARE CLOSELY WATCHED IN CAPITAL

Italians Decide Against Conflict

Mussolini's Cabinet Acts After French and British Mobilization Orders—Hitler Won't Ask Italian Help.

Hitler's Invading Troops Advance in Three Units; London, Paris Mobilize

NEWS MAN IS EYE-WITNESS

Berlin Moves Swiftly to War After Seizure of Danzig Early Today—Bombs Border Cities and Warsaw in First Thrust

RESPONSIBILITY IS ON ONE MAN

On September 1, 1939, Germany bombed Poland and so began World War II. Pres. Franklin D. Roosevelt asked Congress in May 1940 for $1 billion for rearmament. War production began that fall and Congress passed the draft in September. Medical examiners for the Adams County draft board were Drs. George L. Athey, Kent Barber, and C.E. Ericson.

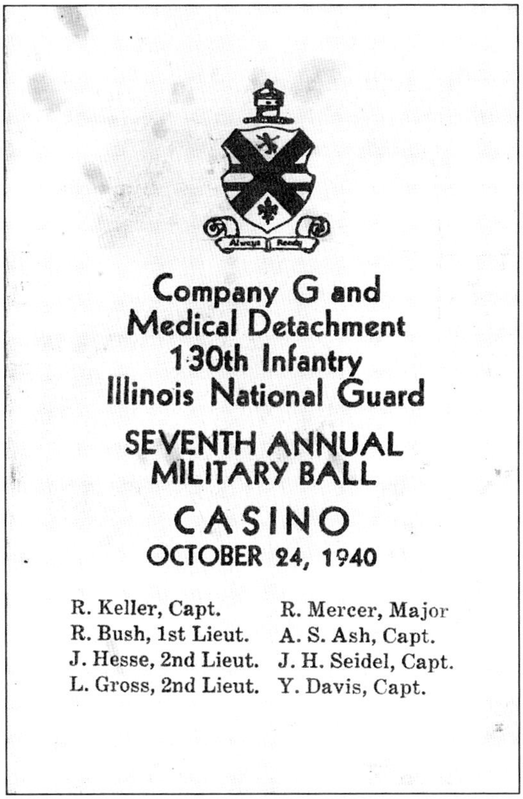

Company G and Medical Detachment
130th Infantry
Illinois National Guard

SEVENTH ANNUAL MILITARY BALL

CASINO

OCTOBER 24, 1940

R. Keller, Capt.	R. Mercer, Major
R. Bush, 1st Lieut.	A. S. Ash, Capt.
J. Hesse, 2nd Lieut.	J. H. Seidel, Capt.
L. Gross, 2nd Lieut.	Y. Davis, Capt.

The Seventh Annual Military Ball of Company G and Medical Detachment, 130th Infantry, Illinois National Guard, was held October 24, 1940, at the Casino. Officers included R. Keller, R. Bush, J. Hesse, L. Gross, R. Mercer, A. S. Ash, J.H. Seidel, Y. Davis; (co-chairmen) First Sgt. T. Einhaus and Corporal E.E. Hunsaker. C. Neubauer, M. Shade, J. Thomas, D. Boden, and R. Snyder were in charge of decorations. R. Hanson, C. Gibson, and E. Howard were in charge of publicity. Many of these men left for service in March 1941.

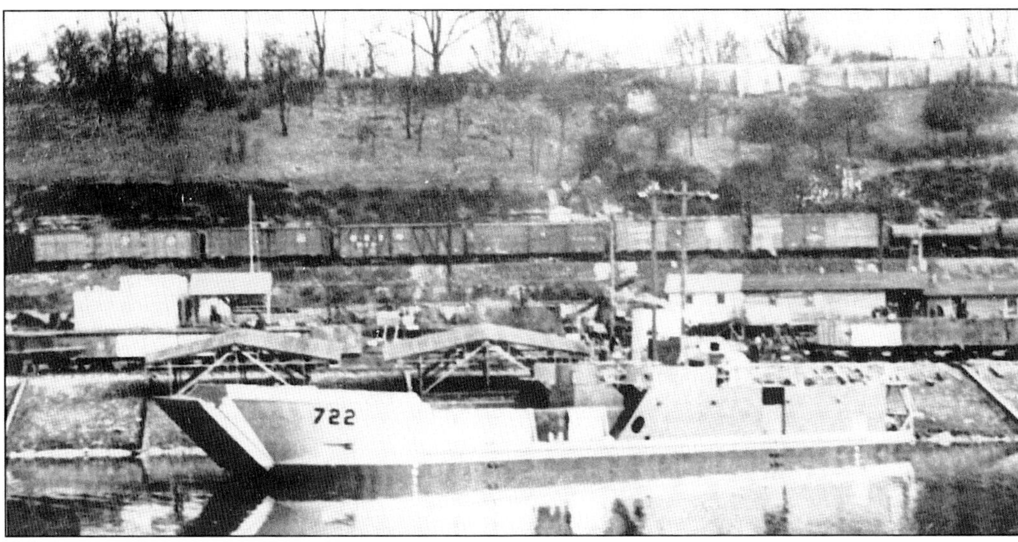

Then came the "Day of Infamy," December 7, 1941, when the Japanese struck Pearl Harbor. The headlines on the *Herald-Whig* newspaper read: "Congress Declares War-Honolulu Loss is 3,000." On December 11, the United States declared war on Germany and Italy. In Quincy, an air-raid warning system was set up. The Quincy Barge Builders on the bay front built the landing craft seen here, starting in the spring of 1942. The craft were sometimes shipped on flatcars to the West Coast in three parts and fully assembled there, while others were completely assembled locally and left Quincy by water.

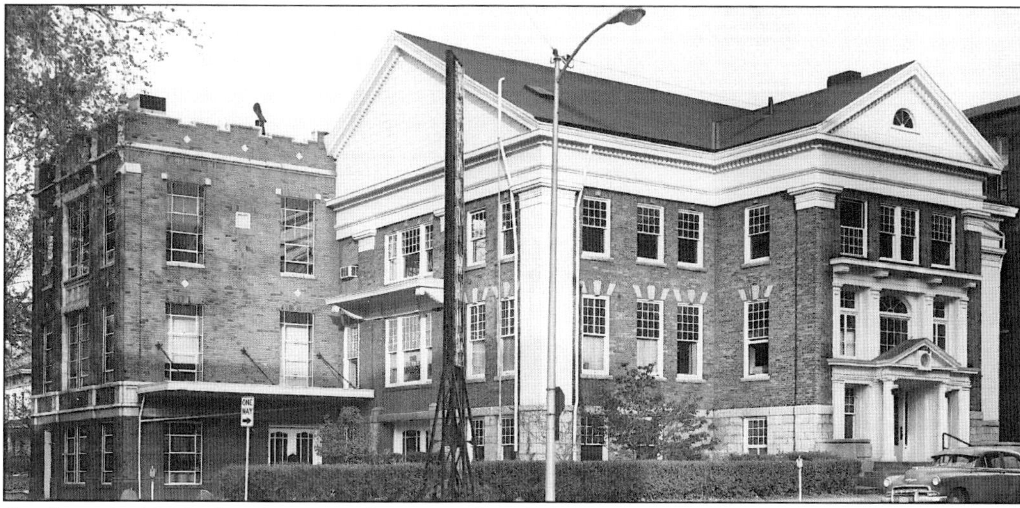

On June 1, 1926, the Quincy *Whig-Journal* and the Quincy *Herald* were consolidated as the Quincy *Herald-Whig*, published by Quincy Newspapers, Inc. Charles F. Eichenauer was editor of the *Herald-Whig* during the days of WW II. He died suddenly on September 26, 1945, and was succeeded by Arthur Higgins, who had come to the *Herald* in 1922. Long hours were required of many at the newspaper to cover the war news, as well as President Roosevelt's death and the tornado that struck Quincy, both of which occurred on April 12, 1945.

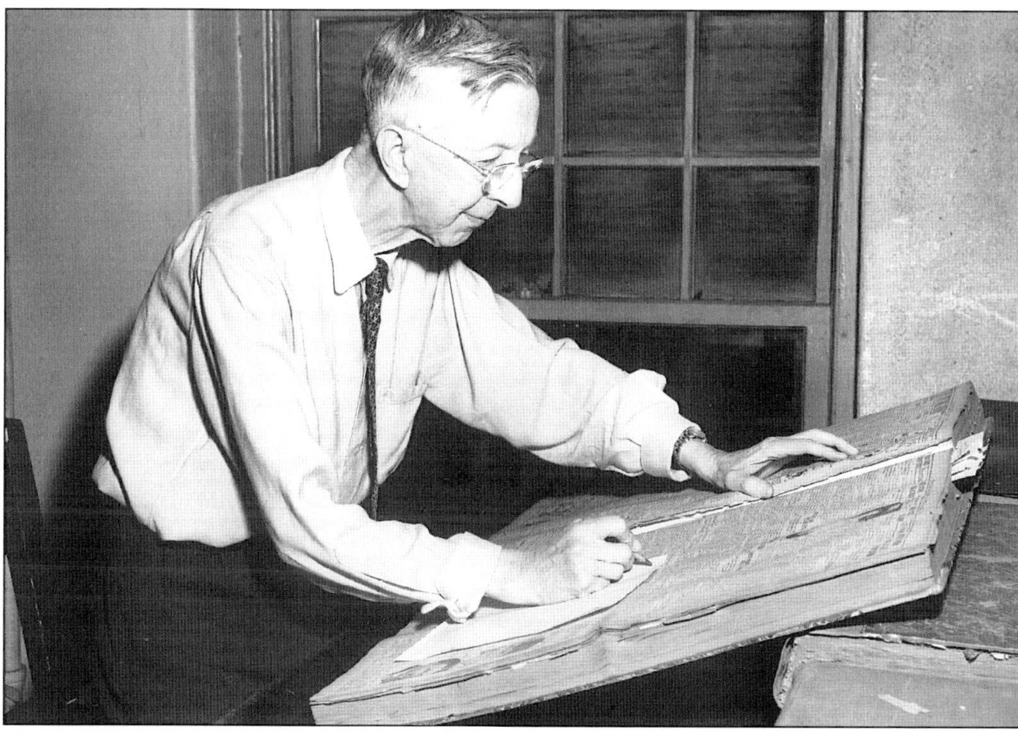

Harry Githens was not an employee of the *Herald-Whig* during the WW II years, although he had been a reporter for both the *Journal* and the *Herald* at one time. In 1952, he was hired as a proofreader, a position he held for some 20 years. He also had a long career working with the youth of Quincy and was in demand for presentations before church groups.

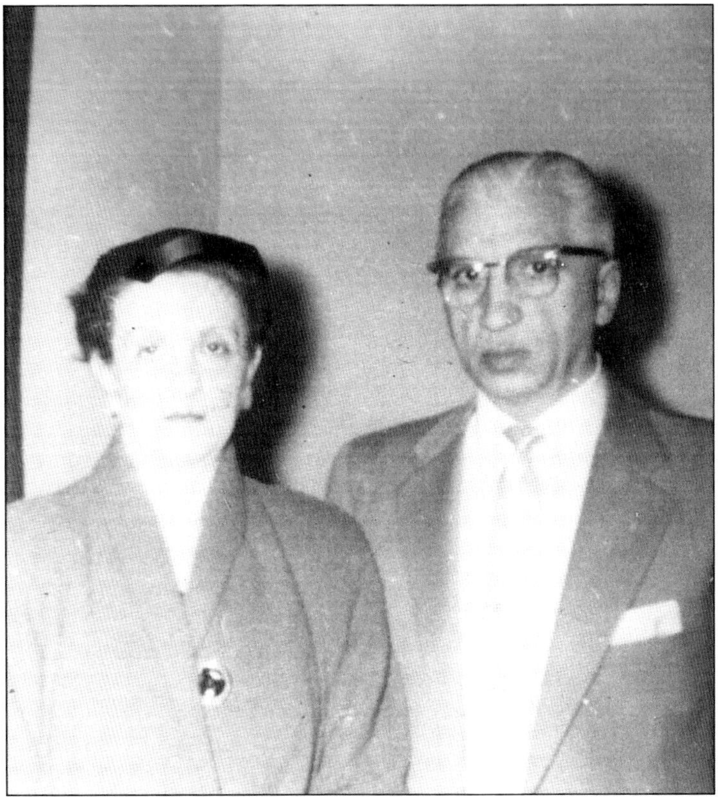

Mr. and Mrs. Frank (Onalee) Malambri and their three sons were called the Musical Malambri Family. Mrs. Malambri played piano in the orchestras of the Empire Theatre, the Orpheum Theatre, and the Washington Theatre, as well as 15 years for the Harriet Musolino Dancing School. Frank Malambri played sax with the Joe Bonansinga Orchestra, the Junior Musolino Orchestra, and the Carl Landrum Orchestra. He also played cello with the Quincy Symphony Orchestra.

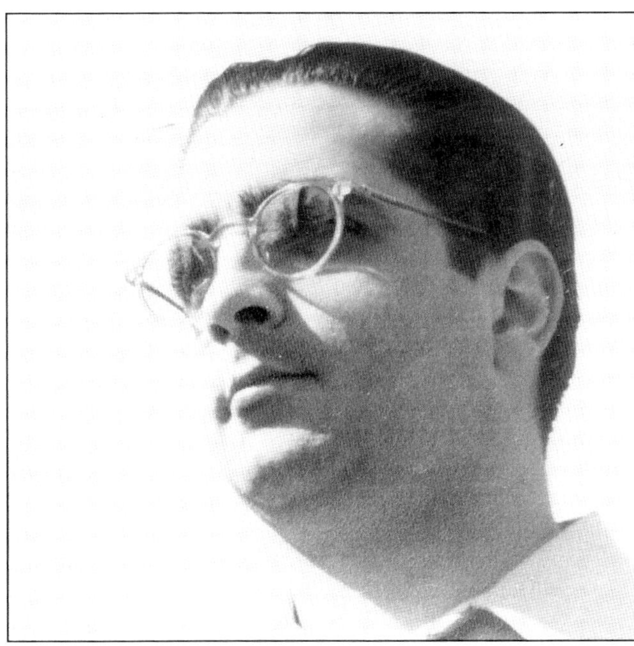

Several Quincy families had five sons in service; the Malambris had three. Before joining the U.S. Army, William Malambri played trumpet and trombone in several Quincy orchestras, and later was Assistant Band Director, Third Army Corps, at Fort McPherson, Alabama.

Frank Malambri Jr. played saxophone in several Quincy orchestras before serving in the Armed Forces. He later became a high school band director in Halstead, Kansas.

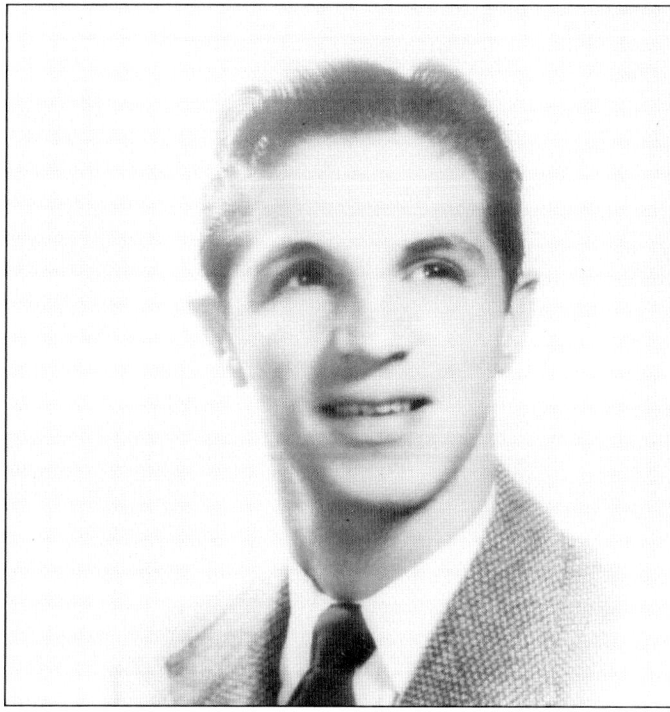

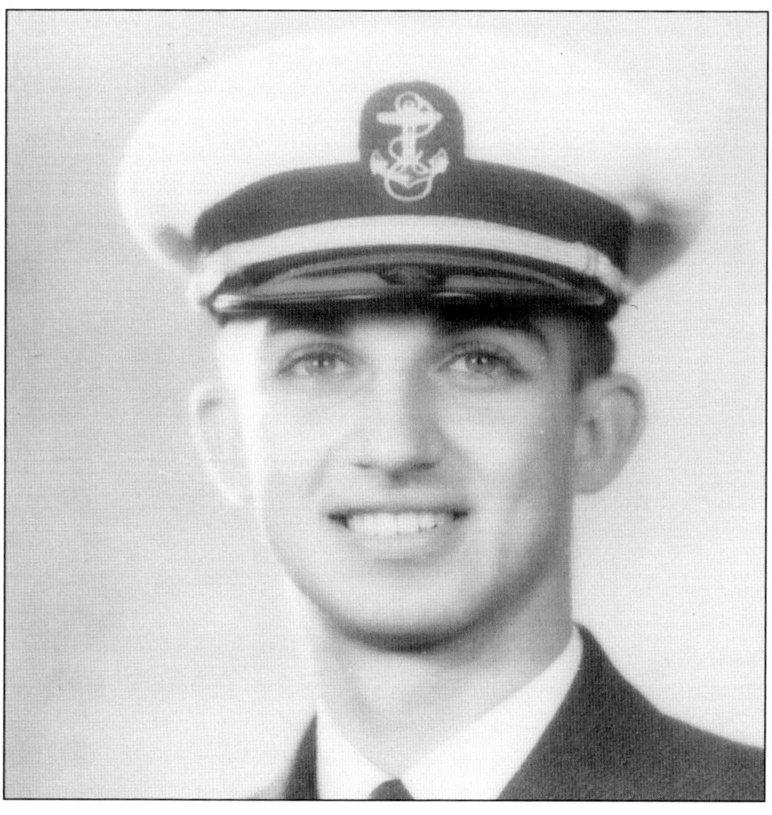

Nick Malambri played with the Junior Musolino Orchestra and the American Legion Drum Corps before serving in the Armed Forces.

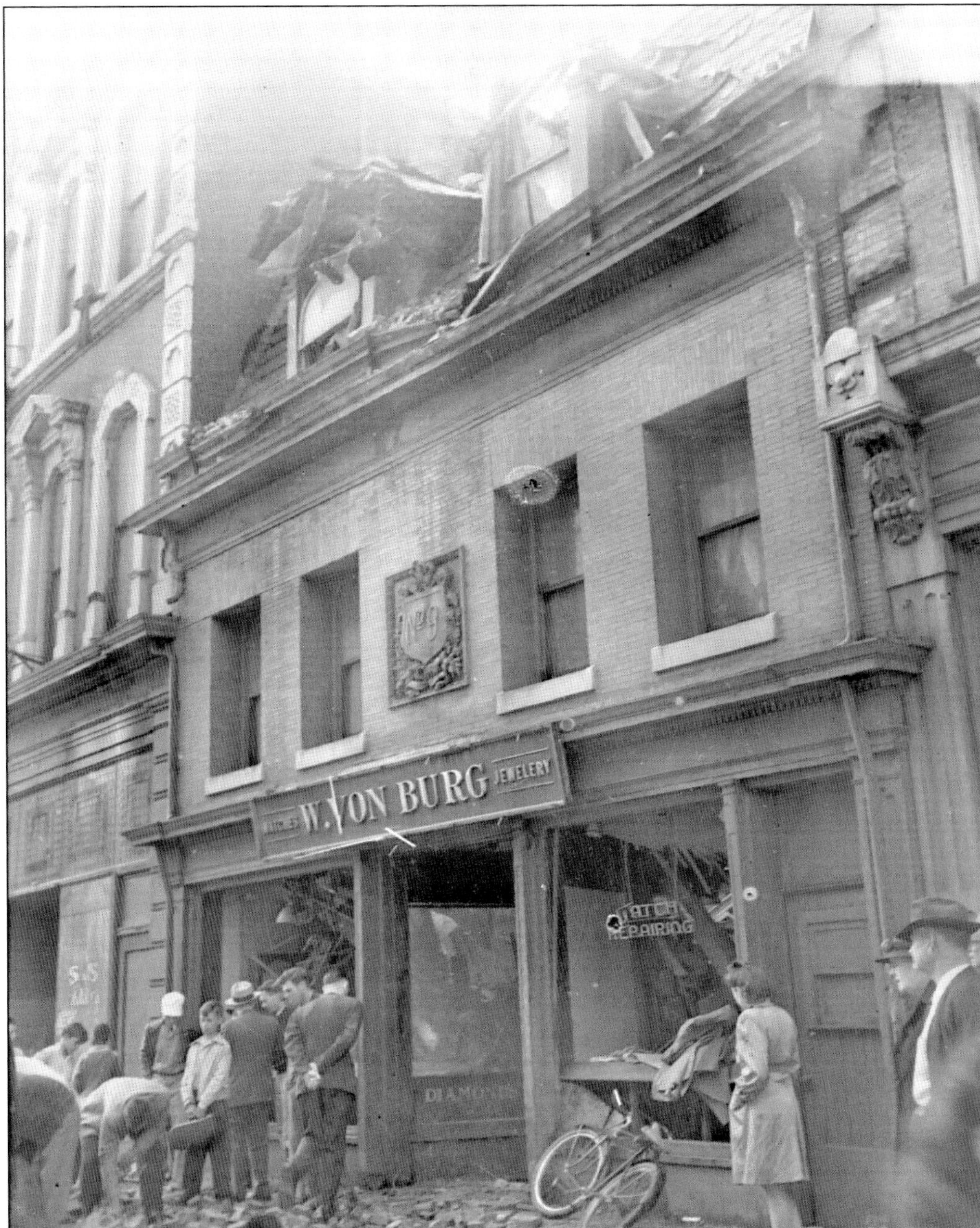

When Pres. Franklin D. Roosevelt died on the afternoon of April 12, 1945, a *Herald-Whig* extra spread the news. That night, about 10:20 p.m., Quincy had its tornado. Coming in from the southwest and spinning northeastward through the city, the storm did $1 million worth of damage, injuring 19 persons, wrecking the courthouse and several churches, and flattening automobiles. Miraculously, it killed no one. The downtown area was the hardest hit. The Von Burg Jewelry Store at 526 Hampshire Street had extensive damage when the safe fell through the floor to the basement.

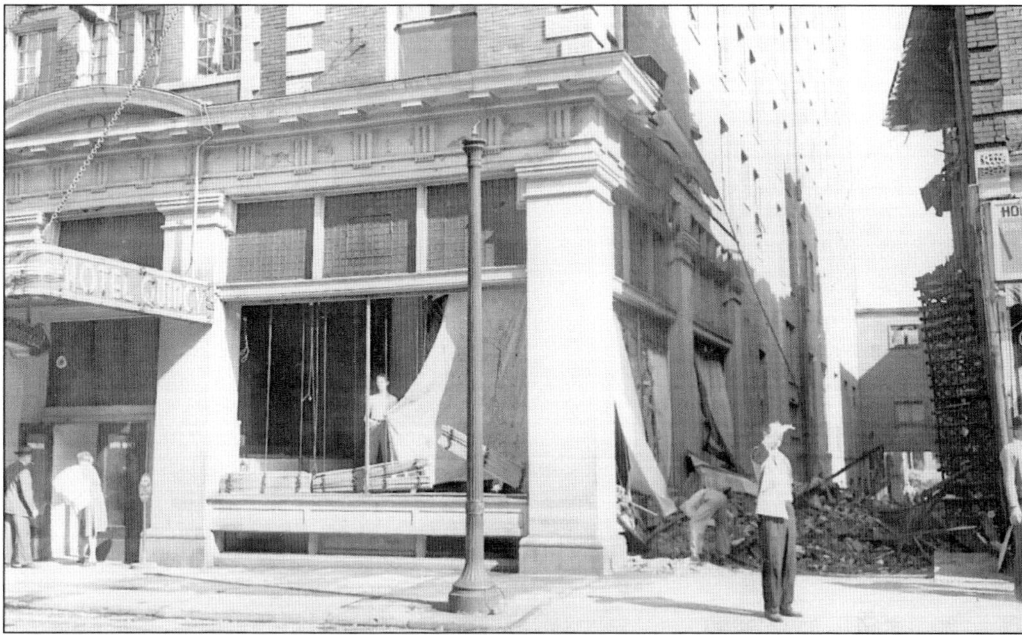

The Hotel Quincy, located at 513 Hampshire Street, sustained heavy damage. The tornado unroofed many buildings, including the old Herald-Whig structure (which has since been torn down and replaced by the current modern building) and the old Adams County courthouse, built in 1876, which lost its dome. The old courthouse was repaired and used for some time, but was later replaced with the current building.

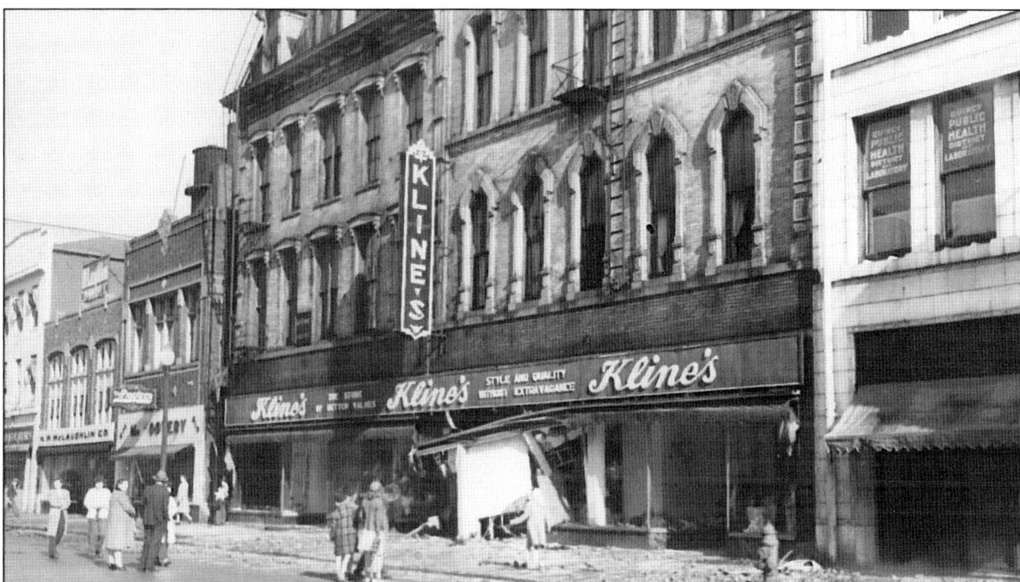

Kline's department store, located on the north side of Maine Street between Sixth and Seventh Streets, also sustained considerable damage, as did St. Boniface Church, located on the northwest corner of Seventh and Maine Streets. St. Peters Church, on the southwest corner of Eighth and Maine Streets, sustained extensive damage. A new church was then built at Twenty-sixth and Maine Streets.

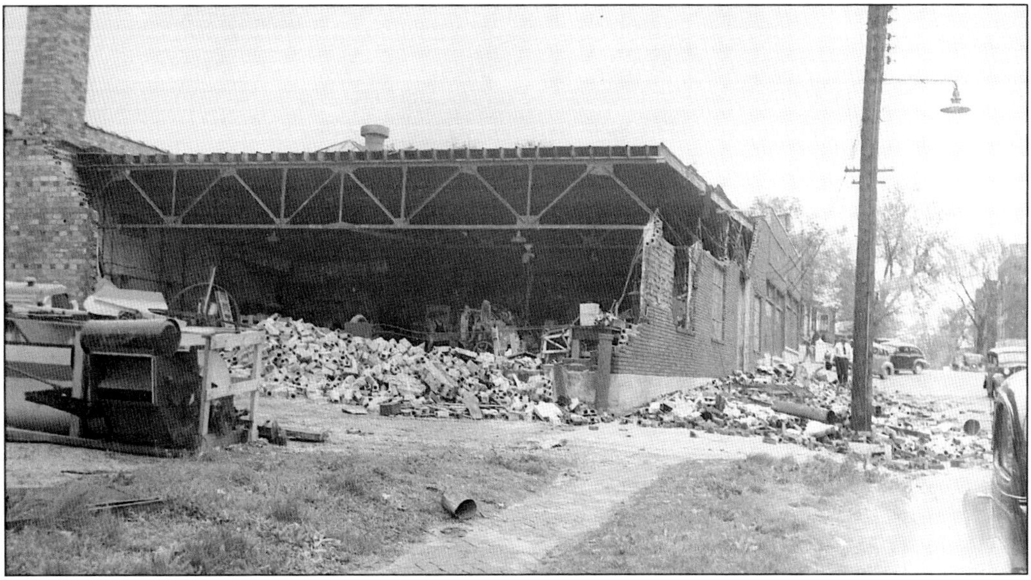

As the storm moved northeastward, it also damaged other areas of the city, including the A&P Super Mart, shown here, located on the southwest corner of Tenth and Broadway and Turner Hall at 926 Hampshire Street.

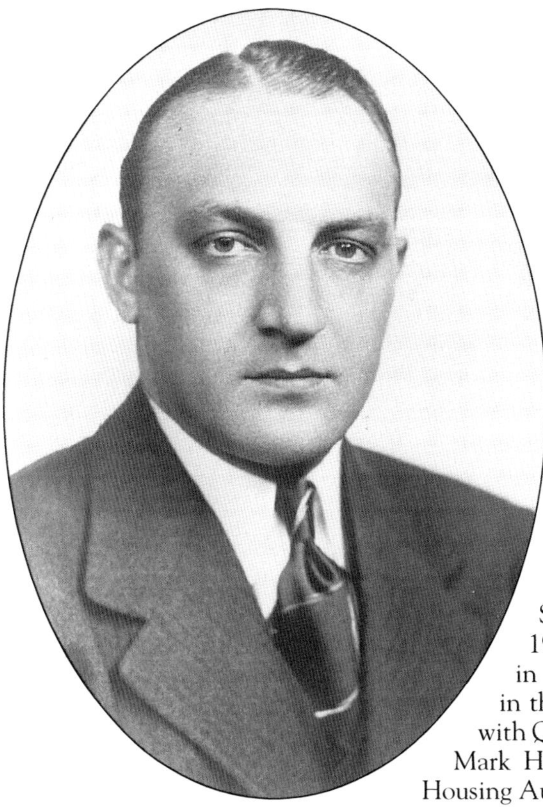

Tragedy struck again in June 1946. Edward J. Schneidman was elected Mayor of Quincy in 1941, succeeding Leo Lenane, and re-elected in 1945. Mayor Schneidman died in Chicago in the LaSalle Hotel fire on June 5, 1946, along with Quincyans Public Engineer James Potter, Ald. Mark Heinen, and Manager of the Quincy Public Housing Authority Emery Sallstrom.

Eight

Post World War II 1960s

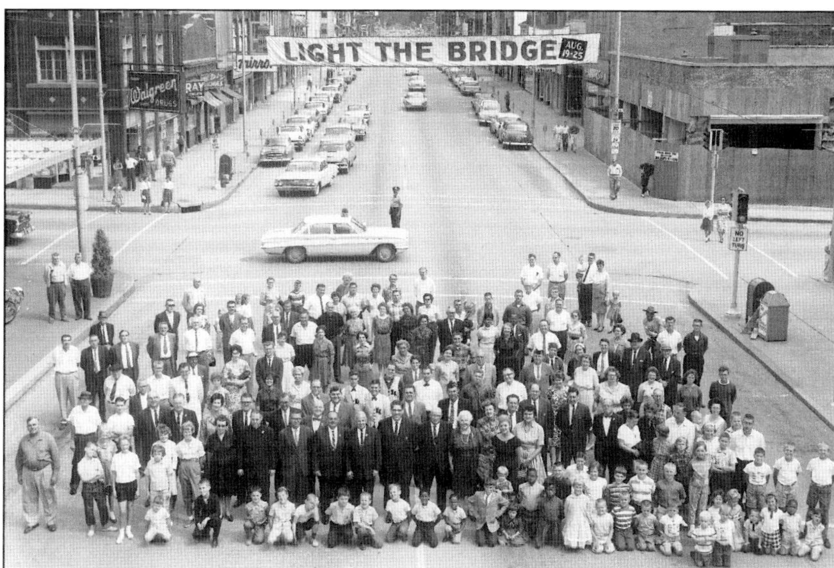

The new Soldiers' Memorial Bridge opened in June 1930 and was dedicated to Quincyans who had served in the nation's armed forces. The first spade of dirt was turned by Mayor Weems on June 16, 1928, but labor trouble, high water, and ice caused delays. It was not until the summer of 1930 that the bridge was opened. The first auto to cross the bridge was on an official inspection trip on May 19, 1930. On May 24, the bridge was opened for pedestrian traffic and Anthony Badamo had the honor of being the first to walk across the new bridge. The bridge officially opened for business as a toll bridge on June 13, 1930, and remained as such until 1945. In 1962, the week of August 19–25 was designated as "Bridge Lighting Week." All Quincy organizations and all Quincy children were called upon to contribute to the $12,000 fund to light the bridge. Memorial Bridge was lighted in a Memorial Day program in 1963.

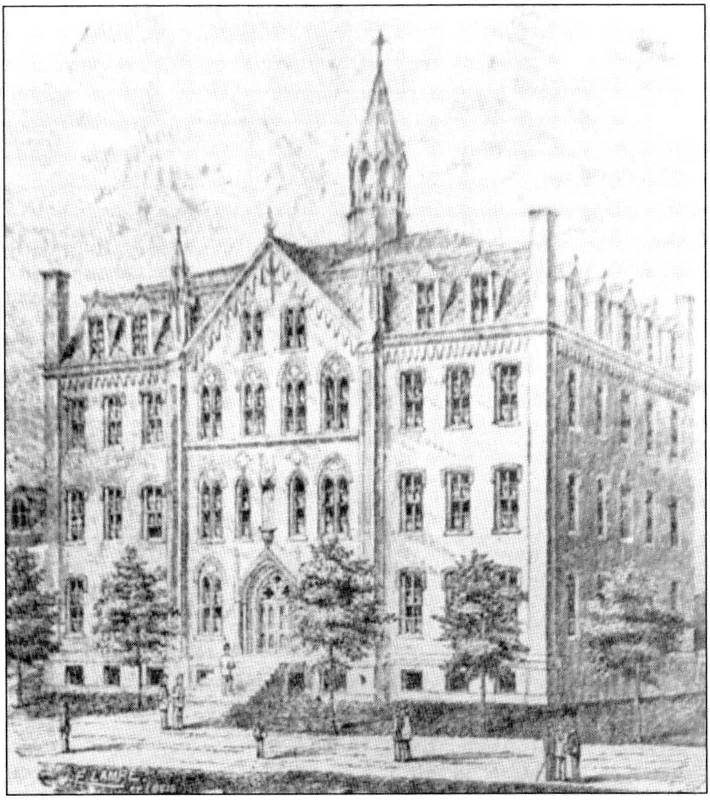

The first Quincy College classes were held c. 1860, in a 3-story brick building known as the Mast building, which was located on the southeast corner of Eighth and Maine Streets. Classes were later moved to the "prairie," at Eighteenth and Vine (College), where classes were held in the friary, the orphanage, and the first parish school. Then permanent buildings were erected on the Christian Borstandt property. This drawing of the first permanent home of Quincy College (then St. Francis Solanus College and now Quincy University), was completed in 1871 and is still in use today.

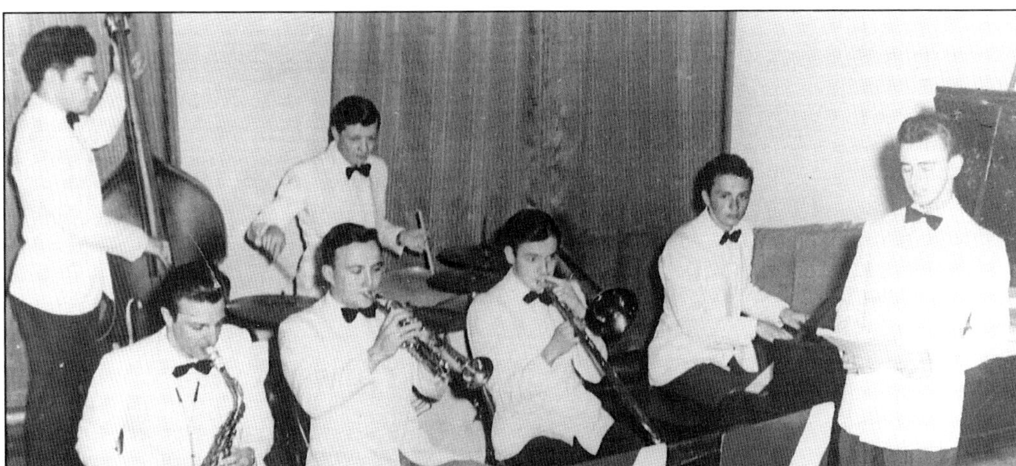

Quincy University continues to present a program of higher learning, with both bachelor and master degrees obtainable. Many musical, athletic, and other groups important to the students, have been formed over the years. One of those groups is seen here in 1948. Members of the Quincy College Sextet are, from left to right, as follows: (front row), Benny DiDia, Allen Hunter, Lynn Lubker, Carl Broeker, and Bruce Whitehead (vocals); (back row) Neal Harvey and Hugh Soebbing. Broeker was the first leader, followed by DiDia, and later Charles Winking.

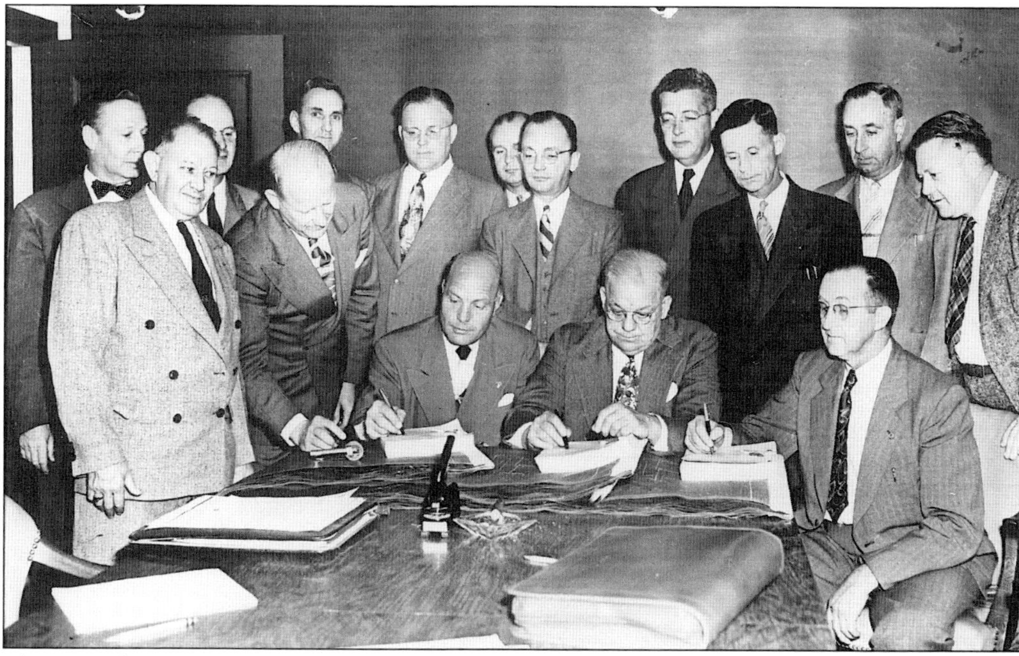

The tornado that struck Quincy on April 12, 1945, caused extensive damage to the courthouse. As a result, a new city-county building was planned. However, the contract for construction of the new joint city-county building did not get signed until 1949. Shown here, from left to right, are as follows: (front row) Mayor George Meyer, Fred Gross, and Vernon O'Brien; (middle row) Oscar King, Lawrence Kuhlman, Montgomery Carrott, Virgil Conover, and Arthur F. Witte; (back row) Joseph Burgee, Arthur F. Stowell, Joseph Latta, William Sass, Henry Pollock, John T. Reardon, and George Miller.

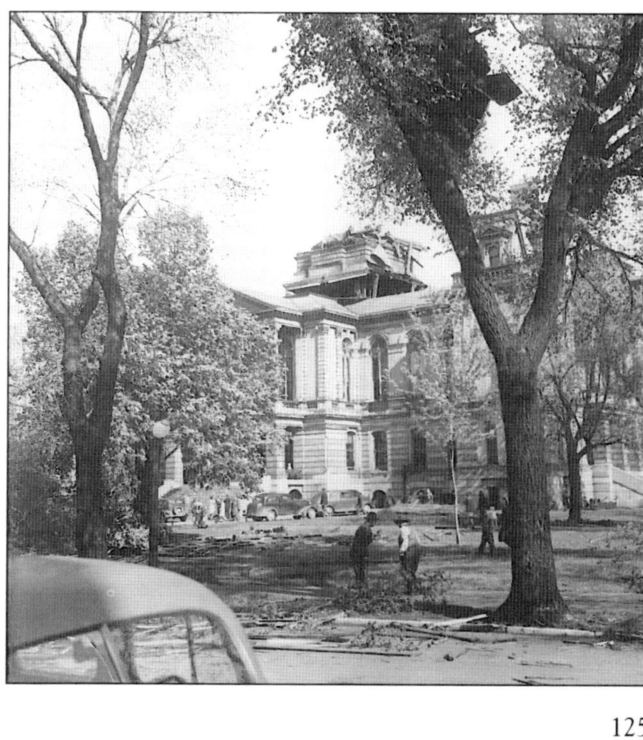

The Adams County courthouse shows some of the damage from the tornado. Extensive damage occurred to other parts of the building not shown in this picture. This was the third Adams County courthouse, erected in 1875–76 at a cost of $260,000. The cornerstone had been laid on July 4, 1876.

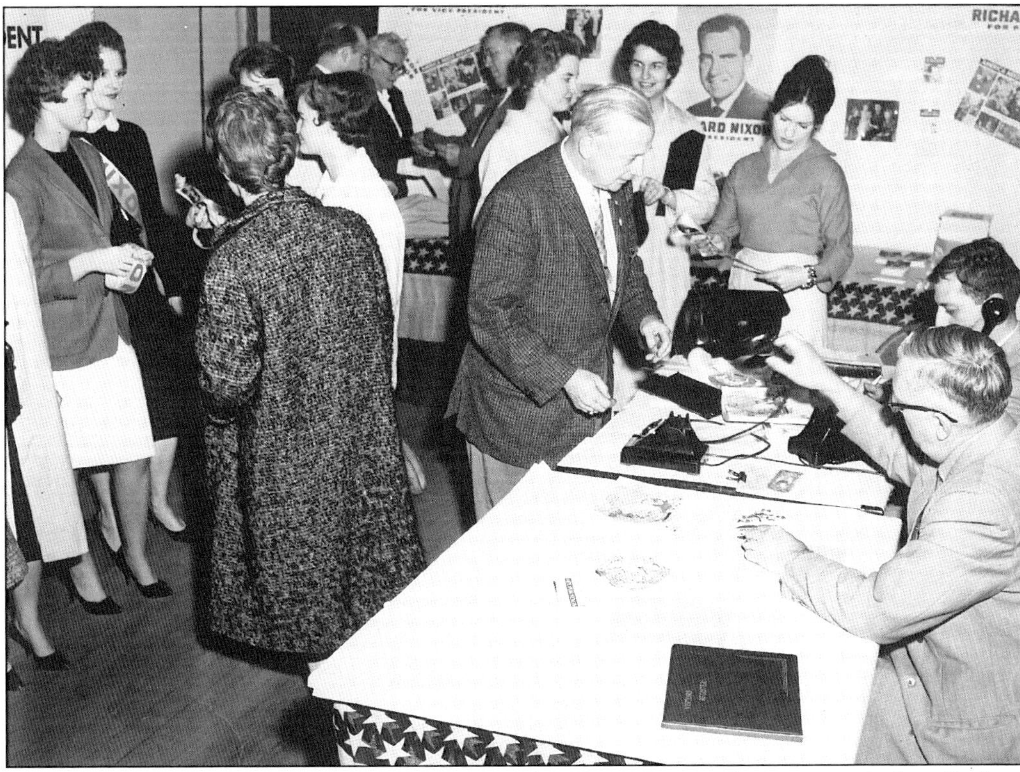

Several presidential candidates have campaigned in Quincy over the years, including Richard Nixon. This is a picture of the Adams County Republicans for Richard Nixon, in 1960, with co-chairmen Art Stowell and Wes Olson. They carried Adams County for Richard Nixon! Henry Cabot Lodge was his running mate.

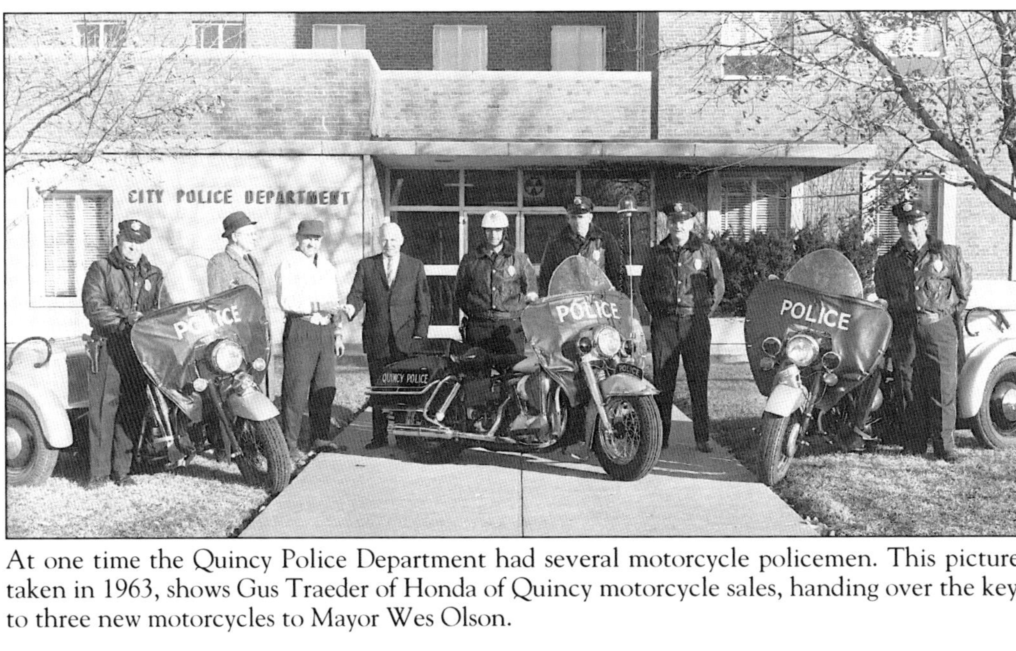

At one time the Quincy Police Department had several motorcycle policemen. This picture, taken in 1963, shows Gus Traeder of Honda of Quincy motorcycle sales, handing over the keys to three new motorcycles to Mayor Wes Olson.

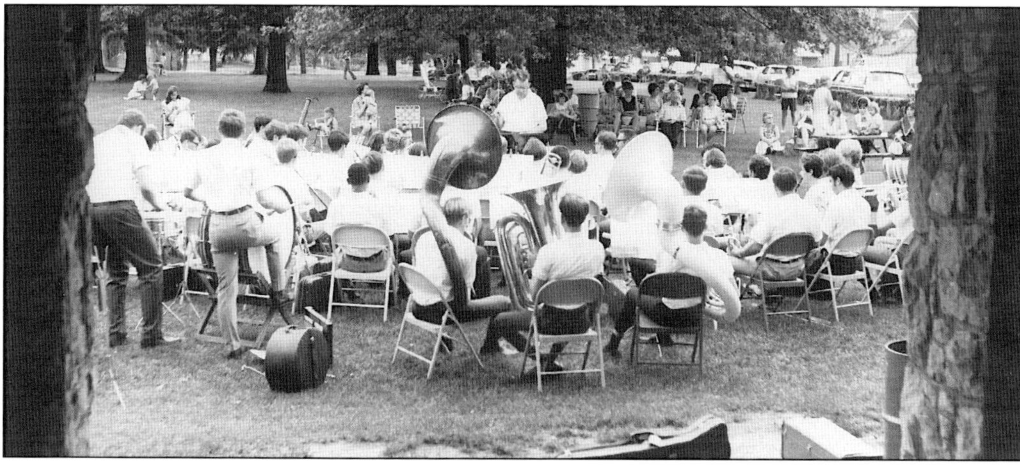

The Quincy Park Band was founded in 1948 by Carl Landrum. He was the director until 1993, when he passed the baton to his associate director, Pam Potter. Although the band has played in many of Quincy's parks, including Reservoir Park, shown here in 1969, most concerts have been played in Washington and South Parks. The band, which plays unrehearsed, has included members of all ages, from high school students to retirees.

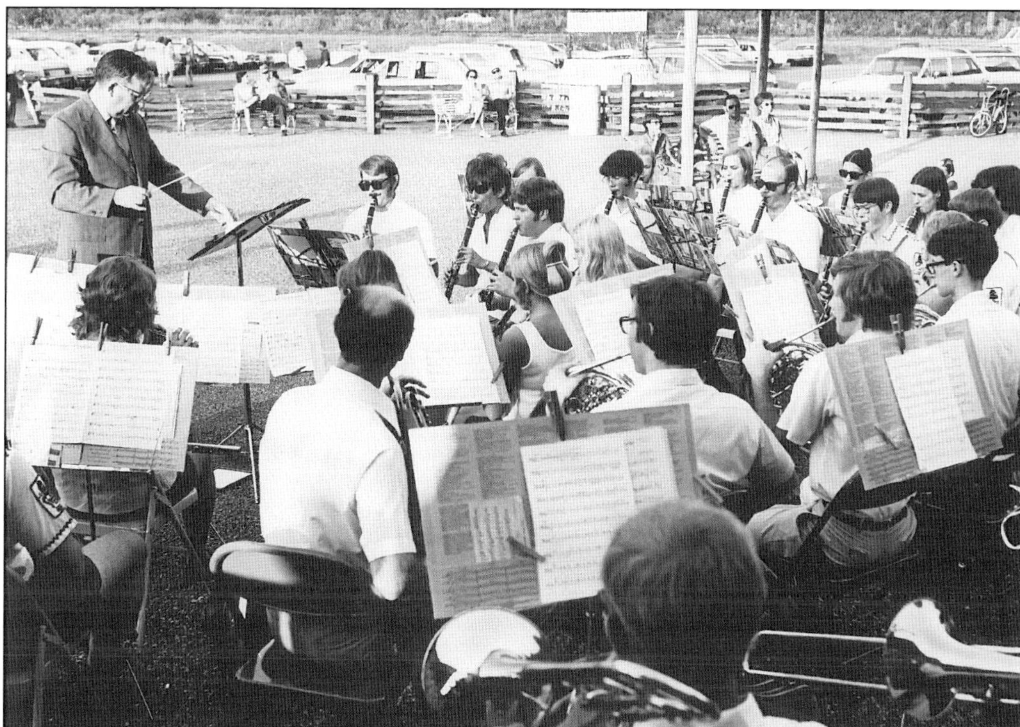

The 25th anniversary concert of the Quincy Park Band was played in All America Park at the Foot of Cedar Street. The 50th anniversary concert was held in 1998 in Madison Park, at Twenty-fourth and Maine Streets. The band, under the direction of Pam Potter, (who may be seen playing clarinet here), continues to play summer concerts in Madison Park, with the exception of Memorial Day and the Fourth of July, when they play at Clat Adams Park on the riverfront. A Christmas concert is now played in Morrison Theater.

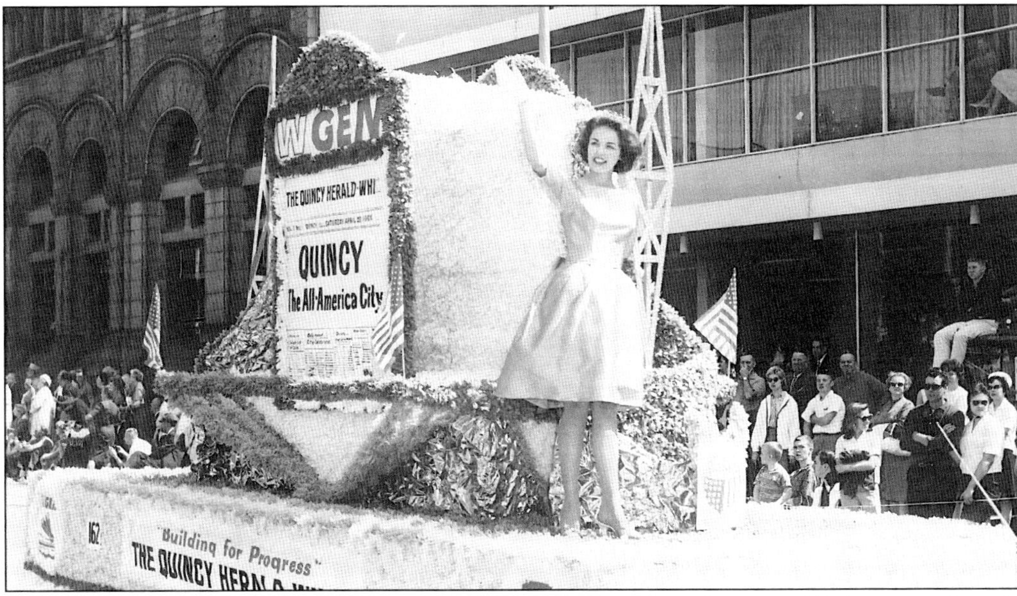

In 1963, the city of Quincy, Illinois, was proud to be selected as an All-America City by the National Municipal League and *Look* magazine. It was selected because it is a city of beautiful parks, excellent recreational programs, superb educational and medical facilities, and exceptionally fine cultural opportunities. In addition, it has many beautifully maintained, grand old homes of another era along and adjacent to Maine Street.

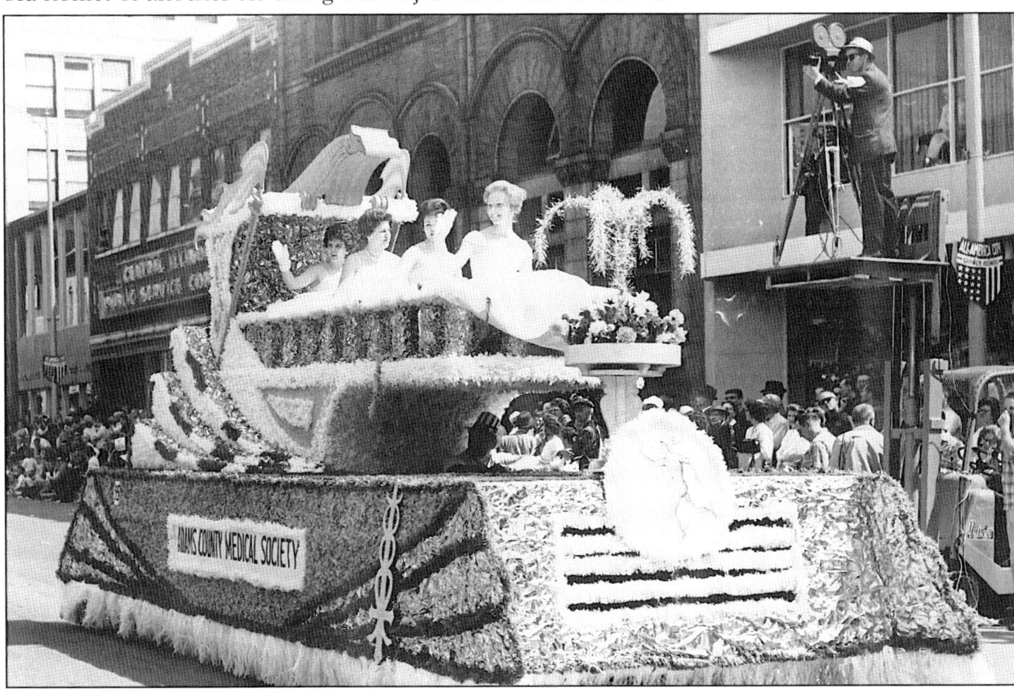

The All-America City Celebration was held April 17–21, 1963, at the time when Quincy's beautiful dogwood and magnolia trees were blooming. The celebration included the appearance of the U.S. Navy Demonstration Team Blue Angels, art shows, street dances, fireworks, concerts, a banquet, and a parade on Saturday, April 20, led by Gov. Otto Kerner.